uppsala to nairobi

524

1968–1975

Report of the Central Committee

to the Fifth Assembly of the

World Council of Churches

David Enderton Johnson

General Editor

Published in collaboration with the World Council of Churches by

FRIENDSHIP PRESS   NEW YORK
SPCK   LONDON

To
EUGENE CARSON BLAKE
in gratitude

contents

Foreword by M.M. Thomas 7

Editorial Note by David E. Johnson 10

Introduction by Philip Potter 13

1. General Secretariat 23

2. Faith and Witness 69

3. Justice and Service 122

4. Education and Renewal 178

5. Communication 210

6. Finance and Central Services 224

Lexicon 243

Index 251

foreword

By M.M. Thomas
Chairman of the Central Committee

Uppsala to Nairobi is a report, commissioned by the Central Committee of the World Council of Churches and issued in its name, which attempts to describe and evaluate the various programmes and activities of the World Council of Churches since its Fourth Assembly at Uppsala, Sweden, in 1968. The volume has been compiled in anticipation of the Fifth Assembly, which is due to take place in Nairobi, Kenya, during the last two months of 1975. It is particularly intended to aid delegates to that gathering (the great preponderance of whom will never before have attended a major WCC meeting) in preparing themselves for active and informed participation in the various sessions of the Assembly. But historians of the ecumenical movement and other friends of the World Council of Churches will also find it a useful assessment of one of the most challenging eras of modern church history.

During the period under review the World Council celebrated its Silver Jubilee. Thus we have experienced a time not only of looking forward but also of looking back, with both gratitude and repentance, of renewing ourselves spiritually for the pilgrim journey before us, and of making sure that we may have accumulated and equip ourselves with whatever suste- that we discard whatever unnecessary and cumbersome baggage we may have accumulated and equip ourselves with whatever sustenance we shall need for the days ahead.

than the mere passage of time or the pursuit of a linear itinerary. For the ecumenical movement is a pilgrim progress in another dimension beyond, as well as encompassing, those of the plane of human existence. At Uppsala Dr. W.A. Visser 't Hooft, the first General Secretary of the World Council of Churches, introduced terms of reference which have frequently recurred in our debates over the last seven years when he declared that "no horizontal advance" of the churches or of humanity was possible "without vertical orientation". His words on that occasion provide the essential link between the celebration in 1968 of the divine promise "Behold, I make all things new" and our joyous acknowledgement in 1975 that JESUS CHRIST FREES AND UNITES:

"When it is said that God makes all things new this means above all that through Christ God re-creates humanity as a family united under his reign. Mankind is ōne, not in itself, not because of its own merits or qualities. Mankind is one as the object of God's love and saving action. Mankind is one because of its common calling. The vertical dimension of its unity determines the horizontal dimension. So Christians have more reason than anyone else to be advocates of humanity. They are not humanitarians in the sentimental sense that it is nice to be nice to other people. They are not humanists in the aristocratic sense that learning and culture constitute a bond between the privileged few of all nations. They are on the side of *all* humanity because God is on that side and his Son died for it."

Therefore no man or woman, as both a temporal and a spiritual being, can be involved in a purely "horizontal" or purely "vertical" activity; the horizontal/vertical, the social/spiritual dimensions meet in human nature and in all human aspirations and activities. Our task as Christians and churches is to "discern the spirits", whether it be the Spirit of God or idolatrous spirits, and to confront them with the Spirit of the God-manhood of Jesus Christ; and Christian theology is a tool of this discernment and confrontation, just as Christian mission is a witness to this insight and challenge.

The World Council of Churches may thus be described as a fellowship of churches founded on faith in Jesus Christ as God and Saviour, and engaged in exploring the meaning of the centrality of Jesus Christ for the unity of the Church, for the Church's participation in the struggle of men and women for their humanity in the modern world, and for the evangelistic witness of the Church in the world of religion, ideology and spirituality; we are also engaged in discovering the proper integration between unity, service and mission of the Church in the contemporary world. *Uppsala to Nairobi* provides some of the details of the ways that we have worked since 1968 at this manifold task.

"No one would claim that this is a popular book", wrote my distinguished predecessor as Chairman of the Central Committee, Dr. Franklin Clark Fry,[‡] in the foreword to a report, similar to this present one, issued for use at the Third Assembly of the World Council of Churches, which met in my own country—India—fourteen years ago. "A volume which is designed to deal with matters of organization, which must treat of technical subjects often in technical language, and which must give an account of achievements and failures in the development of a programme, cannot be a popular book."

Perhaps not, but the work carried out is of far-ranging significance and has elicited wide-spread interest. For these reasons, and also to ensure that *every* delegate to Nairobi will be provided with the necessary information about *every* aspect of the World Council's activities, special efforts have been made to render the contents of *Uppsala to Nairobi* intelligible to the non-expert while remaining intelligent to the expert. For the few occasions when technical vocabulary could not be avoided, for a handy resource in identifying names or events perhaps unfamiliar to many, and to provide the full titles for some of the acronyms employed in the World Council's framework, a short Lexicon has been included at the back of the book, along with an Index.

This report is the work of many hands. The basic material was prepared by the staff of the Unit or Sub-unit most directly concerned. A member of the Central Committee, Mr. David E. Johnson, has served as General Editor and is responsible for the final text in English. Professor Roger Mehl—likewise a member of the Central Committee—was entrusted with the editing of the French version. And Oberkirchenrat Reinhard Groscurth, who served for a number of years on the staff of Faith and Order, has supervised the German edition. To all of these friends and colleagues the Central Committee is indebted.

editorial note

By David E. Johnson

It has been a rare and unforeseen privilege to have served for the past seven years as a member of the Central Committee of the World Council of Churches—and for the last five of them as a member of its Executive Committee. The opportunities for grasping at the heights and groping into the depths of what it means to be a Christian in community, of improving one's theological understanding, of gaining a broader sense of mission, of understanding better what stewardship can mean, of winning warm and abiding friendships, have been overwhelming. I am certain that in my old age I shall look upon the years 1968/75 as among the happiest of my life.

And yet these have been times of dreadful pain and turmoil for humanity. The symptoms and the causes are starkly delineated in the pages which follow. Scattered among the doomsday signs, however, are indications of hope, instances of cooperation, of commitment to fellowship, of compulsion to unity. These senses of ecumenicity are a Paternal gift, sustained by the example of our Lord and Brother Jesus Christ and inspired by the Holy Spirit. The World Council of Churches serves as a backbone and nerve-stream to it all. But yet again this has been a period of trauma for the World Council of Churches. One sees the Council hated in certain quarters as perhaps never before. Magazines and newspapers have gone out of their way to portray the WCC in an unfavourable light. I can remember driving past a conservative and fundamentalist church in the state of Ohio, USA, and seeing the parish notice board proudly displaying the advertisement, "NOT a member of the World Council of Churches". And among the Member Churches these seem to have been what Charles Dickens called "the best of times and the worst of times". In North India and in Britain church union plans were consummated; in Canada and in Britain, again, they were not. Sometimes people in the pews have accepted ecumenically inspired liturgical reforms "because it's nice to do what other Christians are doing". And sometimes these same efforts have been resisted "because it's not the way we're used to doing it". So it goes, subject by subject, instance after instance. It can all be put down to our common human difficulty in doing what *The Book of Common Prayer* calls "giving up our selves to thy service and . . . walking before thee in holiness and righteousness all our days".

My own first direct experience of the World Council of Churches was at the Third Assembly in New Delhi, 1961. My mother was a delegate, and I was along for the ride. My idleness was not long to last, for Eleanor Kent Browne, a stalwart of the WCC New York Office in charge of the Assembly Information Desk, soon pressed me into service. While it was fun to try out my French recently acquired in secondary school, I was more than a bit overcome at the amount of knowledge about the WCC and its delegations that I was expected to dispense.

But that was, nothing compared to the amount of information and parliamentary savvy that it was necessary to muster seven years later when —fate having taken a capricious turn in the interim—I attended the Fourth Assembly at Uppsala as a full delegate of my church. I can scarcely imagine that I acquitted myself properly on either occasion, but I crave the indulgence of the readers for these few glimpses of my own ecumenical past as a means of showing newcomers to the life of the World Council at the Fifth Assembly in Nairobi that they have a genuine sympathiser in the editor of this report.

It is by no means easy to gain a grasp of the programme and activities of so varied and complex an entity as the World Council of Churches. Although the following pages are numerous, they only begin to tell the story of these past seven years. Nor is the report "objective". It is the account of insiders and therefore subjective in the sense that it is a story told by persons who care very deeply about what they have been doing or what has been done on their behalf. Some pains, nevertheless, have been taken to guard against "special pleading". While the first draft of each segment of the report was drawn up by the staff most directly concerned, a specially appointed group of Central Committee members and advisers scrutinized and evaluated the material provided, on the basis of which efforts revisions were made by staff members or, on occasion, by myself.

By such a process no absolute consistency of style was possible or, indeed, desired. How readable the eventual product now is, is a matter for others to judge. I hope that the present report at least matches the standards of its counterparts produced for the New Delhi and Uppsala Assemblies. At any rate there are certain editorial features which have been introduced to make the chores of assimilation and retention of the contents as effortless as possible for the participants in the Nairobi Assembly. First of all the vocabulary and syntax have been kept as simple as was consistent with a minimally attractive style. When a widely popular dictionary, such as *The Concise Oxford Dictionary* or *The American Heritage Dictionary*, does not supply the meaning of an unfamiliar word, name or abbreviation, the Lexicon at the back of the book is at the readers' disposal. A sign (‡) in the text indicates this availability. The contents of the Lexicon are the responsibility of the editor and, except where noted, do not express official views of the WCC. Footnotes, indicated by one or more asterisks (*) in the text, are devoted solely to pointing out where additional information on the particular subject at hand may be found.

Since *Uppsala to Nairobi*, in addition to being general background reading for the Assembly, is the basic document for the "hearings" on the work of the Programme Units and the General Secretariat, some care has been taken to make it easier to come back to a passage that has seemed relevant to the reader. The frequent headlines in the text should help in leafing through a particular chapter, and the Index is partly designed to help a participant get quick access to more information about a particular report, study or even "catch-phrase" likely to be used at the Assembly. Jargon and ecumenical short-hand are maddening diseases to those newly exposed to them. There is no cure, but we hope that we can relieve the symptoms a little.

By common agreement the individual contributions to the text of this report are anonymous, and by and large the names of programme staff have been kept out of it. In one sense this is only fair, but in another it is a pity, for a great deal of time and effort on the part of much over-worked people have gone into it. Also this policy might tend to give the impression that programmes are "things" and not the products of human individuals working together in sometimes difficult circumstances. At any rate I would like to say a word of deep gratitude to all of my wonderful colleagues, especially to those who rewrote and retyped large portions of this report at my request. However, I shall break through the anonymity just once, to give special thanks to the Deputy General Secretary for Programme, Dr. Konrad Raiser, who is in a sense the "onlie begetter" of the ensuing pages and who guided their production through many stages of development. His patience, kindness, wisdom and friendship have been sustaining.

introduction

By Philip Potter
General Secretary, World Council of Churches

This report to you from the Central Committee affords me an opportun-
to reflect on our work in the World Council of Churches during these
ven crowded years. What new emphases have we pursued in carrying out
r traditional tasks? What have we achieved in this period? What issues
ve been raised and what lessons have we learned concerning the ecumen-
l movement?

Perhaps it would be most useful for me to begin my reflections by
inging to your attention some of the major activities and emphases which
 Central Committee has initiated and encouraged since it took up its
ties in 1968. A few paragraphs cannot, of course, adequately sum-
rize all of the ongoing work of the Council: to gain such a perspective
u will need to turn to the Central Committee's report as a whole.

We have, in these seven years, undertaken a wide range of studies and
ogrammes. The Commission on Faith and Order emphasized the relation
 "The Unity of the Church and the Unity of Mankind" in a manner
ich gave fresh relevance to the ecumenical goal. In the course of this
ajor endeavour, other studies like "Giving an Account of the Hope that
in Us" and "Concepts of Unity and Models of Union" have emerged,
ite apart from the ongoing work on the sacraments and the ministry. The
ncerns of the Commission on World Mission and Evangelism (CWME)
ere concentrated on the study of "Salvation Today" which became the
cus of the Bangkok Conference at the end of 1972. The Conference was
l to say that "the salvation which Christ brought, and in which we
rticipate, offers a comprehensive wholeness in this divided life. We
derstand salvation as newness of life—the unfolding of true humanity in
 fulness of God (Colossians 2:9)", a process in which "God's justice
anifests itself both in the justification of the sinner and in social and
litical justice". Church and Society, which had given such a clear lead
 ecumenical social thought in the 1966 Conference on "Christians in the
chnical and Social Revolutions of Our Time", went on to break new
ound in dealing with "The Future of Man and Society in a World of

Science-based Technology''. This study has brought together leading theologians and outstanding experts in various fields of science in order to grapple with some of the perplexing ethical and theological issues posed by the unrelenting march of science and technology. The problems involved in effecting social change also led to a world-wide study of ''Violence, Nonviolence and the Struggle for Social Justice''. A long-standing concern for relating the Christian faith to people of other religions—which has occupied the attention of the world missionary movement since the Edinburgh Conference of 1910 — has now emerged as a special and enlarged programme of ''Dialogue with People of Living Faiths and Ideologies'' (DFI).

In the area of ''Justice and Service'', the Commission on Inter-Church Aid, Refugee and World Service (CICARWS), in a world of continuous emergencies, catastrophes and wars, has been unflinchingly active in meeting human need and in seeing this need in terms of the struggle for social and racial justice. It has also energetically carried out the Uppsala mandate to ''give the needs of development a high priority in its total programme''. Two issues over which the Fourth Assembly agonized have become new independent programmes in the Council: the Programme to Combat Racism (PCR), which was set up in 1969 and was renewed in 1974; and the Commission on the Churches' Participation in Development (CCPD), created in 1970. In this short period, both of these programmes have rapidly broadened their scope of activities and have occupied a very central and controversial place in our deliberations. The Commission on the Churches on International Affairs (CCIA), in addition to its highly significant work of mediation and witness concerning the various trouble spots in our world, has been led to carry out a world-wide study on Human Rights, sponsoring a world consultation on this topic in October 1974.

At the Uppsala Assembly what was then the WCC's Division of Ecumenical Action was charged ''to stir up and equip all God's people for ecumenical understanding, active engagement in renewing the life of the churches, and participation in God's work in a changing world''. The Division was encouraged ''to develop its ministries in terms of the needs of God's people interacting in the world through ensuring love and dignity in the whole community''. As this Division evolved into the Unit on Education and Renewal, several new and imaginative programmes have been developed, in spite of the difficulties which have been experienced in staffing and funding. An action reflection programme on ''Participation in Change'', aimed at finding and listening to groups initiating change in their local situations, has been carried out. Responding to the cries of the dispossessed, the powerless, the silent, the unrepresented, there have been creative consultations and conferences on ''Black Theology and the Theology of Liberation in Latin America'', "Sexism‡ in the 1970's" (discrimination against women in Church and society), as also on the family, the charismatic movements‡, and youth as agents for social change.

The Uppsala Assembly received a report from a Joint Study Commission on Education sponsored by the World Council of Churches and the World Council of Christian Education (WCCE). An Office on Education was set up to deal with education in a comprehensive way: general education, Christian education and theological education. The World Council of Christian Education, which had existed since 1907, was integrated into the WCC in 1971. During these 7 years the Office of Education has had a major impact on the ecumenical movement by focusing attention on education as a process of "conscientization"‡ (a new word in our ecumenical vocabulary), that is, the ways in which people's consciousness is awakened to their true nature as subjects rather than objects, and so become enabled to be active participants in mastering their environment and altering the structures of society for a fuller life in justice and community. This Office, while having an effect on the educational work of Member Churches of the World Council and beyond, has also brought creative influence upon the whole style of thinking and working in all the activities and programmes of the Council. This is particularly reflected in the emphases adopted by the Theological Education Fund (TEF), and by the Christian Medical Commission (CMC) which was created a few months before the Uppsala Assembly.

The Assembly also initiated a study on Humanum‡ as a means of providing "an admirable opportunity for the design and testing of new methods of ecumenical study, especially for experiments using inductive methods, and including the dimensions of biology, psychology, sociology, anthropology and philosophy as well as theology". The study has reflected deeply on the way that theology can and should be done, and has also raised profound questions not only on "What is man?", but also and more directly concerning the humanness of relationships among Christians and within the World Council itself. By its Basis the World Council is committed to live and work "according to the Scriptures", and Bible study has nourished our life and work. In 1971 a Portfolio on Biblical Studies was established with the task of developing different approaches to Bible study in various parts of the world, providing documentation on what is happening in this field, enabling and training persons to lead Bible study, and participating in a series of studies on particular themes. Finally I must mention here the many-sided courses and consultations conducted by the Ecumenical Institute at Bossey, which continues to be an effective instrument for ecumenical education and for courageous confrontation on some of the burning concerns of our faith and of our world today.

All this has been an astonishing achievement, especially when it is remembered that during this period we have struggled with budgetary difficulties which have become worse with the world monetary crisis and with inflation; during these past years we have maintained stringent limits on the size of staff, yet the number of churches and councils to be served has appreciably increased.

And now, before examining the consequences of our activities for the ecumenical movement and for the World Council, we should briefly consider why we have been compelled to go in the direction indicated in these few years. When the Fourth Assembly met at Uppsala in 1968, there was an acute consciousness of a world in which the inequalities of rich and poor, the injustices meted out to people because of their race, sex or class, and the confrontation of nations in wars which threatened the whole human race, had become intolerable. In the words of the Message of the Assembly:

"We heard the cry of those who long for peace; of the hungry and exploited who demand bread and justice; of the victims of discrimination who claim human dignity; and of the increasing millions who seek for the meaning of life.

"God hears these cries and judges us. He also speaks the liberating Word. We hear him say: 'I go before you. Now that Christ carries away your sinful past, the Spirit frees you to live for others. Anticipate my Kingdom in joyful worship and daring acts.' "

In these seven years, we have seen the growth of women's liberation movements, the increasing impatience and unrest of peoples seeking political and racial liberation, the spread of militaristic governments allied to a technocracy hell-bent on increasing the Gross National Product with little regard for the powerless majority; the violation of human rights and the abuse of power everywhere; the ruthless suppression of efforts at people's participation in changing social and economic structures for a more humane existence; the outbreak of war between nations and the confrontations within nations. There have also been signs of hope in the resolution of the civil war in Sudan, the end of direct super-power involvement in Indochina, the changed situation in Portugal, and so on.

During this period, too, the whole economic system which has dominated the world for the past two hundred years began breaking down. The growing pollution of the environment, the population explosion, the world monetary crisis, the world crisis in food and other commodities, the widening gap between rich and poor within and between nations have converged to create a situation which threatens the very future of international society. Human beings have reacted to these threats to their peace and survival in different ways. Three types of response can be discerned in

articular. A first reaction is to seek salvation and security in remaining
ignorant of or evading the issues by such means as pursuing one's own
personal or group interests, by refusing to be involved, by retreating into a
private world of self-indulgence, or drug taking, or of mystical and religious escape. The second reaction is to endeavour to exorcize the dangers we
face by forcing them into the rigidities of a reassuring ideological or
religious system which explains everything and explains it away. The third
reaction is to face the dangers head on with open eyes, deploying all the
resources of vision, imagination, reason and skills at one's disposal in
order to understand and interpret the dangers in their full reality and to be
free to discover and attempt new ways of overcoming them in cooperation
rather than confrontation.

It is, I think, important for us to reflect on these various responses to our
human situation in terms of what we have been attempting to do in the
ecumenical movement and as Christians and churches. Two facts stand out
very clearly as we review the work we have been tackling during these
seven years in the World Council. First, our programmes, activities and
emphases have constantly sought to be relevant to the challenges of our
time. We have strained every nerve of faith and obedience to meet these
challenges. We may not have achieved a great deal, but, in our fumbling
way, we are there in the midst of the travail of our fellow human beings
seeking to discover what God is saying and doing in his world on the
foundation of what he has said and done as disclosed in the Word of
Scripture and the Word made flesh in Christ, and as discerned through the
centuries by his people. Secondly, it can be said that we have tried to
avoid the first two reactions, and have opted for the third response as the
way of faith, hope and love. This is not, of course, an option peculiar to us
in these years. It has from the beginning constituted the ecumenical
movement's very purpose for existence. We are inheritors of the tradition
which is expressed in the words of J.H. Oldham‡: "We must dare in order
to know"; and of Dietrich Bonhoeffer‡: "We shall only know what we
do". The daring and the doing are the effect of faith, the ever-renewed and
tested conviction that the Lord of the *oikoumene*‡, the whole inhabited
earth, has indeed conquered the principalities and powers, and entrusts us
with his strength and wisdom, through the Holy Spirit, to discern his will
and do it in and through the threats and challenges of our time. There is no
way back for us into an escapism either of disengagement or of setting up
theological or dogmatic walls of defence.

What does all this mean for the fellowship of the World Council? The
reality is that in this period under review our fellowship has been profoundly
tested and all sorts of tensions have been revealed. How should we interpret
this experience of testing? What does it say to us about the nature of our

fellowship in the World Council? Let me suggest some concerns which have been crystallizing since Uppsala.

(1) As the peoples of the world have become increasingly interdependent and as the issues facing each nation concern all, so there is a close inter-relationship between the various programmes of the World Council. But these programmes are carried out by different departments or sub-units, serving different constituencies and guided by different committees. It is true that Central Committee is the co-ordinating body of all these programmes. Nevertheless, historic or new concerns have tended to develop according to their own momentum.

Part of the problem is that Member Churches are often not aware of the comprehensive and varied character of the programmes of the Council. Many churches are more aware of some programmes than of others be-cause of their involvement or lack of it. Due to inadequate communication and interpretation and indeed to the fact that the work of the World Council is often known only from the mass media, there is a widespread impression that the work is one-sided, dwelling upon certain aspects (for instance, the especially social and political issues) rather than on others. Of course, it is possible to argue that serving over 270 churches in more than 90 countries, and also different groups within and beyond them, calls for a variety of approaches. But it may well be that the immense challenges of our time and the limited resources at our disposal call for greater concentration of effort in order to facilitate the more widespread participation of the Member Churches of the Council in facing these challenges. As we reflect on what we have been doing and on the ways we have initiated and developed programmes, and as we prepare for the period after the Fifth Assembly, it is essential that we find more effective ways of avoiding overlap in programmes and achieving greater intensification in our work— thus facilitating communication with the churches—without losing the diversity of approaches which are called for.

(2) The concern for coordination and concentration of effort is related to the issue of how the operations of the World Council are funded. The WCC has a General Budget which is supported by the contributions of the central treasuries of the Member Churches. Then there are several other budgets which reflect the structural and funding patterns within the Member Churches: these are the budgets of the Commission on Inter-Church Aid, Refugee and World Service, the Commission on World Mission and Evangelism and its sponsored agencies, the Commission on the Churches' Participation in Development, the Office of Education. These latter sections of the World Council often command more adequate resources than those which must rely on the General Budget and are able to embark on programmes which, while worthwhile, may overlap or be in competition with, and may even be of less priority than, similar programmes elsewhere. Moreover, such

is the tight funding of the General Budget that the programmes of the departments covered by that Budget have to be financed by specially raised Programme Project money. The staff has to spend time soliciting these funds from wherever they can find them. This highly unsatisfactory state of affairs has hindered the effectiveness of the Council and has discouraged the Member Churches from feeling fully responsible for what is being done by the Council on their behalf. Furthermore, the current monetary crisis has revealed the profound weakness of the financial structure of the World Council—an intolerable condition for a body called to do so much and to serve so many.

The Finance Committee has often drawn attention to this problem and exhorted the Council to work towards a coordinated budget. Attempts have been made to meet this demand. However, it must be borne in mind that the structures of funding of the World Council reflect, and have largely been imposed by, similar structures of the Member Churches and their agencies. Any radical changes in the financing of the Council will be ineffectual unless the churches themselves re-examine their own ways of funding and of involving their members.

(3) The issues so far raised deal with matters of structure and finance, though they greatly affect the relationship between the Council and the Member Churches and also the capacity of the Council to meet the challenges of today with the wholeness of the Gospel. But any consideration of the work of the Council must probe deeper into the relations with and between the churches. The Uppsala Assembly and the Central Committee, with the assistance of various councils, committees and the staff, have sought to discern the burning issues of our day, both as regards the life of the churches and their calling to renewal and unity, and the life of society as a whole. We have endeavoured to bring Christian thinking to bear upon them and to be messengers of hope in word and deed. But the question must be asked: Do the Member Churches themselves seek to do the things which their representatives require of the World Council? If there is ignorance, incomprehension or—in a few places—even hostility concerning the work of the World Council, is it because it has little counterpart in what is going on in our churches? The impression I have is that many of our congregations are engaged in styles of worship, Christian nurture and programme activities which are so geared to maintaining a certain "spiritual-security-at-all-costs" that they come perilously near to the first two reactions to the threats and challenges of our time that I have described earlier. Many of our people have been so trained in their faith and life that they find it extremely difficult and even dangerous to face the issues of Church and community openly and fearlessly. It must also be said that, by and large, Member Churches have not found it easy to translate insights hammered out in ecumenical debate and frontier action into the life and thinking of the congregations. This "involvement gap" is widening. We

must find ways of closing the gap, lest it cause incalculable harm to the ecumenical movement and especially to the effective witness of the churches themselves in today's world.

This situation heightens conflict between the rich Northern Hemisphere and the poor, industrially underdeveloped South. There is a sense in which the churches in the South have no alternative but to face the challenges of our time because they are the principal sufferers in our world today. This is not to say that they are more alert and ecumenically active than the churches of the North, because their whole life and structure have been influenced by the churches of the North and they have the same human propensities for seeking to escape from facing the harsh realities around them. But this is less possible for them than for the churches in affluent countries. It is therefore easier for leaders of churches in the South to encourage and give their moral and verbal support to the programmes of the World Council than for those who come from the North, who have to deal with groups and individuals who are suspicious of what the Council is doing. Here, again, is an element which needs to be looked into more closely because it raises questions about the commitment of the churches to the World Council and to one another. What, for example, is the ecumenical significance of churches in the rich North being tempted to curtail their financial contributions to the World Council because of programmes of which many of their members and powerful vested interests within their own countries do not approve? What is at stake here is not simply a policy disagreement between a minority of Member Churches, on the one hand, and the Central Committee, on the other. Rather what is at stake is the meaning of ecumenical commitment for a divided Church in a divided world.

How do the vast majority of our church members learn? How do they distinguish between what is new and creative over against what are novelties and ephemeral? How do they become open to receiving and sharing their faith with people from cultures other than their own? As we take these questions seriously to heart, we face again the recurring problem that membership in the World Council, for many in our constituency, is not perceived as imposing any deep obligation on the churches. I believe that we shall have to give urgent consideration to this matter at the Assembly and in the coming years. Dietrich Bonhoeffer once warned us against "cheap grace". Were he here with us now, he would use equally strong language to denounce the delusion of "cheap ecumenism". Like God's commitment to the *oikoumene* the churches' commitment cannot be cheap and comfortable, for the commitment to which they are called goes the way of the Cross.

(4) The claim made earlier that the programmes and activities of the World Council over these years have been a relevant response to the cries

of human anguish and have been carried out in a bold and open confrontation with the issues puts the searchlight on those who initiate and carry out those programmes and activities—namely, members of Central Committee, other policy-making committees and especially the staff. The mass media and many church leaders and individuals sometimes portray the World Council as though it consisted of committee members and staff over against the Member Churches. This places an intolerable burden of responsibility on us, and particularly on the staff who are often on the receiving end of sharp criticism and innuendoes.

In addressing myself to this matter, I do not wish to be apologetic for our committee members and staff. We represent the diversities of confessions and cultures in our world. We have felt the call to participate fully in this ecumenical movement with all the risks and challenges involved. We have been enabled to be engaged in situations and to acquire knowledge and insights which are denied to most of our church members. We are sometimes tempted to impatience and proud annoyance with our churches for not seeing what we see and not doing what we are endeavouring to do. Moreover, our particular situation within the World Council as staff and committees has perils of its own. We share the contradictions of our world, including the urge to escape from the realities of our own lives into various, perhaps sophisticated forms of security. The strains and stresses of having to shoulder some of the anguished world's burden are bound to take their toll on our spiritual resources.

What I am trying to say is that the World Council and its committees and its staff face fundamentally the same challenges in faith and faithfulness as everyone else. There is no room here for the "we-they" attitude which has become prevalent in some circles and which threatens our usefulness as a Council and as churches. We shall have to learn afresh the meaning of repentance, the turning away of ourselves from ourselves to our common Lord whose we are and whom we serve. This means that we must, in the midst of our ecumenical obedience, relentlessly expose ourselves as a Council and as churches to the purifying Word of the Cross that we may be again and again renewed in mind and heart for real and costly commitment to one another and to the cause of the unity of God's people and of the peoples of the world whom he redeemed in Christ and whom he loves. In the process we may discover a new simplicity and spontaneity of living, a new openness to one another and a new patience with one another which are indispensable for the pilgrim people of God working for radical change in our world towards a more human existence in justice and community.

The issues I have tried to raise point to our preparations for the forthcoming Assembly under the theme "Jesus Christ Frees and Unites". It will be the most representative Assembly we shall have had, bringing to its deliberations all the diversities of faith and culture in our world today. It will be an occasion for coming to terms with the cries of anguish and the harsh realities of our world calling for a variety of responses, and yet in the face of severely limited human and financial resources. It will be an encounter of those who participate in the conflicts, the hatreds, the agonies of our nations: our fellowship, therefore, will be very sorely tested. It will, above all, be an opportunity to explore together our common faith in Christ who breaks our many fetters, who draws us together for the sake of others, who sends us forth as servants of his liberating, reconciling love.

1
general secretariat

The World Council of Churches: A
Fellowship...But What Kind of Fellowship?

When the World Council of Churches came into being in 1948, its founders described their new council as "a fellowship of churches". But what was at first the prophetic endeavour of a closely knit circle of visionary individuals has over the past quarter-century become a movement more fully involving the churches themselves. In the course of this development the World Council has constantly widened in scope. So at several stages it has proved necessary to re-interpret and to re-define the character and aspirations of this fellowship.

Many years have passed since the statement on "The Church, the churches and the World Council of Churches"* was adopted by the WCC Central Committee at Toronto in 1950. That statement—in attempting to define what the World Council was, and what it was *not*—went a long way towards clearing up fears which had arisen in some minds that a Super-Church had been formed, claiming the kind of authority possessed by the Ecumenical Councils of the ancient Church. Yet in many different contexts today the question about the ecclesiological‡ significance of the World Council is being asked afresh. Can the fellowship of churches in this Council be considered as an "ecclesial reality"? What would this imply for the understanding of membership in the Council? The time is far from ripe for a definitive answer to such questions. But the questions are being raised, and they cannot be ignored.

Meanwhile the period since the Assembly at Uppsala has offered particular opportunities to test the Council's fellowship in critical conflict and to advance together towards a fuller understanding of the ecumenical commitment. The question: *What kind of fellowship?* can be seen to underlie many of the discussions in the Central Committee during these years. And one important answer to it has been given in the revised Constitution of the WCC, which will be brought to the Nairobi Assembly for ratification. For the first time, the Constitution formulates in a positive way the basic function of the Council, namely "to call the churches to the goal of visible unity in one faith and one eucharistic fellowship expressed in worship and in common life in Christ, and to advance towards that unity in order that the world may believe".

* The Ecumenical Review, Vol. III No. 1, October 1950, pages 47-53. Available as a separate pamphlet: Geneva: WCC, 1950.

An Inclusive Fellowship

What kind of fellowship? A few figures to begin with. Membership in the World Council has almost doubled since its beginnings in 1948. This growth has continued in the period since the Assembly at Uppsala (see Box). Between the Assembly and the 1974 meeting of the Central Committee 31 churches were accepted into membership. A further 8 churches have been received as Associate Member Churches. Several churches were formerly represented through other churches but have become members in their own right. Seven church unions have been consummated between WCC Member Churches involving 19 churches. Including the 6 Member Churches received at Uppsala, this represents the largest single increase in membership between two Assemblies, bringing the total number of Member Churches to 271 in more than 90 countries.

Among the new Member Churches, 17 come from Africa, 12 from Asia and Australasia, 11 from Latin America and the Caribbean, 3 from Europe and 1 from North America. Thus the extension of the constituency into the Southern hemisphere has continued, with more than half the total membership of the World Council coming from this area. It is especially interesting to note the coming into membership in 1969 of the Evangelical Pentecostal Church "O Brasil para Cristo", as well as the Church of Christ on Earth by the Prophet Simon Kimbangu‡. These two churches represent two quite recent Christian traditions, and they have thereby contributed significantly to the inclusiveness of the World Council of Churches.

Similar developments can also be reported in national ecumenical organizations. Since the Uppsala Assembly, 6 additional National Christian Councils have been recognized as associated with the World Council of Churches, bringing the total number of such Councils to 27. A further 29 Councils are affiliated to the Commission on World Mission and Evangelism, and another 34 Councils maintain working relationships with the World Council, though not formally associated with it. Their number has more than doubled since the Uppsala Assembly. The World Council is thus in relationship with 90 national ecumenical organizations, which means that the great majority of its Member Churches are in fellowship with each other on the national level as well.

The growth and strengthening of Regional Conferences of Churches has also continued in recent years. A new Caribbean Conference of Churches (CCC) was created in November 1973, including the Roman Catholic Church as a full member. In May 1974, the former Near East Christian Council was reconstituted as the Middle East Council of Churches (MECC), bringing into ecumenical fellowship for the first time all the historic Orthodox churches in the area, together with the Protestant

NEW MEMBER CHURCHES 1968 - 1974

UPPSALA 1968

The Evangelical Lutheran Church in Southern Africa--Transvaal Region
The Methodist Church in Kenya
The Moravian Church in South Africa Eastern Province

Associate Member Churches

Eglise Protestante Africaine, Cameroon
    (The African Protestant Church)
Iglesia Metodista en Cuba
    (The Methodist Church in Cuba)

CANTERBURY 1969

Eglise du Christ sur la Terre par le Prophète Simon Kimbangu, Zaïre
    (The Church of Christ on Earth by the Prophet Simon Kimbangu)
Gereja Batak Karo Protestan, Indonesia
    (Karo Batak Protestant Church)
Igreja Evangélica Pentecostal "O Brasil para Cristo"
    (The Evangelical Pentecostal Church "Brazil for Christ")
The Moravian Church in Jamaica
Staro-Katolickiego Kosciola Mariatowitow w PRL
    (The Old Catholic Mariavite Church in Poland)

Associate Member Churches

Iglesia Evangélica Luterana Unida, Argentina
    (The United Evangelical Lutheran Church)
Presbytery of Liberia

ADDIS ABABA 1971

The Church of Pakistan
The Church of the Province of Burma
The Church of the Province of Kenya
The Church of the Province of Tanzania
De Gereformeerde Kerken in Nederland
    (The Reformed Churches in the Netherlands)
Iglesia Evangélica Metodista Argentina
    (Evangelical Methodist Church of Argentina)

churches. The former East Asia Christian Conference has also been reshaped into the Christian Conference of Asia (CCA). This change of name after almost 15 years of existence symbolizes the increased importance of regional ecumenical work in Asia.

An Inter-related Fellowship

Significant as this numerical increase and geographical spread of the WCC's constituency may be, it does not in itself provide an answer to the question: What kind of fellowship? In fact, it raises new questions. How is fellowship maintained on these various levels? How can the increased quantity of association be matched by an enhanced quality and inclusiveness of the fellowship? It is perhaps in the area of relationships with the constituency in the widest sense that the World Council is facing the most critical test of its fellowship today. Far from having found satisfactory answers already, the Central Committee has struggled with these questions repeatedly.

It may be helpful to distinguish three levels of relationships: participation, communication, and visitation—together with the general issue of decentralizing the ecumenical movement—and to discuss the critical challenges as they have arisen in these four areas.

Participation. The World Council of Churches is founded on the principle of representative participation by its constituency in the work and decisions of its constitutional bodies. Significantly, an increasing number of Member Churches are beginning to acknowledge the importance of this representative function. However, representative participation is limited in many ways. The Assembly is the only body in which every Member Church is represented by at least one delegate. Yet many Member Churches very rarely find one of their representatives appointed to a WCC committee. Further, any list of participants in World Council meetings will show that in most cases the Member Churches are represented by church officials or "experts". In spite of serious efforts to make its constitutional bodies more representative of the actual life of the churches and of the world-wide spread of its constituency, the World Council has not been able to break through the limitations which most of its Member Churches face in their synodical life as well.

Representation and participation point to a mutual relationship. Representative delegates should express the voice and the opinion of their churches. At the same time, they are also called to be representative messengers of the ecumenical fellowship within their respective churches and regions. Churches are beginning to recognize this double function and to make provision for it in their own structures. Much more, however, needs

NEW MEMBER CHURCHES 1968 - 1974

ADDIS ABABA 1971 con'd.

Latvijas Evangeliska Luteriska Baznica
(The Latvian Evangelical Lutheran Church)

The Methodist Church in Malaysia and Singapore

The Moravian Church, Eastern West Indies Province

The Nigerian Baptist Convention

The United Church in Papua, New Guinea and the Solomon Islands

Associate Member Churches

Iglesia Evangélica Metodista en Bolivia
(The Evangelical Methodist Church in Bolivia)

Iglesia Evangélica Metodista en el Uruguay
(The Evangelical Methodist Church in Uruguay)

Iglesia Metodista de Chile
(The Methodist Church of Chile)

UTRECHT 1972

Banua Niha Keriso Protestan Nias, Indonesia
(The Church of Nias)

Chiesa Evangelica Internazionale, Italy
(The International Evangelical Church)

The Church of North India

Eglise Presbyterienne au Zaïre
(The Presbyterian Church in Zaire)

Eglise Protestante Méthodiste au Dahomey-Togo
(The Protestant Methodist Church in Dahomey-Togo)

Iglesia Evangélica Metodista en las Islas Filipinas
(The Evangelical Methodist Church in the Philippines)

Igreja Reformada Latino Americana, Brazil
(The Latin American Reformed Church)

The Lutheran Church in Liberia

Associate Member Church

Iglesia Métodista del Peru
(The Methodist Church of Peru)

to be done in order to give delegated participation its proper role in developing relationships between the World Council of Churches and its Member Churches.

The World Council itself needs to examine its processes of decision-making in view of the limited participation by the whole constituency in these decisions. It has always provided room for minorities to express dissenting opinions. However, the more basic question has to be asked: can even a unanimous decision by the Central Committee any longer represent a unanimous agreement of the Member Churches? The pressure for common action by the Member Churches has increased since Uppsala. What is the status and authority of decisions or recommendations agreed on by the Central Committee, and how is the inclusiveness of the fellowship being maintained in the face of dissenting churches?

Communication. One of the basic functions of the World Council is to be an organ of communication. It is clear that communication and participation are two elements in the same process. It is equally clear that extending the World Council's constituency has made effective communication more important and more difficult at the same time. The constant exchange of correspondence between Member Churches and the World Council of Churches, and the distribution of WCC publications and periodicals (including the large number of newsletters issued by various sub-units), are no longer sufficient to maintain close communication between all parts of the constituency.

Any communication starts from listening to one another. Thus, as the Central Committee said in 1972, "We shall have to learn to be better and more humble listeners to one another. Listening is especially needed where the fellowship is rent apart by human tensions and where men can only affirm it in darkness". The Central Committee recognized that what the churches and their members want is more than communication from the World Council to Member Churches and to society at large: "They want more careful listening by the World Council to what is happening in the Member Churches and the world, and they want increased communication among the churches aided by the WCC. Through that process the Member Churches can have broader participation in the ecumenical movement, and the WCC can become a more effective organ of communication to, among and with the churches".

Listen to whom? Where it is recognized that communication begins with open ears, it becomes essential to ask who can speak for the churches and who can speak for the World Council of Churches. For all churches, and even more for the World Council itself, it has become increasingly difficult to speak with one voice. The authority of church leaders and synods is questioned in many places by those whom they supposedly represent.

NEW MEMBER CHURCHES 1968 - 1974

GENEVA 1973

Eglise du Christ au Zaïre: Communauté Lumière
    (Church of Christ in Zaire: Community of Christ the Light)
Eglise du Christ au Zaïre: Communauté Ménnonite
    (Church of Christ in Zaire: Mennonite Community)
Gereja Kristen Protestan Simalungun, Indonesia
    (Simalungun Protestant Christian Church)
The Japanese Orthodox Church

Associate Member Church

Eglise du Christ au Zaïre: Communauté Baptiste Episcopale
    (Church of Christ in Zaire: Episcopal Baptist Community)

WEST BERLIN 1974

Gereja Masehi Injili Sangihe Talaud, Indonesia
    (The Church of Sangihe Talaud)
Huria Kristen Indonesia
    (The Indonesian Christian Church)
The National Council of Community Churches, USA

Associate Member Church

Eglise Protestante d'Algérie
    (The Protestant Church of Algeria)

The World Council is criticized for maintaining communication only on the official level and for not being sufficiently responsive to the experiences and hopes of the so-called "grass roots". This is not a new dilemma, but it has been sharpened in recent years. There are situations where official church structures and ecumenical groups openly compete with each other's claims to be articulating the true voice of the Church in a particular matter. Again, the inclusiveness of the ecumenical fellowship is tested seriously in such cases.

On the other hand, who speaks for the World Council of Churches? It has become increasingly difficult for Member Churches to draw the proper line between official statements and communications from the Central Committee, its Chairman or the General Secretary on the one hand, and reports from consultations or even major papers presented by speakers at World Council meetings. As the critical interest in ecumenical discussions grows, it becomes more important to communicate their results to the various parts of the constituency. Therefore, in a number of cases, agreed reports have been replaced by individual accounts. In this way, communication may be improved, but a careful evaluation and reception of the results in the Member Churches may be rendered more difficult. Furthermore, as the agenda of the Central Committee and the Executive Committee has grown and certain items become more controversial, it has proved necessary for the General Secretary to write to the Member Churches after each meeting, interpreting the major decisions even before the formal minutes are available. These letters are an important link between the World Council and its constituency. More consultation is needed, however, on the questions of how to make such communications more useful for the Member Churches and how to bring them to bear on their own decision-making processes.

In this context, it is important to note that a number of Member Churches have addressed official communications to the World Council of Churches in the period since the Uppsala Assembly. Among these were messages from the Ecumenical Patriarchate‡ and the Holy Synod of the Russian Orthodox Church, to both of which formal replies were given.* Such exchange of messages could offer new ways of communication far beyond the churches immediately concerned. The most important task for the years ahead, however, will be to bring the churches into communication with each other.

Visitation. The experiences of recent years have underlined the fact that, even today, there is no better way of communicating and maintaining

---

* The Declaration of the Ecumenical Patriarchate appears in The Ecumenical Review, Vol. XXV No. 4, October 1973, pages 475-81. The response of the Officers of the WCC may be found in The Ecumenical Review, Vol. XXVI No. 2, April 1974, pages 326-8.

contact than through direct personal conversation and visitation. Thus, the travel of members of the World Council staff to all parts of the constituency has increased in value and importance. Formal delegations have been sent to several churches. In addition, meetings of WCC committees' in particular countries have proved to be invaluable occasions for mutual information, for the establishment of contacts and for the building up of understanding. Visits paid by representatives of Member Churches to the Secretariat in Geneva, as well as special consultations with particular Member Churches, have proved to be of highest value in improving relationships. Two visits by heads of churches in the period since Uppsala deserve special mention. On June 10, 1969, Pope Paul VI visited the Ecumenical Centre in Geneva. Even if the main value of this visit was symbolic, it has deeply influenced the development of further relationships with the Roman Catholic Church. In September 1973, the newly elected Patriarch, Pimen, of the Russian Orthodox Church came to Geneva at an important stage in the development of relationships with this particular Member Church. Further, in June 1974, an unprecedented visit was paid to the WCC by the whole presiding Council of the Evangelical Church in Germany.

Nor should it be forgotten that the Ecumenical Centre in Geneva is regularly visited by about 6,000 people each year. Many of them come in church-related groups with specific interests in the work of the World Council. The value of such contacts for furthering the ecumenical movement cannot be overestimated.

In the years since Uppsala, a large number of visits were made by General Secretaries Eugene Carson Blake and Philip Potter to Member Churches and to their governing bodies. Several of these journeys offered an opportunity to enter also into direct conversations with heads of states and governments. In particular, the visit to several countries in the Middle East in 1969, a visit to Czechoslovakia in 1970 and a visit to Algeria, as well as one to Chile, in 1971, should be mentioned. Many other members of the staff of the World Council have been invited to address meetings of synods, councils, and the like.

The example of the Secretary for Relationships with National and Regional Councils, who in a period of two years visited at least once all of the more than 80 Councils at the national level in all parts of the world, and equally all existing Regional Conferences, merits special note.

Visits of these various kinds—apart from their function of maintaining relationships and communication with the Member Churches and between them—can often fulfil a pastoral role. They offer opportunities for overcoming the sense of personal and spiritual isolation which often accompanies church leadership. They can express encouragement and solidarity to those carrying dangerous and highly unpopular responsibilities. And they are a means of sharing each other's burdens in the spirit of the Gospel. Thus they are one of the living links which maintain the World Council as a fellowship of mutual intercession.

But, even after all that has been said, it is evident that the World Council needs to develop a clearer "strategy of visitation". Only recently have initiatives been taken to plan and coordinate WCC travel in any comprehensive way, and to evaluate travel reports for the benefit of the work of the whole Council. How can the World Council best discover the ways of making visitation a real occasion for sharing in one another's joys and sufferings?

Decentralization. The extension of the World Council's constituency has been parallelled by an intensification of ecumenical work on the national and regional levels. An important World Consultation of Christian Councils was held at Geneva in 1971 under the auspices of the WCC. This was the first consultation of its kind, and regional meetings took place in various continents to follow up its recommendations. In addition, the meetings of the Central Committee have offered regular opportunities for representatives of National Councils to maintain relationships and to explore mutual concerns.

Decentralizing the ecumenical movement, therefore, is no longer an issue for the future, but a fact in the present situation. All the more must it be asked what the role of National and Regional Councils should be within the ecumenical movement and in relation to the World Council of Churches. At present a large proportion of WCC field programmes, staff visits and other activities are being referred to or handled through National Councils of Churches. This has placed a heavy burden on some of these Councils but has greatly facilitated the work of the World Council at the same time. In many countries, however, Member Churches have expressed concern that their needs and interests are not fully represented through NCC's. Even though this problem has to be solved in the first instance on the national level, it is clear that the situation presents a challenge to the World Council as well.

An equally strong challenge arises out of the work of Regional Conferences of Churches. The establishment of regional bodies in Asia and Africa, for instance, has strengthened considerably the voice of churches in these areas within the ecumenical movement. More and more, Regional Conferences assume tasks which were formerly carried out through the World Council. Many WCC programmes have been decentralized and the main responsibility handed over to regional bodies. Regional structures, however, are not yet equally well developed in all parts of the world. Questions concerning the relationships between national, regional and world ecumenical structures will need to be pursued. What are the specific functions of the regions within the world-wide ecumenical fellowship, and how can the inclusiveness of the fellowship be maintained in view of the increasing diversity of regional concerns?

A World-Wide Fellowship

The period since 1968 has been particularly important in recovering the true universality of the Church of Jesus Christ. At Uppsala the earlier emphasis on the unity of "all Christians in each place" was complemented by a fresh understanding of the unity of "all Christians in all places". Thus, the Assembly said that "in a time when human interdependence is so evident, it is the more imperative to make visible the bonds which unite Christians in universal fellowship". And, it added, "the churches need a new openness to the world in its aspirations, its achievements, its restlessness and its despair". This enlargement of the ecumenical vision to embrace the needs of the world and of humankind in its striving for unity and community has characterized the work of the WCC since its last Assembly. It has been affirmed afresh that the word "ecumenical" in its biblical sense refers to the whole inhabited earth, to the universal human community, and not only to fellowship among Christian churches. The emphasis on the unity of mankind as inseparable from the quest for the unity of the church runs through most of the reports from the Uppsala Assembly, and it has remained a predominant feature of the work of the World Council in the years since. The ecumenical movement, which was described at the New Delhi Assembly in 1961 as a truly "pan-Christian movement", has more and more become a movement for the whole world community.

Even a quick look at the programmes of the World Council reveals the considerable extension of the range of activities since the Uppsala Assembly. The Programme to Combat Racism and the Commission on the Churches' Participation in Development were created during these years. Another issue has developed since the Assembly into a major programme and policy item; the understanding, implementation and defence of Human Rights. Mention must also be made of a major study on Violence, Non-violence and the Struggle for Social Justice. In addition, technologists, scientists and theologians have participated in a wide-ranging process of reflection on the Future of Man and Society in a World of Science-based Technology, focussing on such issues as environment, genetics, population and the quality of life. It is no coincidence that all of these programmes have been initiated in the same period in which the World Council has created a special working group for Dialogue with People of Living Faiths and Ideologies. The concern for human community must be guided by respect for the wholeness of human life, including the religious and ideological convictions and the spirituality of men and women.

This widening of scope is also reflected in the area of international affairs. Since its inception, the World Council of Churches has made public pronouncements on urgent political issues of international concern and has maintained relationships with international organizations through its Commission of the Churches on International Affairs. The various statements issued since 1968 on the war in Indochina, the crisis in the Middle East, and the situation in Southern Africa have continued this tradition. However, the experience of the Nigerian conflict demonstrated that the dividing line between humanitarian and political involvement has become more and more difficult to draw. A similar lesson can be learned from assistance given to Palestinian refugees. Whether labelled "inter-church aid" or "international affairs" the World Council's actions have political implications which in recent years have been recognized more and more clearly. But what precisely is its responsibility in this sphere? Regardless of its self-understanding, there are growing indications that the World Council is accepted outside its own constituency as a recognizable and credible fellowship. More and more governments and secular institutions are appealing to the WCC as a moral authority on the world level.* But is this authority accepted also by the Member Churches, and can it have validity without such support? Should the World Council strive at all to exercise any—even very limited—moral suasion in the area of international political and social affairs?

The many controversies which have arisen in the years since Uppsala over positions which the World Council has taken on social and political issues have made it clear that the WCC is a fellowship including churches with frequently conflicting interests, commitments and loyalties. At Uppsala the tension between northern and southern hemispheres was in the forefront of the discussion. Meanwhile, a more differentiated picture is beginning to emerge, and the various regions and continents are asserting their individual identities. The relationships of churches in the ecumenical movement reflect to a large degree the antagonisms and tensions prevailing in the secular world of nations. They are tarnished by the same conflicts of power, access to resources, class, race and ideology. In the period since Uppsala it has become apparent that in many instances the traditional confessional divisions have been replaced by new ones, largely social in origin. Thus, the World Council of Churches is experiencing the divisions of mankind in its fellowship, and any search for the unity of the Church which is not coupled with the desire for true human community falls short of the goal.

This new situation has put the fellowship in the World Council under serious strain. In the letter which the Central Committee addressed to the Member Churches from Utrecht in 1972 on the theme "Committed to

* See The Churches in International Affairs, Geneva: WCC, 1974, pages 151-4., where a number of interesting comments on the WCC made by delegates to the UN General Assembly are reproduced.

Fellowship" two important insights are formulated. First, "we shall have
to learn to speak more openly to one another of the centre of our commitment". Thus we shall have to try again and again to relate our actions in
the social and political spheres to the action of God in Jesus Christ.
Secondly, "we shall have to learn to comprehend the priestly ministry of
liberating reconciliation and the prophetic ministry of liberating conflict".
We have not yet sufficiently integrated our belief and our action. These
two statements are a word of self-criticism'addressed to the World Council
as well as a guide for future action and reflection.

In a time when the conflicts and divisions of the human family find such
an immediate expression within the World Council of Churches and among
its Member Churches, the powerlessness of this fellowship is starkly
revealed. But such a situation has led equally to a new recognition of the
power of prayer and intercession. This spiritual dimension of fellowship is
beginning to receive new and serious attention, and it will have to influence future action and reflection in the WCC even more strongly than
heretofore.

An Expectant Fellowship

The fellowship of the World Council of Churches is open to all churches
which are able to accept its Basis. There are, however, individual churches
and groups of churches which, while being able to accept the Basis, have not
found it possible to join its membership. This is, of course, the case with the
Roman Catholic Church. But in recent years attention has equally been
focussed on the large group of evangelical churches and communities and
their relationship—or lack of it—with the WCC. Various pentecostal and
charismatic‡ churches should also be mentioned in this context. The World
Council will never cease to hope and work for fulfilment of its expectation of
becoming the instrument for the fellowship of all Christian churches. The
ecumenical movement, therefore, cannot and should not be seen as standing
over against the movement of evangelical churches, if for no other reason than
the simple fact that a large part of the constituency of the WCC is of
evangelical persuasion. The World Congress on Evangelization held at
Lausanne in July 1974 has reinforced this position and has opened many new
possibilities of contact and dialogue with those who are afraid of betraying
their evangelical calling by joining the WCC.

On several levels the WCC has tried during the past seven years to
translate its expectation of wider membership into actual dialogue.Two
series of conversations have been held in 1969 and 1971 with representatives of the Reformed Ecumenical Synod. The Commission on Faith and

Order not only has representatives from several non-Member Churches among its membership, it has sponsored a dialogue with representatives of the Seventh-Day Adventist Church. The results are now being studied on national and local levels. A special series of papers, "Ecumenical Exercises", has been published, including presentations of self by churches not in membership of the World Council, for the benefit of wider ecumenical discussion. In a few cases, the preparation of these papers has opened the way for later membership.

The relationship between the WCC and the Roman Catholic Church requires fuller discussion. It is clear that the World Council must not be understood as a fellowship of non-Roman Catholic churches. It is an instrument of the ecumenical movement as a whole, and the Roman Catholic Church has been a major and active part of the movement since the days of the Second Vatican Council at the latest. Therefore the Uppsala Assembly, when discussing relationships with the Roman Catholic Church, welcomed the growing collaboration which had become possible and expressed the hope that future work together would contribute to the further "growth and deeper unity of the ecumenical movement". What have the developments been since then?

The Joint Working Group (JWG) of the World Council of Churches and the Roman Catholic Church, which was established in 1965, has continued to be the main formal instrument of collaboration. After the Uppsala Assembly its membership was expanded from 14 to 24 persons in order to provide for a more representative group both in confessional and in geographical dimensions. The full group has met regularly once a year. A smaller executive body, chaired jointly by Philip Potter and Jan Cardinal Willebrands, President of the Vatican's Secretariat for Promoting Christian Unity, has met between the full sessions to carry out ongoing programme and to settle various matters of detail. From time to time the Joint Working Group has issued reports to its respective authorities on the activities which it has undertaken. The fourth such report is now being prepared and will be presented to the Fifth Assembly in Nairobi.

Collaboration with the Roman Catholic Church has become a normal part of how the World Council of Churches goes about its business. Nearly all of its Programme Units and agencies have established at least some contacts with their respective counterparts in the Roman Catholic Church. Two examples are particularly worth mentioning. As a result of the Uppsala Assembly's decision to invite Roman Catholic theologians to serve as full members of the Commission on Faith and Order, some 10% of the Commission is now made up of Roman Catholics, and numerous national and local Roman Catholic groups are associated with the Commission's work. Preparations for the annual Week of Prayer for Christian Unity are

so a common undertaking of the WCC's Faith and Order Commission
d the Secretariat for Promoting Christian Unity. Secondly, the Uppsala
ssembly approved plans for a Joint Committee on Society, Development
d Peace (SODEPAX), which was established for an initial period of
ree years until the end of 1971. During this time, it developed wide-
nging activities and served in many countries as a catalyst and stimulus
r ecumenical collaboration in the field of development. After the first
riod, however, its mandate was re-defined, and both staff and prog-
mme were considerably reduced. SODEPAX now serves primarily as a
ison between the Pontifical Commission on Justice and Peace and the
CC's Commission on the Churches' Participation in Development. In
cent years it has particularly concentrated its work on questions of trade
d economic justice in Asia, on efforts towards peace and reconciliation
Ireland, as well as on a survey and analysis of local, national and
gional ecumenical collaboration in the areas of society, development and
ace.

In addition to these two examples, the following areas of collaboration
ould be noted: world mission and evangelism; Christian medical work;
urch and society; dialogue with people of living faiths; service and relief
tivities; issues of laity, women and youth; and the field of international
fairs. The forms of collaboration vary from area to area. In some areas it
limited to regular consultations and exchange of information at staff
vel; in others, Roman Catholics are more directly and actively involved
the World Council's work.

Under the direct sponsorship of the Joint Working Group a study on
Common Witness and Proselytism" was conducted. The report which
sulted from this effort was published in 1971 and given wide circulation.
attempts to define the attitude which should inspire the churches in their
tual relations. The Joint Working Group also regularly surveyed and
scussed Roman Catholic involvement in regional, national and local
umenical structures. Under its auspices a detailed report on the subject
s worked out. Although the situation varies from country to country, the
mber of National and even Regional Councils enjoying full Roman
tholic membership is steadily increasing. This development is of con-
derable importance for the future of the ecumenical movement.

But what then, of the possibility of the Roman Catholic Church becom-
g a member of the World Council of Churches? The Uppsala Assembly
couraged the Joint Working Group "to continue to give attention to the
estion", and a study on "Patterns of Relationships Between the Roman
tholic Church and the WCC" was begun in 1969. This exploration was
ven further stimulus by His Holiness Paul VI later in the same year on
occasion of his visit to the Ecumenical Centre in Geneva. "In fraternal
nkness", he declared, "we do not consider that the question of mem-

bership of the Catholic Church in the World Council of Churches is so mature that a positive answer could or should be given.... It requires profound study and commits us to a way that honesty recognizes could be long and difficult''. The results of the study, after two years of intensive work, were published in 1972. The report concludes that there are no basic theological, ecclesiological or canonical obstacles to Roman Catholic membership in the WCC. Obviously, an application for membership would raise delicate problems for both sides, but the report states the conviction that they could be resolved without violating the nature either of the Roman Catholic Church or the World Council of Churches. When the report was published it had already become clear that for the time being the Roman Catholic Church was not prepared to commit itself to the possibility of membership. The preface to the report, signed by Cardinal Willebrands and Eugene Carson Blake, puts the matter bluntly: membership was ''not expected in the near future'' * This does not, of course, mean that the question could not be re-opened at a later date.

Where does this leave future relations between the Roman Catholic Church and the World Council? Collaboration should certainly not be reduced. ''All are convinced'', the preface to the membership report goes on to say, ''that cooperation between the bodies must not only continue, it must be intensified''. Nevertheless it must be recognized that the present pattern of relationship does not meet the Uppsala Assembly's ''conviction that the guiding principle of future effort should be to bring'' the *one* ecumenical movement ''towards complete manifestation''. The World Council of Churches must continue to present to the Roman Catholic Church the challenge inherent in this formulation. As long as the Roman Catholic Church remains outside the membership of the Council there will be limits to the collaboration possible between the two bodies. At the same time, however, the Roman Catholic understanding of the ecumenical movement presents a challenge to the World Council of Churches. Does the Council really live up to its own self-understanding? Is it the ''expectant fellowship'' which it claims to be? These questions will need to be faced in the future.

A Fellowship of Shared Resources

As a fellowship of churches the World Council is dependent on the willingness of its Member Churches to share their resources with each other in pursuing their common goal. The WCC has always included rich and poor churches in its fellowship. The tensions arising from this differ-

* Patterns of Relationships between the Roman Catholic Church and the World Council of Churches. Geneva: WCC, 1972. (An offprint from The Ecumenical Review, Vol. XXIV No. 3, July 1972, pages 247-88.)

ence in access to resources have increased considerably in the period since the Fourth Assembly. The discussions about a moratorium on financial and personnel assistance, the future of Inter-Church Aid, and the Ecumenical Sharing of Personnel, which are reported in detail in later sections of this report, serve to underline these conflicts. The World Council has still to find ways of holding rich and poor together in the same fellowship without endangering their integrity.

However, the World Council of Churches itself is part of this conflict about access to resources. For many of its Member Churches the World Council has become a major channel for the distribution of funds which are essential for their life. It is thus placed on the side of the rich and experiences the ambivalence of financial power. The increasing availability of funds from governments and international organizations for particular WCC activites has only reinforced this situation of ambiguity. On the other hand, the World Council is dependent for its central activities on contributions from Member Churches and thus is affected by their decisions and priorities.

During most of the period since Uppsala the World Council has faced major financial difficulties, for two main reasons. First, the world-wide financial crisis has resulted in a considerable loss in value of certain currencies on which the World Council has traditionally relied very much for its income. Secondly, financial difficulties occurring inside certain Member Churches have led to a decrease in funds available for international and ecumenical tasks.

So far it has been possible to avoid a major financial breakdown in our activities thanks on the one hand to the constant reallocation of the available resources and, on the other hand, to the willingness of certain churches, institutions and foundations to make available special additional funds which had not originally been anticipated. Special mention should be made of the churches in the Federal Republic of Germany, which not only have increased their annual contributions as requested but also have provided funds over and above their normal annual contributions. However, the financial difficulties are far from resolved, and the Fifth Assembly will have to find ways and means of ensuring the financial resources necessary for the work to which it commits the World Council in the years beyond Nairobi.

Re-adjusting available resources has in a number of cases meant cutting programmes and reducing staff. It has also meant restricted participation in World Council activities by representatives from certain parts of the world due to lack of funds for travel subsidies. When the Central Committee met in January 1971, a Committee on Programme Priorities was established to consider procedures by which priorities of programme and activities could be examined and determined. Since income for the General Budget was, and has remained, inadequate to finance the full programme authorized by the Central Committee, the Committee on Programme Priorities was asked to advise how orderly reductions in expenditure could be made and a balance between income and expenditure restored.

The Committee developed guidelines and a number of specific recommendations which were accepted by the Executive Committee in September 1971. The Priorities Committee was then reconstituted as a permanent sub-committee of the Executive Committee, meeting between and in conjunction with meetings of the Executive and Central Committees. It was given the mandate to make recommendations about priorities in the work of the WCC through a continuous evaluation of all activities both present and proposed, without focussing exclusively on financial considerations. Though many of its recommendations have not had to be implemented due to unexpected improvements in the overall financial situation, the work of this Committee has proved useful for the direction, coordination and supervision of all WCC activities. With the experience gained by this Committee, the World Council is in a better position to select programme emphases for the period after the Assembly.

However, no internal procedure for setting priorities can alter the fact that the World Council is dependent on the prior decisions concerning the use of resources taken in its Member Churches. The scarcity or abundance of funds for certain programmes of the World Council of Churches usually reflects decisions about priority which it has little chance of influencing. This may even result in imbalances which can distort the overall programme of the World Council. From a different angle, this raises once again the question: what kind of fellowship? How can and should the ecumenical commitment of the churches be expressed in their willingness to share resources? And, on the other hand, how can the WCC secure the funds necessary for its work and should it be ready to refuse certain funds in order to preserve the integrity of the fellowship?

AN ORGANIZED FELLOWSHIP...
BUT WHAT KIND OF ORGANIZATION?

Until Uppsala, the World Council of Churches followed structural patterns of work which were elaborated by the Second Assembly at Evanston in 1954. In the 20 years since then the size and complexity of the World Council have grown considerably. The WCC is serving many more churches in a far larger number of countries. Cultural and theological diversity has increased within the fellowship of the World Council, and former styles of work and decision-making proved inadequate to the new tasks ahead.

The time had come to consider how the work of the World Council should reflect this change in orientation and activity. The Uppsala Assembly therefore initiated a process which has led to significant changes in the overall structure of the World Council of Churches.

The New Structure

The Fourth Assembly authorized the appointment of a nucleus Structure Committee under the chairmanship of Bishop James K. Mathews. It was asked to study, among other things, the role and composition of the Assembly, the Committee structures of the World Council of Churches, and the organization of the Secretariat in Geneva. The Committee held four meetings and sought continued advice from a consultative group of Central Committee members as well as from staff. Intermediate reports and draft sections of the final report were submitted to the Executive Committee meetings at Geneva and Arnoldshain in 1970. The final report was presented to the Central Committee at its meeting at Addis Ababa in January 1971.

The Structure Committee was guided by two basic considerations. First, the structures of churches and ecumenical organizations clearly need to change as the context and challenges posed by society and by the churches themselves change. And secondly, there is no "right" structure and no such thing as a theology of structure. Any decisions about a new structure of the World Council of Churches must therefore be pragmatic ones.

In assessing the functions of an Assembly in the present complex ecumenical situation, the Structure Committee suggested that the Assembly must "be the occasion for a celebration which will include the conducting of business of the World Council of Churches; for worship and study; and an occasion for common Christian commitment. In its composition it will have to be both a representative body and an occasion for participation of a wider circle among the people of God". These guidelines have implications in particular for the style of an Assembly. As a result, it was decided that the responsibility for the detailed supervision of the ongoing work of the Units of the World Council of Churches should be removed from the Assembly and handed over to the Central Committee. It was further decided that formal programme sessions and plenary addresses should be reduced in number and that small working groups, as well as hearings and forums should be introduced instead. Concerning the composition of the Assembly, the Structure Committee recommended that Member Churches should be obliged to observe certain rules in selecting their delegates to assure a balance of church officials, parish ministers, laymen, women and young people. In addition, it was proposed that 15% of all delegates should be chosen by the Central Committee upon nomination by the churches in order to provide additional opportunities for achieving the necessary balance.

These recommendations reflect not only the insights gained from four Assemblies and many large world conferences; they also reflect some change in the self-understanding of the World Council. The Uppsala Assembly gave the Central Committee special authority to implement the new structure in planning the forthcoming Fifth Assembly. This event will therefore provide an opportunity for testing the wisdom of these recommendations and also the reservations expressed by some Member Churches, especially concerning the procedures adopted for the appointment of delegates.

In its recommendations concerning the administration of the World Council, the Structure Committee departed from the former Divisional structure in favour of three more flexible Programme Units, each grouping a number of sub-units. The titles of the three Programme Units ("Faith and Witness", "Justice and Service", "Education and Communication") were chosen to reflect the major functions of the World Council of Churches as laid down in the Constitution. Among the basic reasons for adopting this new structure were the following:

(a) the creation of administrative units with a broad mandate, with at the same time the possibility of concentrating on a number of very specific issues;

(b) the overcoming of separation between study and action;

(c) the encouragement of greater participation by the various segments of the constituency in the World Council's work.

In each of the three Programme Units, several sub-units were deliberately put into positions of "creative tension". The Programme Unit on Faith and Witness thus includes the Commissions on Faith and Order and on World Mission and Evangelism, and the Working Group on Church and Society as well as on Dialogue with People of Living Faiths and Ideologies. The Unit on Justice and Service includes the four Commissions on Inter-Church Aid, Refugee and World Service; on the Churches' Participation in Development; on International Affairs; and of the Programme to Combat Racism. In its original composition, the third Unit on Education and Communication included three Staff Working Groups on Education, on Renewal and on Communication as well as the Secretariat for Relationships with National and Regional Christian Councils. Since then the Central Committee has decided that the Department of Communication should instead be considered as a specialized unit related directly to the General Secretariat, and the General Secretariat has also assumed responsibility for relationships with National and Regional Councils. The Programme Unit has thus been renamed Education and Renewal, with two Working Groups as its constituent parts. In all three Units, the former Departments were redefined as more flexible sub-units. Each Unit was given a Unit Committee consisting partly of members of the Central Committee and partly of members of the governing bodies of the sub-units. Under the authority of the Central Committee the Unit Committees are responsible for general policy and budget decisions.

The Structure Committee was aware of the need for reflection and coordinated planning across the boundaries of the central objectives of the newly proposed structure. It also felt that the Units should not be conceived of as permanent and rigid structures: as new issues and programmes arose it was proper that they be given organizational expression. The Structure Committee anticipated that the transition from the old to the new structure would take time and that the process might develop differently in each of the three Programme Units. These differences are reflected in the following reports on the work of the Units and sub-units.

Immediately after the adoption of the structure proposals by the Central Committee at Addis Ababa, those which concerned the Assembly and the new administrative organization were put into effect. By the time of the Fifth Assembly, the Unit Committees will have met three times and have gained some experience with the new structure. The staff has begun to work cooperatively within the new pattern, and the suggested collegial style of decision-making has proved successful in most cases. Since, however, the various programmes of the sub-units had been developed before the implementation of the new structure, it is not yet possible to evaluate the results of these changes in any final sense. It is already evident that in certain cases adjustments will have to be made to avoid new complications. In particular, the relationships between the Central Committee, the Unit Committees and the governing bodies of the various sub-units need to be defined more clearly.

These changes have constitutional consequences. The Structure Committee therefore presented a revised version of the WCC Constitution which was provisionally adopted by the Central Committee at its meeting at Utrecht in 1972 and subsequently sent to the Member Churches for their approval. A final decision concerning the Constitution will have to be taken by the Assembly.

The WCC at Work

The *Central Committee* of the World Council of Churches has met five times since the last Assembly. Meetings were held at Canterbury, England (1969), Addis Ababa, Ethiopia (1971), and Utrecht, Netherlands (1972). The 1973 gathering, originally planned for Helsinki, had to be relocated in

Geneva for financial reasons. The fifth meeting was held in 1974 at West Berlin.

In addition to its general business the Central Committee selected one major issue for debate at each of its meetings. At its first meeting, the Committee concentrated its work on developing the detailed guidelines for the programme of the World Council in the coming years. A special communication interpreting the decisions of the Uppsala Assembly and the proposed programme directions was adopted and sent to the Member Churches. For the meeting at Addis Ababa, the theme of dialogue with people of other faiths was selected. At Utrecht, the nature of the fellowship of churches in the World Council was considered, and the Central Committee sent a letter to all Member Churches on the theme "Committed to Fellowship". The meeting at Geneva was marked by the celebration of the 25th Anniversary of the World Council of Churches, and major attention was given to discussing a report on "Violence, Nonviolence and the Struggle for Social Justice". The last session at West Berlin concentrated on preparations for the Assembly.

A number of representatives of World Council Commissions and Working Groups have been able to participate in the meetings of the Central Committee and make valuable contributions to the discussions. Since Addis Ababa a number of younger advisers have also been invited to attend the meetings of the Central Committee.

Meetings of the *Executive Committee* have taken place twice a year. The first meeting was held at Tulsa, USA, in January 1969. Meetings in 1970 took place in Geneva and Arnoldshain, FRG. In 1971 the Committee gathered in Addis Ababa and Sofia, Bulgaria. The meeting at Sofia provided a particular opportunity for contact with the Bulgarian Orthodox Church and other Member Churches in that country. Due to the generous help of the Russian Orthodox Church, the first meeting in 1972 could be held in Auckland, New Zealand, thus offering members and staff a chance to visit congregations in New Zealand and Australia. The second 1972 meeting took place as usual in conjunction with the Central Committee at Utrecht. Meetings in 1973 were held in Bangalore, India, and in Geneva. In 1974, the Executive Committee went to the German Democratic Republic and to West Berlin, using these occasions to strengthen ties with the various German Member Churches. Its January 1975 meeting was scheduled for Geneva.

The six *Presidents* of the World Council of Churches and its Honorary President have issued their traditional Whitsun Message every year. Many of them have participated in meetings of the Executive and Central Committees and have assumed important responsibilities in relation to the ongoing work. After the untimely death of Dr. D.T. Niles‡ in 1970, Dr.

(Mrs.) Kyoko T. Cho from Japan was elected to succeed him in the Presidium.

In the period since the Uppsala Assembly the *General Secretariat* of the World Council of Churches has undergone important changes in its task and composition. The most important was the election of Philip Potter to succeed Eugene Carson Blake as General Secretary, November 1, 1972. As this change in leadership occurred after the implementation of the new structure, certain other innovations were introduced as well. Under the former structure, the General Secretary was assisted in his task by two Assistant General Secretaries on the one hand and the heads of major Divisions in their capacities as Associate General Secretaries on the other. The Structure Committee had proposed instead one or two full-time Deputy General Secretaries with particular assignments from among the total range of responsibilities of the General Secretariat. The Central Committee in Geneva 1973 therefore agreed to appoint two Deputy General Secretaries, Alan Brash and Konrad Raiser, with major responsibility for relationships with Member Churches and National and Regional Councils, and for the coordination of programme, respectively.

Since 1968, the *Staff Executive Group* (SEG), consisting of senior staff members, has acted as an organ of collective reflection and has advised the General Secretary in all major decisions. After the new structure had been put into effect, the Staff Executive Group was reconstituted in order to make it more widely representative, not only of the various regions and confessions, but also of the concerns of women, laity and youth. This enlargement of the Group made it necessary to establish a smaller, cabinet-like body responsible for ongoing administrative matters. The full Staff Executive Group has remained the body to reflect about all long-range issues of policy and to take any major decisions of importance for the entire staff.

To assure the coordination of work in the World Council and to handle issues which concern several Units and sub-units at the same time, a number of Task Forces and Staff Coordinating Groups acting under the SEG have been established in recent years. Drawing their membership from all three Programme Units, these Task Forces have become important instruments for generating policy and implementing programmes. The flexibility of the new structure would suggest a greater use of such teams in the future work of the World Council.

Staff Relationships and Personnel Policy

The years since Uppsala have been marked by major changes in patterns of staff collaboration and in overall personnel policy. Implementation of

45

the new structure revealed a growing desire for more widespread participation and for a broader share in responsibility át all staff levels. Sharp criticism directed against lack of clarity in the processes of decision-making led to the formation of a Staff Representative Group in 1971. The Staff Representative Group, elected annually by all staff members, has helped to improve relationships.

Following an initiative originating in the Staff Representative Group, the Executive Committee authorized a study by a professional consultative firm of the personnel policy and the salary system of the World Council of Churches. The results of the study, submitted to the General Secretary in March 1973, revealed a number of severe shortcomings. The report pointed in particular to:

(a) the lack of an overall remuneration policy;

(b) the disproportionate relationship between basic salary and supplements or allowances;

(c) the often illogical relationship between job content and grade due to inaccurate job descriptions and the absence of uniform job analyses;

(d) the "class"-oriented conception of staff regulations which was contrary to the objectives of the WCC;

(e) the wide possibility for arbitrary and subjective interpretation of the staff regulations, many rules not being properly defined.

The study therefore proposed a single salary scale composed of 10 grades, the grade of each staff member depending on the classification of the post he/she holds, and on his/her ability to perform the functions that go with it. In this way, the basic salary of each staff member is related to job content, allowances being abolished to a great extent and any remaining allowances made the same for staff at all levels.

Following these basic proposals, a Personnel Officer was appointed in February 1973 to a newly created position with main responsibility in the field of personnel management. In collaboration with the Staff Representative Group, staff rules and regulations have been worked out and agreed upon. Job descriptions have been established for all staff, and on the basis of these job descriptions a board, nominated by the General Secretary, fulfilled the delicate task of grading each job in the WCC. With the approval of the Executive Committee the new salary system and the new staff rules were put into force on January 1, 1974.

The recruitment of staff has remained a subject of the greatest importance. During the past years there has been a marked effort on the part of the Executive Committee and the General Secretary to improve both the professional and the geographical balance of the staff. It should be noted that in 1969, 44 churches and 37 countries were represented on the staff.

In 1974, staff came from 49 churches and 45 countries. Within this interval the number of staff members from Africa, Asia and Latin America has in every case been more than doubled. But further improvement is necessary in the recruitment of Orthodox staff members and the appointment of women to leading positions.

Compared with the national structures of many Member Churches, and in the light of the considerable demands made upon it, the World Council works with a very limited number of staff (see Box). By decision of the Central Committee in 1971, no new staff positions have been created and many vacant posts have been left unfilled. The Central Committee, however, also expressed its firm conviction that the present level of staff had to be maintained if the forthcoming Assembly was to have responsible preparation. New directions will have to be given by the Assembly to bring the requirements of programme into harmony with the resources available.

In September 1974 the total staff of the World Council of Churches included 329 persons. The following table shows the movements of staff in the period since the Assembly at Uppsala.

	Arrivals	Departures	Total Personnel
1969	74	51	314
1970	76	58	373
1971	59	67	367
1972	87	75	320
1973	71	82	328
1974	35	34	329

Activities and Services Related to the General Secretariat

Most of the work of the World Council of Churches—as has already been shown on pages 42 and 43 of this chapter—is carried out in one or another of the three Programme Units: Faith and Witness, Justice and Service, and Education and Renewal.

There remain a number of activities and services of the WCC which benefit the Council's work as a whole and are therefore attached to the General Secretariat. Two of these, the Department of Finance and Central Services and the Department of Communication, are given chapters of their own later in this book.

I.   HUMANUM STUDIES

The Fourth Assembly in 1968 noted that among the various programmes of the World Council there was a "large measure of convergence of studies proposed on questions of the nature of man", in view of which it requested "the cooperation of all divisions and departments which share in this convergence, in coordinating studies related to the problem of man"; and it authorized the Central Committee "to appoint (i) a highly qualified full-time coordinator for a minimum period of three years to act as a research consultant or study adviser, and (ii) an *ad hoc* consultative committee to advise the coordinator for the studies on man".

Canon David Jenkins of the Queen's College in the University of Oxford was invited to take up this coordinating post. He was attached directly to the General Secretariat so as to be free to work with any part of the Council's activities as the development of his task seemed to require. He was given the title of "Director of Humanum Studies". The title, however, had little meaning at the time. There were no clearly defined groups of studies—or persons involved in study—to direct. Also, the word "Humanum"‡ was an odd one. Clearly it refers in some way to understandings of the nature of man and to questions about what is involved in being human, but it does not, in itself, point to any particular form or content of enquiry. The first task, therefore, was to identify the factors in the life of the WCC and its Member Churches which led to the setting up of the Humanum project.

Being Human

At the time of the Uppsala Assembly, many pressing concerns seemed to combine in raising two questions: *What is happening to man?* and *How should Christians faithfully understand and respond to these happenings?* In order to understand just how these questions currently arose and to discover clues as to how they could appropriately be faced, it was necessary to begin development of the studies by surveying a broad range of the Council's activities and by taking part in its various programmes.

This work provided material for a more precise reflection about the theological understanding of man. It also made clear that the behaviour and the beliefs of the churches are challenged at many points in the present man turbulence. *Science* and *technology* have put many powers into man hands and posed many problems for human society. These powers d problems have called in question not only what the churches have aditionally believed about man, but also their ability to make the Gospel ard as good news applicable to the present and future of man. In the alm of *politics* there has been an immense awakening of peoples, races d classes throughout the world. They demand the right to a human life d to a share in the resources of the world. This awakening calls in estion the fabric of all existing societies and their interconnections of de and military power. At the same time it challenges the churches nich have preached the Kingdom of God while being in open and hidden iance with various exploitative kingdoms of men. Likewise the very ospel is questioned also. From what source, if any, can men and women ally expect liberation, freedom and fulness of humanity? As to *culture*, it once again obvious that mankind is made up of a great variety of cultural d religious traditions and histories. The dominance of one culture, with nich both Christianity and science as historical phenomena have been ry largely associated, has been a temporary feature of history from nich the human race is emerging. But immense wrong has been done to n-Western cultures and countries. Once again the Church, which inevit- ly has particular cultural embodiments, is sharply called in question. us the concern about the Christian understanding of man reflects a sturbance of the self-understanding of the Church and of the understand- g of the relations between Christian identity and human identity.

A first reflection on the direction of the studies was given in a speech by Director to the Central Committee in Addis Ababa in January 1971. tention was focussed first on the limited nature of our present experience being human and on the structural and relational features which en- ngered human growth or promoted human distortion.

On the other hand, attention was drawn to the many ways in which vileged groups of human beings use power to dominate and distort the nan identity of others. How can Christians understand and receive the wer of Jesus Christ so as to combat the threats to humanity and develop promises of a larger humanity? Surely we must develop the clues presented by Jesus Christ as "the embodiment of transcendence in the dst of human life, Emmanuel, God with us and for us and as us, God sent in, and suffering with, human problems". Thus we should be rching together for "the way through the particularities to the one new n in Jesus Christ where there will be a universally shared fulfilment of our human particularities".

Such a move towards a common search for, and a common development what is involved and what is offered in being human will lead us into

49

both collaboration and conflict. Very sharp questions arise within the churches and the ecumenical movement and in the world at large about how our understanding of being human is in fact being expressed and pursued.

How to Do Theology

The circumstances, therefore, which had provoked the Assembly into appointing a Humanum coordinator to pursue the question: "What is man?" at the same time raised questions about the methods of pursuing theology and about the ways in which the Church expresses her life and calling. This tendency was confirmed by the work done between January 1971 and the meeting of the Central Committee at Utrecht in August 1972.

The Director continued to find the material for this work from the concerns of various departments. For example, a Humanum paper "Concerning Theological Reflection" was contributed to the study on the Role of Christians within Changing Institutions, one on "Problems of Biology and the Quality of Life" (concentrating on issues raised by developments in human genetics) to the study on Science and the Quality of Life, and one on "Human Rights from a Theological Perspective" was prepared for a meeting of the CCIA. Collaboration with the Ecumenical Institute at Bossey produced three consultations on "Human Capacity for Change", "Institutions and Change" and "Doctrine and Change".

Analysis of the above and other work led the Director to report to the 1972 meeting of the Central Committee as follows: "It is not the question: 'What is Man?' which I have been encountering in my studies, but men and women who are asking questions because of what is happening to them or because of what is not happening. How could there be one formulated answer about 'Man' relevant to all situations? The question: 'What is Man?' may, therefore, perhaps be shifted to the question: 'What resources do men and women have, and what resources might they have for living hopefully and creatively with the questions which their life in the world puts to their humanity?' Theology is relevant to this latter question because theology is about God. And the centre of the revelation of God in Jesus is what he has done for men, what he will do for us and, therefore, what he can now be discovered to be doing for us and how it can be part of our living and hoping. But 'theology' in practice all too often does not provide resources relevant for living humanly. So the question becomes: 'How can we do theology so that men and women can discover resources and hopes, corrections and encouragements in all that they have to face?' "

Thus the focus of the Humanum studies shifted to attempting to develop ways of "doing theology" which would set Christians free to share more faithfully and more hopefully, in the various struggles of men and women to be and become human. It is a part of Christian faith that the activity of God which is above all embodied in Jesus Christ offers to those who commit themselves to him an understanding and a promise of what is involved in being human which would not otherwise be available. Hence, in the deposit of Christian experience, understanding and expectation which we call "tradition" and "doctrine", we must expect to find vital clues to the sources and resources for being human at this or at any time.

Practical Ecclesiology

The phase of the studies which then developed had two aims. The first was to continue working within the activities of the Council in pursuit of the problems and possibilities of "doing theology". Examples of this type of work were a contribution entitled "Verbalization and its Limits" to the Faith and Witness study on "Confessing Christ Today" and work with the Language Task Force of the Programme Unit on Education and Renewal. Both of these were concerned with the implications and possibilities of the human being as a language-using animal and the ways in which the domination of one language or language-style distorts expressions of our humanness.

The second concern of the studies was to gather a consultative committee of men and women from as many parts of the world as possible who were particularly interested in working together to discern the results and emphases which should be contributed to the planning for the Fifth Assembly and the consideration of the World Council's studies and activities after Nairobi. It was this group which was charged with pointing to the theological emphases in the understanding of man which seemed of particular importance for the churches in their life in the world at this particular stage of history.

In preparation for the work of the Consultative Committee and as a means of summing up the general direction of the studies a paper was published entitled "Man's Inhumanity to Man" (*The Ecumenical Review*, Vol. XXV No. 1, January 1973, pages 5-28). Here the thesis was advanced concerning the product of the studies "(i) that what the WCC has potentially at its disposal is an extensive case-study relating to human and organizational response to change; (ii) that this case-study indicates many points at which both the WCC (at the level of staff operations, at the level of committee operations and at the level of relationships with churches) and the churches in their own lives need to learn and practice administrative and institutional repentance (which involves a great deal of personal and individual repentance; and which includes a very deep repentance about the ways in which the various traditions 'do theology'); and (iii) that this repentance is urgent because much in our activities and our lives is based on a false doctrine of man which shows itself in the fact that our work is often conducted in dehumanizing ways".

Thus the trend of the studies has been to indicate that concern with the question of man leads us back to a fresh concern with practical ecclesiology. We do not need and cannot have one "doctrine of man". Rather our question is: "What guidance do we obtain *in* the process and *for* the process of being and becoming human?" And this faces us with the question of how the Church can and should be at the disposal of being human, the being in the Image of the God who is love. It is not a question of knowing what it is to be human but of working together, through the Spirit of God, at being and becoming human.

The Humanum studies have been an experiment in a different style of study for the World Council of Churches. This style has been concerned not with its own product but with contributing challenge and help to other studies and activities of the Council. In so doing it may be that something can be learned and shared about the ways "by which the Church must live, bear witness and play her part in the whole humanizing work of God".*

II.   BIBLICAL STUDIES

Although the Portfolio for Biblical Studies was only established in May 1971, this does not mean that the World Council of Churches before that time was not interested in studying the Bible. Bible studies have been central to the ecumenical movement from the beginning. Theological reflection about the Bible has for many decades been carried on, first by the WCC's Division of Studies, and then by the Faith and Order Commission in particular. Bible studies have played a prominent role in programmes of the Ecumenical Institute at Bossey and have been an integral part of most WCC meetings. Finally, it should not be forgotten that the WCC has long collaborated with the United Bible Societies, which for several years appointed Study Secretaries who worked closely together with the WCC staff on special information and research projects, such as the Bible in world evangelism, Bible study methods and the study of the Old Testament.

Why the Portfolio was Established

The WCC claims to be "a fellowship of churches which confess the Lord Jesus Christ as God and Saviour *according to the Scriptures* and

*   These last phrases are taken from the Report of the Humanum Consultative Committee to the WCC Central Committee in 1974. See "The Anguish of Man, the Praise of God and the Repentance of the Church", Study Encounter, Vol. X No. 4, 1974 (SE/68).

herefore seek to fulfil together their common calling to the glory of the
ne God, Father, Son and Holy Spirit''. It was in order to explore more
eeply what it means to live, confess and act ''according to the Scrip-
ures'' as Christians, churches and a Council of Churches that this Port-
olio was inaugurated.

Much of the thinking and action of past and present WCC work is in fact
direct or indirect response to biblical judgement, promise and challenge.
However, no person and no movement can escape the danger of misusing
he Bible, of seeking only a ''biblical rationale''for what is already thought
nd done. One can easily become deaf to biblical judgement, gradually
eplacing the presence of the ever-astonishing Christ, witnessed to in the
Gospels, with a closed system of christology or ideology. The Portfolio for
iblical Studies has as a first task the concern that the voice of the God of
he Bible be heard as a judging and renewing power in the Council's work.

In many churches an important ministry has been left out. The Bible is
anslated, published and distributed, studied academically, preached and
aught. Above all, the Bible is placed at the centre of the Church's
orship. Yet one step more is needed: Biblical texts must become really
perative in the Christian style of life. This means that Bible study
enablers'' must be trained, and that a two-way system of traffic must be
et up, moving from the insights of biblical scholars to the every-day
ecisions of Christians and from the insights of Christians seeking to
ffirm their faith to those working in biblical research. The Portfolio for
iblical Studies has a special task in the field of this missing ministry.

The Portfolio can also become instrumental in building up relationships
ith groups such as conservative evangelical student movements, certain
iblical renewal movements within the Roman Catholic Church which
ften have little or no contact with the Catholic ''ecumenical wing'', with
rge parts of church life in Southern Africa, with staunchly conservative
vangelical churches inside and outside the WCC membership and with a
rowing number of persons and groups who have severed all relationships
ith the organized Church (including organized ecumenical work), but
ho maintain the discipline of Bible study. Churches and persons involved
present in the WCC's life and work can learn much from the above-
entioned groups; and, on the other hand, these groups need the correction
nd support of ecumenical fellowship.

The Work Accomplished so Far

From the beginning it was decided that the Director for Biblical Studies
ould work as a consultant, related to the General Secretariat, and collabo-
te with studies, meetings and work-projects organized by different WCC
its and by Member Churches. The small budget of the Portfolio was

financed from sources outside the regular WCC budget, especially with the help of gifts from churches in Western Europe and from several Bible Societies.

During the initial period of 3 years the needs and priorities with regard to biblical studies in the present ecumenical scene had to be discovered.* At the same time, relationships were established with national and international organizations working in the biblical field (for example, the Biblical Research Institute at the Lausanne University, and other such centres); with the United Bible Societies (with which the Director collaborated in a series of training courses on translation, interpretation and communication of the Bible); with the Roman Catholic Federation for the Biblical Apostolate; with the World Student Christian Federation (especially in their work of training for biblical thinking in the Asian region); with the World Alliance of YMCA's and the World YWCA (for whose 1971 World Assembly in Ghana the Director wrote the Bible study booklet); and with organizations publishing daily Bible reading notes and Bible correspondence courses.

Both in the initial period and later, the major work of the Director for Biblical Studies was concentrated on three tasks: (a) collaborating with ongoing studies and projects of WCC Units, (b) stimulating the training of Bible study enablers in different member churches and (c) carrying out a research project on the role of cultural factors in biblical interpretation.

(a) *Participation in WCC work*. With regard to the Programme Unit on Faith and Witness, the Director took part in the last stage of the Faith and Order study on "The Authority of the Bible" and in its current study on "Giving Account of the Hope that is in Us". Much work has been done in collaboration with the Committee on the Church and the Jewish People.**

The Director was also involved in the preparation for and the carrying through of Bible study at the World Mission Conference in Bangkok 1972/3. In the field of Church and Society there was some collaboration with the study on Violence and Nonviolence.*** Only a few working relationships have so far been established with the Programme Unit on Justice and Service, but for the Programme Unit on Education and Renewal the Director led the Bible studies at the joint WCC-Roman Catholic World Consultation on Laity Formation, Assisi 1974, and participated in the Task Force on Language Policy. For the whole World Council he has of course been involved in preparing Bible study materials for the Nairobi Assembly.

---

* See Hans-Ruedi Weber: "The Bible in Today's Ecumenical Movement" in The Ecumenical Review, Vol. XXIII No. 4, October 1971.

** See the paper by Hans-Ruedi Weber on "The Promise of the Land: Biblical Interpretation and the present situation in the Middle East", Study Encounter, Vol. VII No. 4, 1971 (SE/16), and the report of an enquiry on "Jewish-Christian Dialogue: a North Atlantic Affair?", The Ecumenical Review, Vol. XXV No. 2, April 1973, pages 216-21.

*** Hans-Ruedi Weber: "Freedom Fighter or Prince of Peace?", Study Encounter, Vol. VIII No. 4, 1972 (SE/32).

(b) *Leading Bible studies and stimulating training for Bible study enablers in member churches*. Since 1971 the Director has been asked to lead Bible studies at many ecumenical conferences and in local, regional and national study groups. In this connection three visits were made to Asia, three to Africa, two to the Middle East, two to North America, and several visits in Eastern and Western Europe. However, the emphasis has more and more been laid on the training of Bible study enablers. Information has been gathered about various methods of doing Bible study, the ways in which the Bible functions in worship, the use of audiovisual aids for Bible studies, and so on. A pamphlet on *Experiments in Bible Study*: Suggestions on Why and How to Do Them, was published in 1972. Pilot courses for the training of Bible study enablers were held at Geneva University in 1971 and in many parts of the world since then.

(c) *Research project on the role of cultural factors in biblical interpretation*. In the Humanum Studies and the current work of both the Commissions on Faith and Order and on Mission and Evangelism, the role of culture has been emphasized. What is the role of cultural factors in biblical interpretation? In order to examine this question and thus make a contribution to the above-mentioned studies, a research project was undertaken under the auspices of the Portfolio for Biblical Studies and the Biblical Research Institute of Lausanne University. For this the Director became a research fellow at Lausanne and received a grant from the Swiss National Fund for Scientific Research. The enquiry concentrates on how the event of crucifixion was interpreted in different cultural situations of the first century and is seen in several cultures today. In connection with the latter, local case-studies were conducted in different cultural situations, especially Korea, Indonesia, South Africa, Egypt, Italy, Czechoslovakia and the USA. The research will be concluded early in 1975, and a report will be published with the title, *The Cross of Christ and Culture*: Tradition and Interpretation of the Crucifixion Event in the Hellenistic Culture of the First Century and Different Cultures Today.

Decisions to be Taken for the Future

The Central Committee, when reviewing the work done by the Portfolio for Biblical Studies during its initial period, urged "the continuation of the Portfolio" and therefore requested "that every possible effort be made to secure adequate funding for the Portfolio". The Nairobi Assembly will have to decide whether it wants to endorse the Central Committee's views. It will also have to advise the staff whether the present style of work and the present priorities—collaboration in ongoing work of different WCC units and stimulation of the training for Bible study enablers in the member churches—are the right ones. Finally, the Post-Assembly Guidelines

Committee at Nairobi will have to decide whether the present rather haphazard way of financing the work of this Portfolio should be continued or whether its budget should become a normal part of the WCC General Budget.

III. THE ECUMENICAL INSTITUTE

During the period between the Fourth and Fifth Assemblies the Ecumenical Institute at Bossey continued its work as an ecumenical centre and as a meeting place for different cultures, continents and traditions. Its programme has given over 3,500 people from all over the world an opportunity to live, study and worship together, to discover the significance of the ecumenical movement for their lives and to reflect on the ways in which the Christian faith can be present in today's rapidly changing societies. Bossey is a centre of education within the WCC constituency where young people, especially students, can be introduced to the study of ecumenical topics in the context of an intercultural and international community. The already existing close relationship with other parts of the WCC staff has been further developed during these last seven years, and it is hoped that cooperation will progress further in the period after the Nairobi Assembly.

Encountering Modern Trends

The whole work of the Institute can be termed frontier work. This is true in particular for the so-called "specialized consultations" with scientists, sociologists, politicians and ecologists. The Institute has continued to organize this kind of meeting at least twice a year, often in close cooperation with different sub-units of the WCC. Through these consultations the educative programme of Bossey is fed with topics and new people, and Bossey is kept in touch with the new and ongoing trends in the scientific, social and political world. Some of the following topics give an idea of these consultations: "Industrial Democracy in a Technocratic Age", a consultation with representatives from managements, trade unions and government departments; "Alternatives to War"; "Man the Steward of Power" with specialists in cybernetics, scientists and biologists (1969); "Penal Policies", with criminologists, psychologists and prison administrators; "Law and Social Change", with lawyers and sociologists; "Man as a Physical Being", with psychotherapists, and physiologists (1970); "Industrial Production" (1971); "Capacity for Change", with scientists, psychologists and specialists in cybernetics; "Institutions and Change", with sociologists and planners (1972); "The Price of Progress", with ecologists, sociologists and philosophers; "Law in the Service of Human Needs", with lawyers, judges and legal specialists in international organi-

56

zations (1973); "Power and Property in the Use of World Resources", with economists and ecologists; "The Struggle for Fundamental Human Rights", with lawyers and politicians (1974), and so forth.

Included among the participants in these consultations were theologians with special expertise on the particular topic. In addition, a series of three special consultations was held on theological methodology today, with systematic theologians and a limited attendance of scientists. Further, two consultations with young people took place on the problem of the generation gap.

Ecumenical Training

Throughout these past seven years, ecumenical training has been carried on through the regular educational courses: (a. for pastors, priests and missionaries, b. for lay people, c. for theological students, d. on Orthodox theology and worship) although each year the themes, as well as the leaders (teaching staff) and guest speakers, changed. The courses profitted from the specialized consultations in terms of the selection and preparation of subjects (new trends in science and socio-political life, as well in systematic theology and ongoing experiments in church renewal). Here are examples of the topics which were studied: by theological students, "Futurology as a Challenge to the Churches" (1970); by pastors, "The Meaning of Transcendence Today" (1972); by lay people, "Decision-making in a Violent World" (1973). An attempt was also made to study one major topic from different perspectives in all regular courses during one year (for example, on "Change" in 1972) so as to achieve a concentration of efforts by the organizing staff. For two successive years the pastors' course studied the increase in charismatic‡ communities within and outside the normal church structures. Both attempts have had positive and convincing results.

The pattern of the training course for lay people has been slightly altered. A special effort was made to bring together non-theological students and young lay people, since those with a particular professional background were attending the specialized consultations. This meant, however, that a number of non-specialized lay people were excluded, a group for whom Bossey should also provide basic ecumenical training and experience. The Board therefore advised the staff to re-open the training course to this type of participant.

Academic Ecumenical Education

The Graduate School of Ecumenical Studies continued its work throughout the winter semesters, organized in collaboration with the Theological Faculty of the University of Geneva (in which the Bossey students are matriculated).

The following topics have been studied: "The Future of the Church" (1969/70); "The Bible: Contested and Contesting" (1970/71); "Participation in Change" (1971/72); "Dialogue on Salvation with People of Living Faiths and Ideologies" (1972/73); and "God's Action in a World Planned by Man" (1973/74). For the 1974/75 semester the subject of the Fifth Assembly of the WCC has been selected: "Jesus Christ Frees and Unites". The Graduate School, which is in session for 4½ months (from mid-October to the end of February) has increasingly emphasized seminar and group work as methodology for academic teaching. A closer relationship has been established with the Theological Faculty of the University of Geneva, and plans are under discussion to appoint a Roman Catholic professor of ecumenics and a Protestant research fellow, specially entrusted with the preparation of doctoral programmes, to serve both on the Faculty in Geneva and in the Graduate School. Due to this close cooperation and owing to the fact that well-known academic teachers have lectured in the Graduate School, the School, which in 1976 will have completed 25 years of existence, has won recognition for providing a new type of higher ecumenical education.

A field work programme is organized by the Graduate School for interested students who can spend a three-month period in a local situation, be it in a church (of other than their own denomination) or in an urban or industrial setting. The field work programme usually takes place in Britain, France, Germany or the Middle East.

It should also be mentioned that participants may acquire their doctoral degree "mention oecuménique" from the University of Geneva through the joint doctoral programme of the Graduate School and the Theological Faculty. During this period from Uppsala to Nairobi four Graduate School students have been awarded the doctoral degree.

Participants—Budget—Staff

The number of participants has increased over the past seven years. In 1969 and 1972 maximum figures were attained due to the addition of some extra consultations and courses, which were more fully attended than in other years. The course for lay people experienced a decrease in participation, but the seminar on Orthodox Theology and the course for pastors have shown a gradual increase in numbers. From the point of view of geographical representation, there is still an imbalance between participants from the North-Western quadrant and other parts of the world. This is due mainly to financial reasons: it is not possible to finance trips from Asia, Africa and Latin America for the summer programme of shorter courses. Participation in these courses consisted of people who happened

58

to be in Western Europe. From the point of view of confessional representation, an increase was seen in Orthodox and Roman Catholic participation.

Bossey continues to increase its work on a limited budget, but financial problems have forced the Institute to seek (with success) additional funds for its general budget and for the salaries of two of the four members of its teaching staff. However, this financial factor remains one of Bossey's major problems, due to the increase of its educational programme and the need to grant more study scholarships to participants from overseas countries.

The last seven years have seen many changes in the staff, the most important being a change in leadership of the Institute. The continuity of the work has been maintained, and these changes have allowed more people from different cultures, traditions and professions (including a biologist and a lawyer) to bring their specific contribution to the programme of studies.

Future Perspectives

In 1972/73, by invitation of the Executive Committee of the WCC, a five-member Committee made up of people from different areas, churches and cultures was asked to study and make recommendations about the future of the Ecumenical Institute. The Committee's report was adopted by the Board and endorsed by the Central Committee of the WCC. The report proposed that work at Bossey should be further supported by the WCC; that there should be more cooperation between the Units of the WCC and the Institute regarding the organization and running of the programme; that the study programme should concentrate on one topic for two consecutive years; that the Institute's activities should be more "mobile" to allow Bossey to function outside Europe; that links with the University of Geneva be maintained and further developed through the Graduate School; that there should be only one Director, one Associate Director and further members of the teaching staff (engaged on a short mandate of a minimum of two years); that the specialized consultations be continued in closer cooperation with the WCC Units; that there should be one Board of the Institute (instead of two) and that this Board should form a small academic committee to look after the administrative matters of the Graduate School. These recommendations are now being carried out.

In spite of changes during this period, the Institute has remained alert to new areas of interest and new trends of education which characterize the student world in contemporary society. There was greater flexibility in the programme of courses, and several attempts were made to introduce new learning patterns based on group dynamics and other processes of mutual sharing of knowledge and experience. This method of work should be further explored in the future in order to ensure a renewed and fresh approach in the field of ecumenical education.

IV.   THE LIBRARY

The Library at the Ecumenical Centre has now existed for almost thirty years, and it remains the most complete and best equipped ecumenical library in the world because of its relatively long existence and first-hand experience. The number of professors, students, pastors, priests, laymen and women within and outside the WCC Member Churches working in the WCC library does not diminish. Each year a dozen doctoral dissertations are started, continued or finished in the Ecumenical Library. The building in which it is housed, located within the Ecumenical Centre complex but set slightly apart from the main blocks of offices and meeting rooms, is a most congenial place to do research, catch up on the latest ecumenical periodicals or simply escape from the daily hustle and bustle.

At the end of 1968 the total library collection consisted of approximately 37,500 volumes; at the end of 1974 the total came close to 57,000 volumes, an increase of almost 20,000 volumes since the Uppsala Assembly. The WCC Library currently receives 600 periodicals and 200 mimeographed ecumenical serial publications. Besides a general annual acquisition budget of $7,000 the Library continues to purchase materials through special funds placed at its disposal. The United Presbyterian Church in the USA Fund and the Browne-Mayers Fund, which have become available since the Uppsala Assembly, deserve particular mention. Practically all periodicals are currently received through exchange with WCC journals. The Library's reference collection is now more than adequate and serves a great variety of needs. The Library possesses at present well over 150 doctoral dissertations on ecumenical subjects; these are mainly on microfilm.

The WCC archival collection now consists of approximately 11,000 boxes containing an estimated total of 16 to 18 million sheets of paper. Recently the archives of the Commission of the Churches on International Affairs London Office and parts of the archives of the WCC New York Office were shipped to Geneva. Also the World Student Christian Federation has transferred more of its archives to the WCC Library. The collection of various materials from National Councils of Churches has been greatly expanded. The Librarian published an article on "Treasures in the World Council of Churches Library" (*The Ecumenical Review*, Vol. XXII No. 2, April 1970), which describes in some detail the various archival collections of the World Council of Churches and its major predecessors in this century.

In addition to enhancing the WCC's own collections, the Librarian and
assistant Librarian have been active in sharing their expertise with other
institutions. The Librarian has had the privilege of serving as a consultant
to the Ecumenical Institute of Advanced Theological Studies at Jerusalem,
which is building a large new ecumenical library; to CERDIC-Publications
of the University of Strasbourg, who are publishing annually a Biblio-
graphical Repertory of Christian Institutions on computer; to IDOC, an
international documentation centre in Rome; to the "Interuniversitair Instituut voor Missiologie en Oecumenica" in Utrecht, Holland; and to
various other institutes and church organizations establishing or reorganiz-
ing an ecumenical library. The Assistant Librarian served as a consultant
to the "Centre Saint-Irénée" in Lyon, an ecumenical institute directed by
Father René Beaupère. The Librarian also made an extensive trip to Asia
in 1974, collecting Asian ecumenical materials and serving as a library and
archive consultant to various Asian churches and their ecumenical organizations.

A major event in the recent history of the Ecumenical Library was the
publication of a *Classified Catalogue of the Ecumenical Movement*, published in two volumes by G.K. Hall and Co. of Boston, USA, in 1972.
This catalogue lists and describes the most complete collection of literature
on the ecumenical movement in the 20th century, collected systematically
since 1946. It contains full documentation on several organs of the movement since 1910 and on the World Council of Churches since 1948. It also
includes a very complete collection of theological books and pamphlets
related to the ecumenical movement, and this in all modern languages.
Approximately 19,000 titles are fully described. And for the past five
years Dr. Charles Graves, Editor of the International Ecumenical Bibliography, has been working in the WCC Library. So far 8 volumes (1962 -
1969) have been published. This bibliography is the most scholarly and
comprehensive tool for ecumenical research. Each annual volume contains
600-700 pages. There are 60 contributors from all parts of the world.

Whatever new directions may be set for the World Council of Churches
after the Nairobi Assembly, the WCC Library will remain an indispensable
centre of international information and resources for studying the past,
present and future of the ecumenical movement. The Library's staff is
aware of its great privilege in rendering continuous service to a world-wide
constituency.

V.   THE NEW YORK OFFICE

Early Days

The World Council of Churches has maintained an office in New York
City throughout all the years of its existence. In fact, the history of the

office dates back even further. An American bureau of the Life and Work Movement—one of the ecumenical strands later woven together to form the WCC—was established as early as 1930. During the Second World War, what had in the meantime become the headquarters of the American Committee for the World Council of Churches (in Process of Formation) proved to be a vital link in the chain of fellowship and trust binding Christians caught on one side of the conflict or another.*

For a number of years after the WCC was founded in 1948, the Member Churches in the United States of America were in a unique position. They made up well over 30% of the World Council's constituency. At home they were growing in size and influence as never before in their history. Abroad their missionary endeavours took on a renewed vigour. And they were rich. Income was plentiful for the local and national activities of the churches, and little difficulty was experienced in finding funds for Christian projects overseas. In 1949 the American Member Churches were able to provide 83% of the income for the General Budget of the World Council. Yet at the same time, American public opinion was undergoing one of its periodic bouts of isolationism, given impetus by fears of communism. The WCC, having membership on both sides of the "Iron Curtain", was viewed with suspicion in some quarters. Further complicating the situation was the vastness of the nation and the diversity of the Member Churches within it.

Thus when the Second Assembly met in Evanston, Illinois, in 1954, few people doubted the wisdom of having a very active and fairly large office in New York, which was "at a long distance from Geneva" and was important "as a point of contact with extensive missionary and ecumenical interests". By the Uppsala Assembly fourteen years later the executive and programme staff of the New York Office had risen to a total of eight, with a supporting staff of fourteen.

But Why Maintain a New York Office Now?

Since Uppsala the situation has changed considerably in some respects. The most obvious difference, as far as the office itself is concerned, is that by 1970 members of the WCC Executive Committee were seriously questioning whether an office in the United States continued to be justified. And even if that were the case, could the World Council still afford so large a staff in New York? The answer to the second question turned out to be "no", and the programme staff was immediately reduced by half and later halved again. But the first question still remained, and the reduced

* The Memoirs of W.A. Visser 't Hooft (London: SCM Press; Philadelphia: Westminster Press, 1973) give a lively account of this period.

size of the office made it even more relevant and posed several other questions as well. Was it fair to have a regional office at all? In most countries liaison between the WCC and the Member Churches was carried on through the National Council of Churches. Was New York all that far away from Geneva? Jet aircraft and telecommunications were readily available. What functions of the office were really essential? And could they be performed by so small a staff? Satisfactory answers to all of these questions and others have proved difficult to formulate. Groups in Geneva and in New York have been working hard at them, but the process is far from complete, and it will not have been concluded by the time of the Fifth Assembly in Nairobi.

The American Scene

Changes in the New York Office have been merely symptomatic of changes which have taken place in the world, in American society and in the Member Churches in the United States. In the 1970's church growth has fallen behind that of the population. Some WCC Member Churches have suffered substantial losses in membership. Often this falling away is the direct result of prophetic social action by the churches in the struggle for racial justice and outspoken criticism by church leaders of American involvement in the Indochina War. The engagement of the churches in these two issues did not win many friends and did make many enemies. Other losses may be attributed to an anti-institutionalism which has spread throughout the country. In 1973, a survey was taken of the confidence which Americans had in their institutions: only 36% expressed confidence in organized religion — twice as high as their confidence in the White House but substantially lower than their confidence in local trash collection.

In all of these changes the New York Office of the World Council has been challenged. It has sought to understand what has been happening and to offer assistance. At the same time, some of the reasons why the Member Churches have lost popularity apply with equal force to any acceptance of WCC programmes. The New York Office is especially aware that no ecumenical activity has the same acceptance as it had five or ten years ago. Isolationism is once again on the rise in the nation, and a new and well-documented regionalism has swept the churches. Opposition to national and international participation has more than doubled in the last two years. The World Council of Churches is both less acceptable and more needed.

These things have meant that there is also less money being given in the American churches for work outside the USA. A typical denomination reported in 1974 an increase in total receipts of nearly 6%, but this was less than the rate of inflation, and most of the gain was siphoned off at the congregational or middle judicatory level. The national budgets of the churches, on which the WCC chiefly depends, have increased by only 2%. Nevertheless, the Member Churches have done reasonably well in maintaining, and sometimes increasing, their giving to the World Council and its programmes. The same is true of individuals who support the American share (one-half) of the budget of the New York Office through contributions to the United States Conference for the WCC and the Friends of the WCC.

The Essential Functions of the New York Office

Thus one of the principal tasks of the New York Office in the past seven years has been to raise financial support for the World Council. The importance of this function has increased at the same time as its performance has grown more difficult. Contacts with church leaders at all levels have had to be maintained and improved. New strategies have had to be devised. In 1974 plans were developed for a "pilot project" intended to whet interest in the World Council and seek support for it at the local level in various parts of the country. This idea was the result of proposals placed before the WCC Central Committee in 1973, where it was pointed out that "in every section of our constituency" there are groups and individuals "who, although they are not in contact with us, work in some of the fields we are concerned with or are sympathetic to the World Council stance".

Getting to know such people is an equally important task of the New York Office. For this reason the office maintains a publications department which distributes WCC books and periodicals; the demand for these continues to increase. It publishes a newsletter, *The Ecumenical Courier*, four times a year. It provides resources to the information media. The recent appearance of Philip Potter on network television drew a large volume of favourable response. Many viewers who wrote to the office had not before been aware of many of the Council's activities. They were curiously surprised that it was made up of men and women like themselves, and many were touched by the breadth and depth of the fellowship which it serves and enjoys.

Helping to preserve the ties among the American Member Churches and with the World Council is the third essential function of the New York Office. One way by which this is done is the annual meeting of the United States Conference for the World Council of Churches. All delegates to the most recent WCC Assembly are members of the Conference. Its yearly session provides the members with the opportunity of keeping up to date with ongoing programmes and recent developments in the Council, often learning of these directly from specially invited members of the Geneva

taff. Since 1971 annual meetings of the U.S. Conference have been held
n cities beyond the New York metropolitan area where important local
cumenical work is going on. This new development has greatly improved
ne contacts between the World Council and some of its constituency.
Another way by which the New York Office tries to preserve and improve
elationships with its American membership is cooperation with the Na-
onal Council of the Churches of Christ in the USA. Both bodies have
ffices in the same building in New York, and close involvement by
elated units of both Councils is a long-standing practice. Considerable
lanning is taking place in order to eliminate unnecessary duplication in
ne services rendered by them to the American constituency. In the near
uture it may be possible for the NCC to perform a number of the functions
vhich are now a part of the New York Office. At the same time, restruc-
uring in the NCC and in some Member Churches has sometimes made it
ifficult to know what agencies are now dealing with which WCC issues.

Towards the Future

In spite of all the changes which have taken place in these past few
ears—often very disturbing changes—there are many grounds for hope. A
ecent report on the state of one American church said that while it
ertainly was "changing" it was "not collapsing". There are still 131
nillion people in the country who are members of churches. Their atten-
ance has declined, but only by 9% among adults. These Christians, when
hey act, are now likely to join forces for action across denominational
ines. Young people are interested. Often they are not committed to a
articular church, but they are very serious about Jesus of Nazareth. The
harismatic movement‡ is present in most denominations. It is an indica-
ion that people are hungry for warmth and personal involvement. And the
Vatergate scandals have revealed how desperately America needs renewal
f the spirit to undergird standards of personal and national morality.

The New York Office and the United States Conference for the WCC
ave committed themselves to whatever reorganizations or new divisions
f labour may be necessary to make more effective use of a limited staff
nd volunteer resources so as to be ready to communicate and follow up
ne actions of the Nairobi Assembly among the American Member
Churches, with their new structures, new leaders and new sense of mission
n a society which changes even faster than the Church does.

VI.   ASSEMBLY PREPARATION

"An Assembly of the World Council of Churches", the Central Com-
nittee observed in 1971, "is necessarily a complex event. As a total

experience within the fellowship of the Member Churches and of the whole ecumenical movement, it should be an occasion when the nature of Christians' joyful and yet painful community in Christ in this world is experienced and celebrated''. It is in this spirit that the Central Committee, as has been noted earlier in this chapter see pages (41 - 42), proposed a number of basic changes in the style, programme and composition of future Assemblies. The ever-varying needs of the World Council and its Member Churches, it was felt, "take priority over 'the way we did it last time , and over some of the things to which we have become accustomed''. The plans for the Fifth Assembly in 1975 reflect these intentions.

The process of preparing for the Fifth Assembly was begun in 1971. The date was set, and the search for a suitable meeting-place was started. Choosing a location for an Assembly of the WCC is no easy task. Even with the deliberate attempt that has been made "to meet in conditions of the greatest simplicity compatible with effective working'', seeking a "reduction of the amount of business and a slower pace than in the past'', the need for fairly elaborate physical facilities could not be avoided. Large numbers of people have to be housed, fed, given transportation and provided with adequate meeting halls equipped for simultaneous interpretation. There should be an invitation from churches in the country concerned, and the active involvement of the local Christian community is essential. Assurance is needed that the Assembly will be able to do its work without restrictions on its freedom of speech or refusals of entry to participants from certain countries. Moreover, such gatherings must deliberately be spread around the globe, to make clear that the Council is in fact as well as in name a *World* Council of Churches.

In response to an invitation from the churches of Indonesia, Jakarta was chosen in 1971 as the site of the Fifth Assembly. By mid-1974, however, there were signs that the Assembly might unintentionally have an unfavourable impact on the national unity of Indonesia and jeopardize relationships between the country's Christian and Muslim communities. Emphasizing that "it is the policy of the World Council of Churches to work for constructive relations with people of other faiths in the common service of mankind'', the Central Committee in August 1974 decided "with deep regret not to make use of this invitation in 1975, but instead seek an alternative location for the Fifth Assembly''. An invitation to hold the 1975 gathering in Nairobi was immediately brought on behalf of the churches of Kenya. It won unanimous and enthusiastic acceptance from the Central Committee, and the way was opened for the WCC's first Assembly in Africa.

Since a deeper understanding of Christian commitment to fellowship has been one of the ecumenical movement's principal goals in the period following Uppsala, it was appropriate that the Central Committee agreed in 1973 that the theme of the Assembly would be JESUS CHRIST FREES AND UNITES. Bible study at the Assembly, presentations in plenary session and the topics of the Assembly's six Sections (Confessing Christ Today; What Unity Requires; Seeking Community—The Common Search of People of Various Faiths, Cultures and Ideologies; Education for Liberation and Community; Structures of Injustice and Struggles for Liberation; Human Development—The Ambiguities of Power, Technology and Quality of Life) were all determined in the light of the central theme of the freedom and unity which God the Father offers in Christ through the power of the Holy Spirit.

Clearly the affirmation that Jesus Christ frees and unites must not be made in a glib, facile or triumphalistic way. Does not Christ also judge and separate? What are the special insights of the people among whom the Assembly will be meeting? How can liberation and community be *lived* rather than just talked about? To enable the Assembly to "come together in humility and hope, penitent about our failures of the past, hopeful of being renewed from what other cultures have to teach us, trusting in the forgiving Christ and the renewing Spirit", two special groups were appointed to carry forward the preparations: A Consultative Committee on Assembly Programme and an Assembly Worship Committee. A secretariat for Assembly preparations was established in October 1973 at the Geneva Headquarters of the WCC.

Much as the planning of the Assembly's programme and worship reflects a desire to overcome inherited patterns of work, a number of innovations have been tried in the production of preparatory material for the Assembly. For example, there is no "authoritative text" for the study booklet *Jesus Christ Frees and Unites*. Raw material was prepared in English, French, German and Spanish by four specially invited authors, each working in his own language. Although the writers consulted one another, their manuscripts turned out all quite different. These were then circulated to National Councils of Churches with the exhortation that they adapt the material to suit the needs of their own cultures. Results have proved fascinating: within the galaxy of editions being published no less than four separate versions (British, North American, Indian and Nigerian—with little resemblance among them) have appeared in the English language alone! Instead of trying to draw up "drafts" for the reports of the Assembly Sections, as was done in the past, the Geneva staff compiled dossiers of background papers on each of the Section topics. Contents, deliberately, were varied, and selections necessarily somewhat arbitrary, but these have served to stimulate advance work on issues scheduled to come before the Assembly. The volume you are now reading, like its predecessors an account of the retiring Central Committee's stewardship since the previous Assembly, has for the first time undergone final editing by members and advisers of the Central Committee itself.

One justification for these departures from the past has turned out to be that the vast majority of the participants at Nairobi will be newcomers. Indications are that only about 30% of the delegates will have had any previous experience of a WCC Assembly, a result in large part of the Central Committee's insistence on the increased presence of women, laymen, parish clergy and young people in the churches' delegations. The prospect of so many new faces complicates the business of preparing for the event, but, more significantly, it makes it almost impossible to predetermine what course the Fifth Assembly will set for the World Council of Churches in the years beyond Nairobi.

2
faith and witness

The Unit on Faith and Witness is a grouping of programmes which represent major concerns of three of the great movements which have formed the World Council of Churches—the International Missionary Council; Faith and Order; and Life and Work. All of these movements were formed in response to the challenge posed for the churches by the world from the early years of the century onwards. How are we to witness to the Gospel today? How do we manifest the unity given in Jesus Christ? What is the role of the Church in modern society? Though they are different, these questions are intimately connected. The recognition of this connection led to the integration of the three movements in the World Council of Churches.

Developments since the Uppsala Assembly have made it even more imperative to demonstrate the inseparability of these three fundamental ecumenical questions. In the course of the last seven years, the world scene has changed considerably. The horizon of the ecumenical movement has widened. Individual churches are increasingly faced with problems which can only be dealt with in universal fellowship with other churches. The national structures of churches have proved less and less adequate. And thus the ecumenical movement has become the place for discovering the role of the Church in a world which is growing more and more inter-dependent. The past years have been marked by an intensified experience of rapid change. The future will clearly raise up new tasks of enormous magnitude, and it is becoming obvious to all churches that many aspects of their faith and life will need to be reviewed and renewed. Confronted with all these challenges, the churches cannot pursue separately the concerns of mission, unity and witness in the quest for a more just society.

This insight has led to the creation of the Programme Unit on Faith and Witness. Though the three formative movements have long been incorporated into the WCC, it was felt by the Central Committee that they still remained too separate from one another. In bringing together the sub-units Mission and Evangelism, Faith and Order, Church and Society and Dialogue with People of Living Faiths and Ideologies, the resulting Unit was to be a forum where their common concerns could be discovered and debated; where an exchange of views and mutual correction could occur; and where impulses could be given for the churches to face, at one and the same time, the three basic questions which gave rise to the ecumenical movement and which are still the main challenge it presents to them. Obviously this does not mean that the distinct concerns of each of the movements will disappear. No productive work will be achieved if the programmes do not retain their specificity. But there is no doubt that it was a wise decision to provide the opportunity for interaction between the programmes, and the experience so far achieved clearly shows that the direction indicated by this decision needs to be followed in the future as well.

Four examples may illustrate the common emphases which have emerged:

(1)*The Common Expression of Faith*. The ecumenical movement is characterized by a dilemma. Since the churches are still divided on many issues of faith, they cannot speak with one voice about the Gospel they are called to proclaim. Yet under the pressure of developments and events, they are often led to act together. Collaboration is in fact often more advanced than the common understanding of the Gospel seems to permit. Ecumenical conferences have often not been able to speak as clearly as would be desired about the basis of action to be taken. Therefore, a common effort is required to overcome this dilemma. The Central Committee of the WCC stated this quite clearly at its meeting in Utrecht in 1972: "We need to learn to speak more clearly about the centre of our faith". The four sub-units of Faith and Witness have all been led to a stronger emphasis on the common expression of faith. Earlier hesitations have been overcome. CWME has engaged in the study "Salvation Today"; Faith and Order in the study "Giving Account of the Hope That Is Within Us"; Church and Society has given sustained attention to the theological implications of its study on the future of humanity; and the sub-unit on Dialogue with People of Living Faiths and Ideologies has sought to respond to the questions of how the Christian faith needs to be advanced in dialogue.

(2) *The Proclamation of the Gospel*. The basic inspirational text of the ecumenical movement is "that they may all be one . . . that the world may believe" (John 17:21). According to the Bangkok Conference on "Salvation Today" (1973) Christian mission is: "To call men to God's salvation in Jesus Christ; to help them to grow in faith and in their knowledge of Christ in whom God reveals and restores to us our true humanity, our identity as men and women created in his image; to invite them to let themselves be constantly re-created in this image, in an eschatological community which is committed to man's struggle for liberation, unity, justice, peace and the fulness of life". The Faith and Order study on "Giving Account of the Hope That Is Within Us" not only seeks a common expression of faith, but encourages a diversity

of accounts relevant to the local context. The ethical questions raised by Church and Society in relation to technology, power and the quality of life demand of all those concerned with the future of mankind a witness at a deeper level to the quest for meaning and spiritual direction. The open attitude fostered by the sub-unit on Dialogue is an essential part in keeping our proclamation from an attitude of superiority towards our neighbours and helps to clarify the promises and demands of the Gospel. In all of this the message of the cross and the resurrection emerges as relevant to the human predicament.

(3) *The Church in the World.* The constantly growing concern for justice in society has raised sharply not only the issue of methods and strategies for change, but also the theological and ethical basis for the Christian contribution. Underlying the pronouncement and the action, there must be some new common conceptions of justice and of human destiny. But this demands understanding on a number of issues. The Church, as the Body of Christ and as "the Church for others", must continue to examine the relation of faith to the ideologies of the present era. In a technological world new insights need to be gained into the meaning of the human being and of Christian hope in history. While the search for justice is an essential element in mission it also calls the Church to a much deeper pastoral concern for all those caught in the toils of injustice—as oppressed or oppressor.

(4) *The Unity of Mankind.* In many contexts, the Uppsala Assembly stressed the unity of humankind and the need for international political and social justice. This emphasis continued to be a major concern in the following years. Church and Society discussed the theme in connection with its study on the future of man. In the work of the sub-unit on Dialogue, the search for world community emerged as one of the common concerns to be considered in the encounter between people of different faiths. Faith and Order and CWME were more concerned with the role which the Church is called to fulfil, understanding the nature of mankind and working towards a viable form of international community. Faith and Order, in particular, has studied the inter-relation between the unity of the Church and the unity of mankind. And CWME has been concerned about the extent to which the missionary imperative could avoid being a disruptive factor in the search for unity. The implications of these individual studies have been repeatedly discussed at the level of the Unit, and this discussion will need to be pursued in the future.

These four examples may serve to illustrate the obvious connection between the programmes which have been brought together in the Unit. Many other examples could be given, but readers will certainly discover them for themselves as they go through the accounts of the work accomplished by the different programmes in the course of the past few years.

I. COMMISSION ON FAITH AND ORDER

The Quest for the Unity of the Church

The Uppsala Assembly represents a definite shift in the search for the unity of the Church. The introduction to its report on "The Holy Spirit and the Catholicity of the Church" points to the fact that, while great strides had been taken in overcoming the confessional differences between the churches, new divisions had occurred, often separating Christians within the same church or across confessional boundaries. Obviously, the Assembly was thinking of tensions caused in the churches by the emergence of new movements—new commitments to the struggle for political and social justice, the search for cultural identity, a fresh emphasis on charismatic‡ celebration, and the like. The report clearly stated that, in subsequent years, unity had to be sought not only by clarifying the historical differences among the churches but also by maintaining the fellowship in the face of the pressures and conflicts of our own generation.

The new emphasis does not mean that the Faith and Order Commission has entirely changed its objectives. Theological conversations on controversial issues and analysis of dialogues and church union negotiations have continued. The Uppsala Assembly enabled the Commission to deal with this task more effectively by electing an enlarged and more representative membership. The size of the Commission was raised from 100 to 135 to include a wider range of confessional traditions; with the agreement of the Holy See, Roman Catholics were elected for the first time as full members. This made it possible for the Commission to face the full range of confessional differences. Thus, the traditional tasks have acquired new meaning.

The activity of the Faith and Order Commission has therefore been characterized by the tension inherent in a two-fold task. This challenge has not been easy to meet. There was even some uncertainty as to whether this dual emphasis should be pursued. Was the Commission not in danger of losing its specificity by spreading its concern beyond the confessional divisions to practically all of the problems affecting the unity of the Church? The hesitations were finally overcome, but there is still the unresolved question as to how the double task can best and most effectively be fulfilled. What are the priorities in the vast field of possible themes? What are the most appropriate methods of work? How can a gher degree of implementation be achieved?

In the period since the Fourth Assembly, the Commission has held two
meetings—the first at Louvain (1971) and the second at Accra (1974). Its
main activities can be summarized under three headings: (a) enabling
communion among the churches; (b) clarifying the nature of unity; (c)
ying the ground for common witness.

Enabling Communion among the Churches

(1) *Agreement on major controversial issues.* In the period since Upp-
ala, much time and energy have been devoted to the elaboration of agreed
statements on controversial issues such as baptism, the eucharist and the
ministry. Obviously, if communion among the churches is to be realized,
agreement on these themes is required. In the course of the Faith and Order
Movement's history, most conferences had dealt with these subjects, and
me had been able to formulate at least partial agreements on certain
pects. In more recent years, the growth of bilateral conversations be-
een individual churches had led to the emergence of unexpected common
ews. Was it not possible, therefore, to summarize this "emerging con-
nsus"? Obviously, one could not hope for more than a preliminary
atement. The time had not yet come for a full consensus, but the agreed
atements scattered in the different reports amounted to a much higher
gree of agreement than most churches were prepared to admit. The Faith
d Order Commission has attempted to bring these common perspectives
to sharper focus and provide wider opportunities for sharing in them.

Work in this direction had already begun before the Uppsala Assembly.
he Faith and Order Commission furnished the Assembly with a first text
the eucharist, summarizing major statements made by ecumenical con-
rences. In the following years, a parallel effort was undertaken on
ptism. The two texts were discussed again by the Commission at its
71 meeting in Louvain and subsequently were communicated to the
ember Churches for reaction. They were later revised in the light of the
mments received and discussed once again by the Commission three
ars later at its meeting in Accra.

It proved more difficult to arrive at an agreed text on the ministry. This
eme was given central attention at both Commission meetings. Several
nsultations were held, and the reports were shared with a great number
theologians and ecumenical groups. This persistent effort resulted in the
port "The Ordained Ministry in Ecumenical Perspective". All three

reports have been published and sent to the churches for their information and response.*

The statements have been supplemented by an analysis of the present practice and discipline of the churches. To what extent can they recognize each other and extend sacramental fellowship? What changes are required to enable them to take these steps? The two study reports "One Baptism" and "Beyond Intercommunion", as well as that on the ministry, are attempts to respond to these questions.

(2) *Bilateral conversations and union negotiations*. Though the general multilateral debate on the unity of the Church is indispensable for the advance of the ecumenical movement, the actual divisions can be clarified and overcome only in direct conversations and negotiations among the churches. Only the churches themselves can do justice to the specific, particular issues which separate them; only they have the authority to make and to implement decisions. Real progress towards unity—and even more its fulfilment—lies with them. But the general ecumenical debate can inspire and direct their efforts. It can uncover perspectives not yet sufficiently recognized. It can help the churches not to lose sight of the totality of the ecumenical movement. It will remind them constantly of their task to work for the unity of *all* Christians.

The active participation of the Roman Catholic Church in the ecumenical movement has given a new impetus to bilateral conversations. The need was felt for direct dialogue in order to clarify the new situation created by the Second Vatican Council. A whole network of international and national relationships was established. Several of these dialogues have led to remarkable results. Some have issued agreed statements on certain controversial issues. Others have at least produced new descriptions of the different outlooks which keep the Roman Catholic and other churches apart. The Faith and Order Commission has followed these developments closely and tried to analyse their implications for the benefit of the ecumenical movement as a whole. Working in close contact with the Annual Conference of Executive Secretaries of World Confessional Families, the Faith and Order Secretariat collaborated in a process of evaluating the bilateral conversations, and in 1972 and 1975 surveys of these were published. The World Confessional Families were invited to be represented by a "liaison officer" at the meetings of the Commission in order to facilitate the discussion.

At the same time, contact with united churches and with union negotiations

---

* All three have been issued under the title, <u>One Baptism, One Eucharist and a Mutually Recognized Ministry</u>. Geneva: WCC, 1975.

was maintained and deepened. A World Consultation on Church Union Negotiations—the second global endeavour of its kind—was held in 1970 at Limuru, Kenya. The debate at this meeting showed the clear need for closer relations between the united churches and the union negotiating committees in various countries. In particular, the question was raised as to how in the future the united churches should express their world-wide fellowship. To provide opportunity for further thought on this matter, plans were developed for a conference to which all united churches would be invited to send delegates. The conference has been scheduled for June 1975 at the invitation of the United Church of Canada. Furthermore, the Secretariat made an effort to improve the communication between the Faith and Order Commission and the negotiating committees and to keep them informed about developments in different parts of the world. Every other year, surveys on church union have been published in *The Ecumenical Review*.

One particular involvement of the Commission deserves special mention. For many years it was responsible, together with the Lutheran World Federation and the World Alliance of Reformed Churches, for the conduct of "Lutheran-Reformed Conversations at the European Level". These conversations led in 1973 to the so-called Leuenberg Agreement, a consensus statement which is to enable the Lutheran and Reformed churches in Europe to establish full communion. The text has been submitted to the churches for ratification, and by the end of 1974 more than 60 churches had given their approval.

(3) *The danger of over-complication and ineffectiveness*. In the years since Uppsala, the ecumenical movement has become more and more complicated. On the one hand, efforts towards unity are multiplying. Dialogues and conversations, official and unofficial, are being conducted in different compositions and at different levels of the Church's life. On the other hand, more and more people are expressing doubts that dialogue, conversation and negotiation will really help the one Church to come to life. They base their hope instead upon the common response of Christians to the challenges of our time. Common experience and common witness, cutting across inherited divisions, can possibly lead to a re-grouping of Christians more nearly corresponding to the realities of the present age. Under these circumstances, how can the churches advance towards the goal of visible unity which the ecumenical movement seeks to reach? Won't these different efforts inevitably compete with each other? Won't the divergent views tend to paralyze any real progress? The danger undoubtedly exists.

In view of these circumstances the Commission has repeatedly reflected on the pressing question: How can the different efforts all serve the one goal? Each effort has its value, and each also has its limitations. There-fore, in order to hasten the ecumenical advance, each effort must be related to the whole. Each must profit from what is being undertaken in other contexts. Something like a coordinated plan or an "ecumenical strategy" is required. Recognizing this need, the Faith and Order Commission initiated a study on "Concepts of Unity and Models of Union" (1971). While the proposal arose from a discussion of the relationship between bilateral conversations and union negotiations, the subject soon became wider. How can the oneness of the movement be maintained? The study culminated in a consultation in September 1973, at Salamanca, Spain (see the discussion of "The Church as Conciliar Fellowship", page 79).

There has been much talk in past years about a growing ecumenical malaise. Many feel that the ecumenical movement has ceased to "move" and that the ecumenical cause no longer inspires the same enthusiasm as in former decades. Why is this so? Has it lost its urgency? Or has the ecumenical movement perhaps passed beyond the stages of being a naive enthusiasm or of enjoying support as a pet project of individuals and now has come to the point of demanding hard decisions from the churches? Whatever the answer may be, there is an obvious need to move from the level of ideas to that of implementation. In the period since Uppsala, the Faith and Order Commission has increasingly been called to assist churches in the problems that they actually face. It is significant, for example, that the Commission is under mounting pressure to give more attention to those issues which are described by such terms as order, constitution and canon law. The lessons to be drawn from this development are, for the moment, elusive. It may be that a climate of trust has been achieved among the churches sufficient to allow scrutiny of one another's principles and methods of governance. Or it is possible that these latter elements, rather than doctrinal differences, have been the greater stumbling block in the way of unity all along. Nevertheless the phenomenon reflects the recognition that the call to unity ultimately requires a reconsideration of the existing structures of the churches.

(4) *Wider contacts*. One of the tasks of the Faith and Order Commission is to cultivate contacts with churches not belonging to the World Council of Churches. About one-fifth of the Commission's members represent such churches. Their participation makes possible many precious contacts and dialogues. This is particularly true of the Roman Catholic Church, whose theologians have made a significant contribution to all Faith and Order studies of the past period.

A number of other specific efforts deserve mention. From 1965 to 1972 the Commission organized yearly meetings with representatives of the Seventh-Day Adventist Church. The results have been published in a ooklet issued under the title of *So Much in Common* (Geneva: WCC, 973). Descriptive articles on other non-member churches have been published in *The Ecumenical Review* from time to time.* In each case, the rticles were checked with representatives of these churches to ensure that he description was correct and acceptable to them. (A new series of such escriptive articles is currently in preparation.)

The Faith and Order Commission, together with the Secretariat for Promoting Christian Unity of the Roman Catholic Church, continues to be nvolved in the preparation of the Week of Prayer for Christian Unity. very year a small group, named by both agencies, works out a leaflet uggesting some material for prayer and meditation. In the last few years, he first draft of the leaflet has been made by a mixed group in one ountry, the task of the international group being to edit the material eceived. This pattern will probably be maintained in coming years.

Yet another project has proved to be a particular challenge and delight or the Commission and its Secretariat. *Cantate Domino* has served as the ymnbook of the ecumenical movement over many decades. Its first two ditions were published by the World Student Christian Federation. At the equest of the Uppsala Assembly the Faith and Order Secretariat has upervised the compilation of a third edition, which was published in December 1974. The 200 hymns it contains, while including a number of "old favourites"** of Western hymnody, represent musical and liturgical tyles of different parts of the world in greater variety than ever before.

Clarifying the Nature of Unity

All churches engaged in the ecumenical movement agree that God wants is Church to be one. But they do not yet share one common vision of the goal they have committed themselves to reach. What does unity mean? What kind of unity is to be realized? The answers to these questions are perhaps more important than any other answers which Faith and Order tudies may provide.

Both the Third and Fourth Assemblies devoted primary attention to this problem. New Delhi emphasized the local unity of "all in each place". Uppsala developed the concept of catholicity and placed complementary emphasis on the universality of the Church. Perhaps even more important was the insistence that the term "catholicity" was to be understood as

---

* These include the African Brotherhood Church in Kenya, the Old Believers in the Soviet Union, the Church of the Lord (Aladura) in West Africa, and the like. All of this material is available from the WCC in Geneva upon application.

** Cantate Domino. Kassel, Basle, Tours and London: Barenreiter Verlag, 1974 (available rom WCC Publications in Geneva and New York).

expressing a quality of the Church, as referring not only and not even primarily to its quantitative geographical extension but rather to its capacity to reconcile all people and to draw them into the one fellowship. Catholicity is shown forth when human barriers are overcome and people of different cultures, races and classes begin to praise the Lord together. Catholicity becomes manifest when the Church acts as a ferment to overcome the power of sin and injustice in alienating people from one another. Catholicity is God's gift. Since it has been given this gift, the Church *is* catholic, but at the same time, no church can claim to *be* catholic. The Church is constantly on the way to *becoming* catholic. Catholicity is a task yet to be fulfilled, and it can be fulfilled only if the churches together engage in a movement of renewal.

These insights proved to be of great importance in the years which followed. As no Assembly before, Uppsala had underlined the task of working towards a viable form of world community. It was characterized by a sharp awareness of the growing interdependence of humankind and the inevitability of the problems arising from this evolution. It called upon the churches to face the problem of justice in its world-wide dimensions and launched programmes to make possible some contribution on their part. Obviously, this new commitment also had consequences for the unity of the Church. The Faith and Order Commission, therefore, decided to initiate a study on "The Unity of the Church and the Unity of Mankind". How is the Church to give theological interpretation to the growing interdependence of humanity? What role is the Church called to play in this new situation? What self-understanding results if this calling is taken seriously?

The theme was thoroughly considered at the meeting of the Commission at Louvain (1971). Is the Church really a uniting factor in the crucial life situation of today's world? How does it gather together people who are divided by different political commitments? How does it overcome barriers of race and culture? How does it go about including in its fellowship the handicapped, who are normally excluded from participation in the fulness of life? The debate could not be concluded at Louvain. It remained one of the main concerns in the following years and is still on the Commission's agenda. What insights have been gained in this process?

(1) *The Church as the Sign of Christ's Presence.* In the course of the study, the designation of the Church as sacrament and sign became more and more important. The Uppsala Assembly had already spoken of the Church as the "sign of the coming unity of mankind", echoing one of the key phrases used by the Second Vatican Council. The terms "sacrament" and "sign" proved to be particularly suitable in the context of the study because they express at the same time the rootage of the Church in Jesus Christ and its calling to

reflect him in the world. God has revealed himself in Jesus Christ. He offers God's communion to the world. Partaking in this communion, the disciples are called to be a living sign of Christ's presence. They proclaim him not only by their words but also by their being and acting. The divided churches will grow together as they aim to become the sign which they are called to be.

(2) *The Church as Conciliar Fellowship*. Ever since the Uppsala Assembly, this term has played a significant role in Faith and Order discussion. The concept recommended itself in the first place because it enabled a clearer understanding of the universality of the Church. Each local church lives in fellowship with the others, each depending on the others, each responsible for the others. Though each retains its individuality, they together form one body throughout the world. The ecumenical movement must seek to fulfil this vision. But the concept recommends itself also because it gives an adequate description of the Church seeking to respond to the challenges of the present world. The Church as a conciliar fellowship is one in a dynamic way. It is capable of facing new issues because it is prepared to take them up in conciliar exchange. Since each part is committed to being accountable to the whole fellowship, it need not be afraid of diversity and even conflict. As long as the segments are open to the guidance of the Spirit, they will be held together in "reconciled diversity".

After much detailed discussion, the consultation of Salamanca (1973) formulated the following description of conciliar fellowship: "Jesus Christ founded one Church. Today we live in diverse churches divided from one another. Yet our vision of the future is that we shall once again live as brothers and sisters in one undivided Church. How can this goal be described? We offer the following description to the churches for their consideration: The one Church is to be envisioned as a conciliar fellowship of local churches which are themselves truly united. In this conciliar fellowship, each local church possesses, in communion with the others, the fulness of catholicity, witnesses to the same apostolic faith, and, therefore, recognizes the others as belonging to the same church of Christ and guided by the same spirit. As the New Delhi Assembly pointed out, they are bound together because they have received the same baptism and share in the same eucharist; they recognize each other's members and ministries. They are one in their common commitment to confess the Gospel of Christ by proclamation and service to the world. To this end, each church aims at maintaining sustained and sustaining relationships with her sister churches, expressed in conciliar gatherings whenever required for the fulfillment of their common calling".

At the meeting of the Commission in Accra the debate was carried further. It centred in particular upon the relationship between "conciliarity" and ' organic union". The two concepts, it was made clear, do not exclude one another. They are complementary. Only as a conciliar fellowship can the Church be truly and organically one at *all* levels of its life.

(3) *New Perspectives for the Faith and Order Commission.* The debate of the Louvain meeting raised a host of new questions for the Commission on Faith and Order. If the unity of the Church is to be studied in crucial life situations, the agenda of the Commission needs to be considerably enlarged. A whole range of interdisciplinary studies with historians, politicians, sociologists and psychologists is called for. At Accra the Commission singled out two areas of concern in which the divided state of humankind and the consequent challenge presented to the unity of the Church are most acutely felt: the issue of racism and that of dialogue with partners of other living faiths and ideologies. It is hoped that these collaborative efforts will contribute greatly to realizing the full potential of the study of unity in day-to-day contexts. Obviously, the resources are limited, and the efforts will, therefore, always remain fragmentary. But the study has made clear that the issue of unity must be related to the witness and the life of the Church in the context of today's world and its problems.

A second new perspective for the Faith and Order Commission came into view at Accra and has to do not so much with the intellectual concept of the work to be carried out as with methods of thinking and styles of work and presentation. The African setting of the meeting was important to the achievement of this new insight. Louvain (whose sessions took place in the shadow of a great Roman Catholic university and thus made abundantly clear that Roman Catholic participation was now integral to the work of the Faith and Order Commission) might be characterized as "White theology" at its best. Accra, three years later, may be seen as marking the transition from "White theology" to "colourful theology"—a theology infused with the contributions of the whole spectrum of cultures, races and communities. The Accra meeting proved to be a real encounter of the Commission with the aspirations, fears, demands and hopes of the Third World. The Ghanaian hosts, the church leaders and theologians of Africa greatly helped the Commission to see its theological concerns in the framework of a non-Western cultural and political setting. There were drums, dances and hymns, there was a worship life wholly permeating the theological deliberations. The session underlined the necessity for Faith and Order to keep the issue of unity steadily before the churches, but it attempted to spell out more fully what this unity means in the contexts of new divisions between rich and poor nations and in the struggles for a more just interdependence between peoples, races and sexes.

Laying the Ground for Common Witness

How is the Church to confess the Gospel today? All efforts towards unity will be in vain as long as the churches are not able to answer this question. The one community is a confessing community, and the churches will, therefore, find the way to unity only if they learn to speak together of their common faith. In order to assist them in this task, the Faith and Order Commission decided in 1971 to initiate a new study process under the title "Giving Account of the Hope That Is Within Us". This project is an attempt to lead the churches and individual Christians to a fresh and common articulation of their faith. It is obviously a new departure for the Commission. Of course, most studies and activities have had as their ultimate aim to make possible common witness in today's world. Some studies, such as those on "The Authority of the Bible" and on "Common Witness and Proselytism", have sought quite explicitly to facilitate this task. But no study has so far dealt as directly with confessing faith today.

The title of the study, borrowed from the first Epistle of Peter, has been chosen to avoid the false impression that the study aims at writing a new ecumenical creed to take the place of the ancient creeds. It aims rather at the kind of answer invited by the author of the Epistle. The Christians to whom he is writing find themselves surrounded by people who are surprised by the hope radiating from them. These people want to know the reasons for it, and the Christians among them need to give these reasons. Why do we hope even if humanly speaking we have not much reason to hope? Just as their answers had to be cast in terms understandable to their contemporaries, so ours need to take account of those who question us. The Gospel needs to be communicated to people of our time. Though we may be divided by our traditions, we may find ourselves surprisingly united when we face this task.

A new method was chosen for this study. Instead of calling an international consultation, the Faith and Order Commission issued a general invitation to participate in the study. Churches, movements, groups and even individuals were asked to articulate their faith. The primary initiative was to be with the churches and groups which were responding to questions inherent in their own particular situations. The task of the Commission was to begin only in a second stage. As soon as a sufficient number of responses were available, an attempt was to be made to evaluate their significance and to reflect on their meaning for the Church, its unity and its witness. Obviously, these two stages could not be sharply separated in time. The reflection had to begin relatively early, and many groups discovered that their task required more time than they had originally anticipated. The invitation found a very encouraging echo. Churches and groups in more than 40 countries decided to participate.

At its meeting in Accra the Commission engaged in a full discussion of the study. First the Commission examined a number of "accounts of hope", originating in different contexts and situations. The examples were chosen so as to indicate the diversity (and even contradictions) of the responses received. After extended deliberation in ten sub-sections the Commission produced an interim report on the theme. A brief affirmation adopted by the Commission points to the source of the one hope in Jesus Christ. The report then summarizes some of the tensions and apparent contradictions arising from the different accounts. A third chapter begins to discuss the ways by which we can speak together about the one hope given in our Lord. The final section contains some illustrative affirmations of hope. The document does not conclude the study process but aims at encouraging churches and Christians to express their hope in prayers, liturgies, manifestoes and the like. At the same time the document invites the churches to pursue the task of expressing their faith together. The Commission lighted upon the phrase "prisoners of hope" as descriptive of the situation in which Christians find themselves in today's world and decided to continue the study in the conviction that the communion of hope in which we are already living can be made more visible in the future.*

II. COMMISSION ON WORLD MISSION AND EVANGELISM
UPPSALA TO NAIROBI VIA BANGKOK

The Bangkok Conference on "Salvation Today", coming as it did midway in the period from Uppsala to Nairobi, has been central to the life of the Commission on World Mission and Evangelism during the period under review,** and perhaps, when viewed from the perspective of a greater span of years, pivotal in the history of world mission. Far more than a conference productive of reports and findings, the Bangkok meeting had a profound personal effect on participants, and echoes of it continue to reverberate among those grappling seriously with the question of how we are to witness to the Gospel today. The refusal at Bangkok to separate the human being into body and soul, or to resolve the tension between the personal and the social aspects of salvation has given rise both to much

---

* Material arising from the Accra meeting has been gathered in two volumes: Uniting in Hope, Accra 1974. Geneva: WCC, 1975. Accra 1974, Minutes of the Faith and Order Commission Meeting. Geneva: WCC, 1975.

**. For a fuller report of the period 1963-1972 see From Mexico City to Bangkok. Report of the Commission on World Mission and Evangelism. Geneva: WCC, 1972.

misunderstanding and great hope for the future of world mission. New understanding of the comprehensiveness of God's will for the salvation of men and women, greater appreciation of the cultural diversity in which salvation in Christ is proclaimed, and the need for radical revision of the relationships among churches as they work at this task together were the imperatives felt at Bangkok.* It is under these three aspects that we look at the work of the Commission.

The Comprehensive Nature of Salvation

At the Bangkok meeting the participants sought to understand together the meaning of salvation in relation to the variety of situations from which they came. Lengthy periods spent in small Bible study groups or group meditation gave participants an opportunity to share in depth with one another their personal faith as well as their commitment to service in the world. In doing so, they were led to say that "the salvation which Christ brought, and in which we participate, offers a comprehensive wholeness in this divided life. We understand salvation as newness of life—the unfolding of true humanity in the fulness of God" (Colossians 2:9) a process in which "God's justice manifests itself both in the justification of the sinner and in social and political justice"

The *study process on "Salvation Today"* in preparation for Bangkok had attempted to clarify some of the issues. During the first two years following Uppsala groups in different parts of the world were asked to comment on different aspects of the theme. Their reports indicated that it was not possible to confine the study, and thus the Bangkok conference, to the discussion of theological concepts. Therefore, during the two years prior to the conference the study concentrated on ways in which the theme could be approached in close relation to one's actual experience.

In the tradition of the early Christians (who surely did not choose an ancient text and then apply it to their experience of the Lord's living among them) the usual study procedure of selecting Bible texts and then applying them to contemporary experience was deliberately reversed. Camilo Torres, the Colombian revolutionary priest, Antonio José Santos, a humble Brazilian itinerant lay preacher, Kalagora Subba Rao, the Hindu Christian, Halina Bortnowska, a Polish Catholic teacher struggling to find new forms of Christian presence in her society, were some of the voices heard in the collection of contemporary texts published for the study.**A

---

* See Bangkok Assembly 1973. Minutes and Report. Geneva: WCC, 1973.

** Most of these have been reproduced in Tell Out Tell Out My Glory: RISK, Vol. 9 No. 3, 1973

series of Bible studies prepared by a consultation of biblical scholars was used at the Conference and since Bangkok by groups working with the "Salvation Today" study materials. In addition a group of Orthodox theologians contributed a statement during a consultation organized by CWME.

The concern for the comprehensiveness of the Christian message and mission is especially true of the desk for *evangelism*. Contacts have been sought and maintained with persons and groups holding different views on evangelism. Following the Bangkok meeting, which offered the services of CWME for the holding of the International Congress for World Evangelization in Lausanne, staff relationships with the organizers of the Congress were maintained, and a WCC staff delegation of five persons attended the meeting. In the latter part of 1973 a symposium on evangelism was held, including a number of Conservative Evangelicals, which revealed a wide spectrum of views but also significant lines of convergence. Recent issues of the "Monthly Letter on Evangelism", which have carried such articles as an interview with Manoel de Mello, the well-known Brazilian Pentecostal, and responses from publishers and editors to the question: "How can we overcome a narrow evangelization concept of literature work and encourage publishing activities which have in view man as a whole?", have met with widespread response.

In addition, the discussion about the ways of expressing the Christian faith today is now also taken up by other programmes of the World Council, notably the Commission on Faith and Order, and will be discussed in the Assembly Section devoted to the topic "Confessing Christ Today".

Mission in Context

While the emphasis on the comprehensiveness of mission has been growing there has also been a marked growth of the awareness of the diversity of situations in which the faith is proclaimed. The assumption that the Gospel is a neatly packaged collection of concepts which can easily be transported from one cultural context to another has lost conviction.

The shifting scene is reflected in the new CWME *Constitution*; which was revised at Bangkok and comes before the Nairobi Assembly for final approval. The revised aim of the Commission makes clear that both "word and deed" are valid aspects of "proclamation". It locates the CWME fully within the structures of the WCC, making the integration of the World

Council of Churches and the International Missionary Council complete, and at the same time enlarges the possibilities of affiliation to the CWME, thus recognizing that groups of Christians other than official ecclesiastical structures can and do play an important role in mission.

Two studies in the CWME have, during this period, focussed particularly upon the problem of diversity. One is the series of *World Studies on Churches in Mission*, which was brought to a close in 1970. Thirteen book-length studies of 15 churches in 12 countries on five continents have been published. Five persons meeting together have analysed the whole series and, after reflecting on analyses of churches in Fiji and Michigan, Uganda and Japan, published their reflections in a research pamphlet "Can churches be Compared?". They formulated seven clues to re-thinking mission which can be grouped under two headings. (a) The first group stresses the basic diversity of churches, especially in the degree of self-awareness, and their interaction with the surrounding community. This diversity means that external criteria—especially those derived from Western theological concepts—are inadequate to assess the vitality and inner dynamic of particular churches. (b) The second group of clues relates to the traditional role of the foreign missionary and the mission agency in the development of churches. Placing the emphasis on the interpretation of the Gospel in a particular culture by those who belong to that culture, and questioning the undue stress laid on structural links between churches in one place and in another, it asserts that the primary strategy of mission belongs to God himself and that the details of his strategy when he chooses to reveal them to us may surprise and humble us.

The other study was commissioned by the Uppsala Assembly. It focussed on *The Role of Christians in Changing Institutions*. The study was undertaken by some thirteen local task forces in different parts of the world. Each of them sought to discern the nature of institutional change to which its members were related and the particular task and Christian responsibility which arose from involvement in that change. The task forces considered such diverse situations as the impact of USA television programmes in Mexico, an "Ujamaa"‡ village in Tanzania, the politico-social role of the episcopate in a Middle Eastern country, or the involvement of three North American mission societies in Angola. An international Advisory Committee met periodically to hear reports from the task forces and to seek to draw some conclusion from this diversity. The latter task proved to be a quite difficult one, for the situations could not easily be compared. Nevertheless, when the final report on the study was made to the CWME in 1974, a number of conclusions could be presented. They concern four areas: (a) The importance of the Church as a sustaining community in situations of conflict. (b) The need for the Church to reflect on its use of power and hence the need for a political theology. (c) The sharing of Christians in the transformation of institutions. (d) The relation of the proclamation of the Gospel to the process of conscientization.‡

Another aspect of the CWME study programme in which consideration for the context plays an important role is the desk for *Orthodox Studies and Relationships*. The purpose of the programme is two-fold. On the one hand, it endeavours to introduce into the ecumenical discussion on mission and evangelism the contribution of the Orthodox churches. This has notably been the case for the study on "Salvation Today" and the Section on "Confessing Christ Today" of the forthcoming Assembly. Both contributions were the result of major consultations of Orthodox theologians, organized by CWME. On the other hand, the programme seeks to foster closer relationship and association of the Orthodox churches with the totality of the ecumenical concern for mission.

The consultation held in Bucharest on "Confessing Christ Today" grappled with three questions for Orthodoxy.* While the quest for unity has been and continues to be of major theological concern to Orthodox churches, mission as the inevitable consequence of the living continuity of the tradition assumed greater importance in the discussion. New awareness of the crisis of faith in which the increasingly secularized contemporary believers find themselves impressed upon participants the need for mission to such modern men and women, in spite of the tensions that mission inevitably creates in the relationship of churches to their societies. And, third, the growing strength of the Orthodox churches of the diaspora posed the theological question to participants: What is the mission of the Church in a diaspora situation?

To encourage the pursuit of these and other issues there have been undertaken, following Bangkok, a series of CWME visits to countries of major Orthodox churches, with a particular concern for understanding the mission and witness of Orthodox churches in a socialist setting.

The programme of *Helping the Churches in Evangelism* must also be mentioned in connection with the concern for the context of mission. Especially during the first three years after the Uppsala Assembly the programme endeavoured to make clear that evangelism aims at communicating to all men and women the "Word made flesh", that is, in relation to the particular context. An important part of the programme during these years consisted, therefore, of intensive contacts, especially in Latin America, with pentecostal churches in order to discover ways in

---

* See Dossier Section I, pages 53-68.

which they, in their own setting, communicated the Gospel to one another and to the world around them.

Confrontation with government, economic and church structures has come about almost inevitably in many localities where groups engaged in *Urban Industrial Mission* are taking seriously the Bible's demands for faithful witness to the Gospel among urban peoples of low economic and social status. Clergy and lay people in Chile, Argentina, Korea, the Philippines, Thailand and Zimbabwe (Southern Rhodesia), among other places, have suffered physical abuse, harassment, imprisonment, loss of jobs and even exile for their part in urban and industrial mission activities. Their stand springs from sustained reflection on the biblical basis of their faith. The CWME has tried to provide a framework for international exchange of information and mutual encouragement of the some 500 local UIM groups on all six continents through regional contact groups and an international advisory group.

The emphasis on Urban Industrial Mission inevitably led to a concern for the mission of the Church in a rural and agricultural setting, since the rapid urbanization created problems in non-urban areas for both society and the Church. A desk for *Rural Agricultural Mission* was established in 1973 with the purpose of assisting the churches in their involvement in rural community organization and in fulfilling their pastoral role in a changing rural scene. To that end RAM has encouraged seminaries to offer courses initiating seminary students into the problems of community development in rural areas; urged churches to give more attention to the agricultural training of the peasant women who form the backbone of most rural communities; and encouraged them to take a more active part in the creation of programmes for those leaving school and for rural public health care delivery.

An example of the CWME's concern with mission in relation to the cultural and religious context has been the development of *study centres* in different parts of the world. There are now some 19 such centres in existence, with CWME maintaining contact with them and helping them to find support. Programmatically they are closely related to the sub-unit on Dialogue with People of Living Faiths and Ideologies. This sub-unit (see part III of this chapter, below) was established in 1971 to develop the concerns arising from the earlier CWME study on "The Word of God and the Living Faiths of Man". In 1971 a consultation of study centre directors was held in Hong Kong in cooperation with the sub-unit on Dialogue.

It is increasingly recognized that the context is important not only to the practical aspects of mission, but also to the theological reflection about the nature of missionary action. This recognition has led to the call for the "contextualization" of theology (compare the programme of the Theological Education Fund as described in the section on Sponsored Agencies later in this present part of the chapter) or to the plea for a "theology in action". An adequate theology of mission and evangelism cannot be stated in universal terms (even when couched in biblical language) in the hope that these will later be applied to particular contexts. The process of formulating such a theology might more validly be arrived at the other way around: starting consciously with the immediate context, and then, through theological reflection, relating it to a wider context.

The importance of the cultural context for the understanding of missionary proclamation and obligation was also introduced as a challenge to the Bangkok conference. Under the heading "Culture and Identity" the conference considered the challenge in three ways. Concern for the context challenges Christians (a) to enter into serious dialogue with people of other faiths; (b) to face (especially for Western white Christians) any hidden assumption of racial and cultural superiority in the presentation of the Gospel; and (c) to relate the experience of conversion to the conditions and developments of the particular culture in which conversion takes place; or, as a phrase from Bangkok puts it: "Culture shapes the human voice that answers the voice of Christ".

The Churches in their Relationships

The Bangkok conference challenged the churches to seek new relationships among each other and to re-examine their relationships to the secular powers. A strong plea was made in favour of truly mature relationships between churches which would overcome the patterns of domination and dependence where these still exist. The conference considered one promising attempt at providing a model for mature relationships in mission: CEVAA (Communauté Evangélique d'Action Apostolique – Evangelical Community for Apostolic Action), which unites churches in Europe, the Pacific and Africa in a community dedicated to common reflection and joint action in mission. But the models are not many, and the problem is an intractable one.

The responsibility for exploring ways of changing relationships between the churches, or between churches and mission agencies, has become the major focus of the programme on *Ecumenical Sharing of Personnel*. This programme, which was asked for by the Uppsala Assembly, is carried on cooperatively by CICARWS and CWME (compare Chapter Three, pages 175-176). Partly because of the nature of the problems with which it has been asked to deal, the ESP Committee has had a double task. (a) There are those who have hoped that the WCC would move quickly into a

arge-scale operational programme for the recruiting and placing of people
rom all parts of the world in other parts of the world at the request of the
eceiving churches. While refusing to become a super-mission agency the
SP has arranged for the exchange of a limited number of people. It has
one this more in the role of a facilitator, taking care to see that both
eceiving and sending churches were involved. (b) Others have seen the
SP Committee primarily as a forum for discussion and analysis of some
f the problems involved in sharing personnel across frontiers. How does
ne develop a true sense of mature partnership between "receivers" and
"givers"? Is it possible to separate the channels along which people and
noney flow so that people will be received for what they are and not for
vhat they represent? A small group of Africans and Asians serving in
uropean churches met in 1974 to compare their experiences and see
vhether they saw any possible way forward for the rectification of rela-
onships so that the right to engage in mission might truly become the
ght of all Christian churches.

The question of power was recognized as basic, and the Bangkok
neeting proposed that for the sake of a mature relationship in mission,
nere might be situations where a limited moratorium on the sending of
ersonnel would be desirable. The ESP Committee is concerned about
asic guidelines which may be mutually agreed on by the churches in the
ommitted ecumenical fellowship and which may influence the churches'
titude and actual decisions on sharing their resources, both human and
aterial, with partner churches around the world. In seeking to arrive at
ese "principles of mutual responsibility", the ESP Committee is aware
at it is dealing with one of the most crucial and touchy issues in the field
f ecumenical cooperation in which the regional ecumenical bodies are
xpected to play an important role.

In the light of the changing relationship between the churches, the
WME's programme on *Education for Mission* has changed its emphasis.
riginally, the chief concern was the preparation of those who were going
om one church to serve in another (missionaries). With the growing
wareness that the whole Church was called to mission everywhere, the
nphasis has shifted to the preparation of the whole people of God for
iission wherever they live. The shift from one emphasis to the other calls
r a shift in the type of educational material needed by the churches to
ake their members aware of the universal as well as the immediately
cal scope of mission. CWME is at present cooperating with the WCC's
ffice of Education in helping the churches to face this problem.

The question of the relation of the churches to the secular powers has
sumed new urgency since the conference at Bangkok. Christian groups
d individuals in a number of countries have come into conflict with the

government of their countries because of their involvement in Christian mission. This grim trend, which seems to be increasing, makes it all the more urgent to pursue the theme of "Power and Powerlessness", as recommended by the Bangkok Assembly. Other sub-units of the WCC are also deeply involved with the problem, especially the Commission of the Churches on International Affairs, the Programme to Combat Racism, and the Commission on the Churches' Participation in Development. CWME maintains close contacts with them on the staff level and in the case of the former two has consistently given financial support.

Looking towards the Future

The Bangkok conference has given new directions to the work of CWME, and in the period since then these directions have been explored. The main points have briefly been touched upon in this report. They can be summarized as follows:

(1) *The nature of the proclamation* of the Gospel demands continuous emphasis. The study and the conference on "Salvation Today" have merely begun a process which is becoming increasingly central to the missionary enterprise of the Church as well as to other aspects of the churches' life. The meaning of evangelism and of the evangelistic dimension of the Church will need attention. What will it mean, following Nairobi, to confess Christ today?

(2) During the period under review the emphasis upon the context of proclamation has been growing, and it is reasonable to expect that it will continue to grow, with the further development of such tendencies as Black Theology, African Theology and Latin American Theology of Liberation. This should help greatly in promoting *unity in context*. Close attention must be paid to these developments and to the process of relating the various *particular contexts* to each other, thus enabling groups and persons not only to see themselves within a *universal context* of mission, but also to seek that unity which holds the different contexts together.

(3) *Relationships between the churches* must be developed in the coming years to a degree of maturity which will allow the world-wide ecumenical community to participate in mission together with greater integrity and freedom. The churches need to develop the instrumentalities necessary to arrive at such maturity, and CWME, especially through the programme of Ecumenical Sharing of Personnel, will have to play a crucial role in helping the churches to achieve this goal.

(4) Experiments in relating programmes of the different sub-units in the Programme Unit on Faith and Witness have already been made in several areas. These include links between the CWME study of "Salvation

Today" and the study "Giving Account of the Hope that is in Us" undertaken by the Commission on Faith and Order, and cooperation with the Church and Society sub-unit (as well as elements of the Programme Unit on Justice and Service) in confronting the issue of Human Settlements. The ecclesiological implications of the ESP programme have also been mentioned as needing exploration in relation to concerns of Faith and Order. But there is need to explore further *the role of CWME in relation to other programmes* of the Unit in order to make the fullest use of resources and ensure the widest possible scope for programme activities. Such experiments, as they are continued and broadened, may possibly lead to new working arrangements within the Unit as a whole.

SPONSORED AGENCIES

During the last fifteen years, three "Sponsored Agencies" have been established by CWME with the approval of the Central Committee. These agencies have been created in response to specific needs in the field of mission.

A.   Theological Education Fund

The Uppsala Assembly, with its focus upon him who makes "all things new" struck a chord for those involved in theological education, who saw the need for renewal and the urgency of the search for what was authentic. It also brought a deeper awareness in the cry for human development and social justice from the Third World—the cry which was to grow louder and louder until it became the prayer of the Bangkok Assembly: "Out of the depths I cry unto thee, O Lord".

The Theological Education Fund, established in 1958, is now working under its third mandate. The first mandate, given at the Ghana meeting of the International Missionary Council, had an undisguised thrust towards the raising of the level of scholarship and the striving for academic excellence in theological training in the Third World. The second mandate emphasized a missionary orientation and thrust, calling upon the Fund "to respond wherever evidence is found of creative development", particularly "that kind of theological training which leads to a real encounter between the student and the Gospel in terms of his own forms of thought and culture". The third mandate was formulated in response to the spreading crisis in theological education and the search for renewal perceived at Uppsala. The over-all goal was the missiological imperative "that the Gospel be expressed and ministry undertaken *in response to*" three major issues in the contemporary context: (a) the widespread crisis of faith; (b) the issues of social justice and human development; (c) the dialectic between local cultural and religious situations and a universal technological civilization.

There can be seen both continuity and discontinuity in these various mandate emphases, as each was a serious attempt to direct the TEF's effort to the contextual issues in the Church and in the world at the time. Continuity is seen in the concern common to all three mandates, namely, the advancement of theological education in the Third World. Discontinuity arises from the fact that the context changed rapidly and radically in the respective periods, necessitating changes in response.

In order to carry out its third mandate the Theological Education Fund undertook a two-year study, which drew to a close in 1972. At this time it was decided that the "main focus" of its efforts was to be "on Africa, Asia, the Caribbean, Latin America and the Pacific" although it was clear "that the questions with which it is dealing are vital for the churches in all six continents".* The Fund was authorized in 1972 "to seek $3,300,000 during the period from 1970-1977". The booklet *Ecumenical Responses* gives in summary form the 1972-1973 grants, which amounted to a total of $1,095,315. In 1974 over 150 further projects were presented for funding. These grants are intended to help in the reform and renewal hoped for, both among the over 840 institutions now listed in TEF's 1974 Enlarged Directory and the many more institutions not listed—because one of the characteristics of this period is that the horizon of theological education is now widened, and the search for new and alternative patterns must reach beyond the institutions with which the Fund has hitherto been involved.

In producing its working policy for the carrying out of its mandate, the Theological Education Fund introduced two hitherto unfamiliar words which have since become guidelines for discerning evidence of reform and renewal in theological education, namely *contextuality* and *contextualization*. The terms are a kind of shorthand for what has been expressed in various other ways during the study period; for example, by a consultation in Indonesia which had the theme "Double Wrestle": wrestling with God's Word and with this world. This wrestle must be such that we are not only able to discern the contextuality in a particular historical moment, but also be so renewed as to be able to respond to that discernment not only in words but in deeds.

It is a notable feature of the third mandate that nearly all of the projects receiving support from the TEF have been developed and evaluated in

---

* The mandate and the two-year study are contained in <u>Ministry in Context</u>, Bromley, Kent: TEF, 1972. Also relevant is <u>Learning in Context</u>. Bromley: TEF, 1973. Available from WCC Publications, Geneva and New York.

terms of re-defining theology in context. For example, in all of the current faculty development scholarships, clear priority is given to those programmes which are centred in the cultural area of the candidate (whether for study leading to a degree or for a "non-degree" programme). Similarly, a much greater emphasis has come to be placed upon projects for programmes growing out of local attemts to deal with theological education in a "grass-roots" context. A number of these, involving continuing education, laity training, and education by extension, have been given priority in the third mandate period. Again, a growing number of projects has been developed under the category of "alternative" forms of theological education: involving urban or rural mission, groups reflecting on liberation theology, and others which go beyond the boundaries of traditional residential seminaries.

An encouraging example as to how one element in this thrust has developed may be given: in 1964 the TEF made a grant to support an experiment in a Guatemalan school. This was for a new way of teaching which has now come to be known as theological education by extension. The concept has been described in *Ministry in Context*: "Though largely operated from a seminary basis, 'extention' is a mobile training programme allegedly centred around the learner, his specific needs, his availability to study amid his other normal occupations and his skill to do auto-didactic [self-teaching] work on any academic level that best suits him. It caters mainly for people already exercising some sort of leadership, reaches a wider number of students and seems to be financially more viable in poor areas than the residential pattern". This undertaking spread beyond Guatemala into Latin America, then into Asia and parts of Africa; and in spite of certain controversial aspects it attained a position of recognition, so that now, in the third mandate period, it has become a category for TEF support.

But the chief concern—which has been growing more urgent, almost from the first mandate onwards—remains the viability of theological education in the Third World. The Third World has inherited very expensive patterns of theological education, which originated in the context of Western history and cultures—where Christians were in the majority—and were developed in an affluent society. Can such patterns be viable in the contexts of the Christian community when it is in a minority, amid the poverty which is characteristic of the Third World? One of the glaring conclusions of a recent study is that, by and large, the theological institutions of the Third World can count on the local community for only 20% of the necessary financial support. Therefore, to continue the inherited patterns may condemn theological education in the Third World to a "dependency" mentality. This may serve as another existential impetus for the search for alternative patterns; but then, will the quality be endangered? What is *authentic* excellence?

This question leads to larger and deeper issues: What *is* theological education? And what is it for? If we are to be set free to search for alternative patterns, we must go back to these basic questions. In this connection it should be noted that a task force has now been set up by the CWME to assess the place and role of theological education in the total concern and structure of the WCC.

B. Agency for Christian Literature Development

During the period under review, the mandate of the Christian Literature Fund, which was established in 1964, came to an end. In its five years of existence, it had raised and disbursed some U.S. $2,750,000 for the development of Christian literature in Africa, Asia, Latin America, the Caribbean and the Pacific.

In 1970 the CLF became the Agency for Christian Literature Development (ACLD), with a mandate running up to 1975. It has sought to "promote significant advance in the provision of literature addressed with Christian concern to man in his total situation and speaking the language of contemporary society" and to "continue the shift in decision-making from the supporting agencies of the West to Asia, Africa and Latin America". A two-tiered committee structure was established: one in which policy and guidelines were laid down and the other which sought to coordinate the total giving of supporting agencies in the light of this policy. Both committees were constituted in such a way that there was participation in decision-making at all levels by all agencies involved in literature work.

Since Uppsala, many new insights have been gained. Among these may be listed a better-informed professional awareness and the emergence of a group of people with competence in publishing, editing and book-selling; a growing emphasis on self-reliance; a search for communicating the Gospel in indigenous thought-forms and a more readily intelligible style; a concern for relevance and for the necessity to relate the unchanging message to national and social changing attitudes and aspirations. All these are bearing fruit, as is evident in the quality and variety of ACLD publications and the changing emphases in the operations of its bookshops and distribution centres.

Many new and important developments may also be noted.* For example,

---

* These various trends and developments have been summarized in greater detail in ACLD Newsletter; copies available from Agency for Christian Literature Development, 7 St. James's Street, London SW1A 1EF, England.

along with books reflecting the evangelistic thrust and secular outreach, there is a growing body of literature which seeks to discern Christ's presence amidst the longings and struggles of the world's peoples. Dialogue and development have thus received a good deal of attention. There is also a new attempt to relate Christian writings to what is usually called "secular" literature, which forms the every-day reading of people all over the world. This exposure to the creativity of secular writings and providing of a theological critique of such literature is full of possibilities.

"The development of viable publishing concerns must be a major objective of grant-making, but attention will be given to areas where economically viable operations will be difficult if not impossible", says the ACLD mandate. Evaluation of the latter type of operation is to be in terms of the extent of communication achieved in relation to resources used.

The implication of this statement is that if guidelines are suggested for the content of the literature to be published, one cannot expect commercial viability in all ventures. Books on dialogue; periodicals which are not popular in the commonly understood sense but nevertheless put across a creative minority's prophetic point of view; books for the development of the marginal sections of society—all these may not be self-supporting, but are nevertheless necessary.

The investigation into the content of Christian writings and the forms they should assume is an aspect of work that must continue. The fact that all publishers have to deal with is that most congregations are not reading congregations. What can literature agencies do towards promoting a congregational commitment to reading and discussion?

Communication, after all, is the fundamental task of the Church, and a commitment to literature is an essential aspect of this total task. Therefore the ACLD mandate also required it to negotiate with the World Association for Christian Communication (WACC) and to cooperate with it in ways that will lead to other fruitful forms of working and growing together. Christian literature understood as "literature [which] the Church needs to do its work" cannot exist in isolation from the other media of communication used by the Church. This calls for a sustained coming together and the continued cooperation of people working in the various media. It is hoped that the WACC will enable the WCC to be more effective in the communication of the message of Jesus Christ, through mutual sharing and enrichment. At present it is proposed to have two media development units within the Association, Print and Electronics, with provision to include other media when possible. This step marks a new era in the history of the Church's involvement in communication.

C. Christian Medical Commission

The Christian Medical Commission (CMC) was established in 1967 by the World Council of Churches to coordinate church-related medical work on the six continents. Because of the urgent need to deal with the legacy of medical missionary work in the new situation of the 1960's and 1970's its programme has been chiefly related to Africa and Asia and, to a lesser degree, to Latin America. How was this work, carried out through 2,500 church-related hospitals and many more health centres and dispensaries, to be related to the mission of emerging national churches as they sought the best means for proclaiming the Gospel in their particular national and cultural context?

Because of the dependent nature of the relationship of churches in developing countries to overseas mission organizations and church-related supporting agencies, the Commission's involvement in these countries naturally extended to a corresponding involvement with groups of this kind in Europe, North America, Australia and New Zealand. Although the activities of the Commission were largely geared to giving assistance to developing countries, many of the issues it raised were found to be relevant and applicable to the churches in the more affluent world.

Church-related medical work and that of the CMC are influenced from two sides: first, by developments in medicine, health care thinking, and health planning; and secondly, by developments in theology and the practice of Christian mission. Thus, CMC activities have been determined, on the one hand, by an emphasis on providing basic health services for the large proportion of the world's population which is still deprived of such care, and, on the other, by the fact that this emphasis on health care is an expression of the healing ministry of the "Church for others". Taking the Incarnation and the call to mission seriously makes it necessary to look at *what* is being done in the field of health care and medical work and also at *how* it is done. This has led the CMC to question and challenge one-sided medical programmes which do not meet the needs of people in their community and therefore constitute a negative witness for the Church. In practice, this has been done through project evaluation, participation in health planning, study and reflection, as well as through support to experimental projects.

The CMC has seen its role as primarily one of helping churches and their medical institutions to re-think the whole question of the Christian responsibility for the development of health care to the total population of the area they serve. This has made it necessary to stimulate and help establish national agencies for the coordination and joint planning of health care offered by both Protestants and Roman Catholics. These coordinating odies, which have had the approval of National Christian Councils and National Conferences of Catholic Bishops, have been able to work effectively with governmental health authorities in the framework of national health plans. There have also been working relationships between the CMC and the World Health Organization. Close and continuous cooperation with the Roman Catholic Church has also been assured by the presence of a Roman Catholic Sister, who is also a doctor, as a Consultant on the CMC staff.

Re-thinking the delivery of health care and the use of limited Christian resources has inevitably led the Commission to involvement in the question of total community development and thus to the ethical implications in determining priorities for who should get health care, the nature of health care, the nature of health, and the role of the community in promoting health. This has led on to theological discussions about health and salvation, health and social justice, and the role of the Christian community as a healing community.

A specific example of work in health promotion encouraged by the CMC is the Chimaltenango Development Project in rural Guatemala, under the direction of Carroll Behrhorst, M.D.

"In Chimaltenango", Dr. Behrhorst has written, "we felt that we must begin by knowing the people—what they were like and what they thought they needed. This is easily said, but not so easily done. . . . When we first began, I did nothing but walk around the town and get acquainted with the people and play with the children. Gradually I would be invited into their homes to have coffee with them or to sit down to a meal of tortillas and beans. This went on for three months until I was well known in that town and accepted. Then we rented a building for $25 a month, so there was no investment. One hundred and twenty-five patients came that first day, and we have never had less than that number since. They now average 200 per day. . . .

"Curing is not the important thing. It is much more important to encourage life; and this is not very difficult in Guatemala because the Indians themselves are dedicated to life. After some experience working with these people, we came to realize that they were in need of other services besides health care. The following list represents our present estimate of priorities: social injustice; land tenure; population control; agricultural production and marketing; malnutrition; health training; curative medicine".*

Behrhorst's account of the project appears in full in Contact, 19, February 1974, published by the CMC. Contact, an occasional bulletin of the Commission, includes both descriptions of specific projects and case studies and also papers of a theoretical character. Available from CMC, Geneva, and WCC Publications, New York.

The most innovative features in the Chimaltenango project are of special interest, namely, that health care should be made available to people on their terms; that the provision of basic health care requires a multifaceted approach to development; and that it also requires a liberal experimentation in personnel training of those selected for this purpose by the communities to be served. The project seriously challenges many of the presuppositions on which health care systems are designed—and it works very successfully.

III. DIALOGUE WITH PEOPLE OF LIVING FAITHS AND IDEOLOGIES

Dialogue with people of living faiths and ideologies has been a long-standing concern in ecumenical history. If it is understood as an attempt to establish two-way traffic along what was previously a one-way street, then early signs of it can be seen in the attempt to discover "positive values" in religious and secular culture. However, what is decisively new since Uppsala is the increasing recognition by the churches of the fact of cultural pluralism and the way in which this has been reflected in the structural changes, the more recent statements and the activities of the World Council.

Originally dialogue emerged out of missionary considerations of the proper Christian attitude to adherents of other religions. Since Uppsala, it has no longer been confined to the particular sphere of mission. It has become one of the main concerns of the ecumenical movement and is recognized as a continuing Christian obligation in a world of various faiths, cultures and ideologies. What are the theological implications of this shift of emphasis? What issues have emerged for the churches in their actual experience of dialogue? What are some of the areas of common concern for various parts of the WCC in the coming years? These are some of the questions that must be considered.

New Directions

The change in theological emphasis may be brought out by reference to the various descriptions of this concern. It is no longer "The Gospel and Non-Christian Religions" or "The Word of God and the Living Faiths of Men". It is now "Dialogue with People of Living Faiths and Ideologies". Giving an adequate description of the complex relationship between people of various faiths and ideologies is a difficult undertaking. Nevertheless, there are certain points to be recognized. The present formulation avoids the description of the other as "*non*-Christians". The concern deals with *people*, not with religions or ideologies as systems. It is not discussion *about*, but dialogue *with* the partners. It recognizes that there are responses other than Christian to the mystery of human existence. It is more open to others but not less committed to Christ. It is less aggressive and more humble. These new approaches reflect theological virtues, not opportunistic attitudes.

The change is also reflected in the official statements of World Council Assemblies. For example Evanston (1954), referring to "the renaissance of non-Christian religions and ideologies", said: "It is not so much the truth of these systems of thought and feeling which makes the appeal but rather their determination to change the oppressive conditions of life". In New Delhi (1961), even though there was a reference to "the truth claims of the partner in conversation", the report saw dialogue within the framework of communication and spoke of it "as a useful means of evangelism". At Uppsala (1968) the paragraph on dialogue, described by Carl F. Hallencreutz, Study and Research Secretary, Church of Sweden Mission, as "diplomatically balanced", comes in Section II, "Renewal in Mission":

"In dialogue we share our common humanity, its dignity and fallenness, and express our common concern for that humanity. It opens the possibility of sharing in new forms of community and common service. Each meets and challenges the other; witnessing from the depths of his existence to the ultimate concerns that come to expression in word and action. As Christians we believe that Christ speaks in this dialogue, revealing himself to those who do not know him and [correcting] the limited and distorted knowledge of those who do".

The *Interim Policy Statement and Guidelines* received and adopted by the Central Committee at Addis Ababa in 1971, and which is the mandate for the present programme on dialogue, goes further than any of these statements. It bases itself on our faith in Jesus Christ "who makes us free and draws us out of isolation into genuine dialogue into which we enter with faith in the promise of Jesus Christ that the Holy Spirit will lead us into all truth". It further states that dialogue offers "the promise of discovering new dimensions of understanding our faith", opportunities for "new relationships between Christians and men of other faiths", and possibilities where our "Christian faith can be tested and strengthened". It also envisages cooperation with people of other faiths and ideologies on specific issues which "will involve not only study but also common action".*

At Bangkok in 1973, for the first time at a world conference of the Commission on World Mission and Evangelism, the local people, in this

---

* This text and other important discussions of the dialogue concern may be found in *Living Faiths and the Ecumenical Movement*. Geneva: WCC, 1971.

instance the Buddhists in Thailand, were represented by a specially-invited group who were asked to present *their* understanding of salvation in a plenary session. The section on dialogue at that conference acknowledged that people of other faiths also have "mission" and that "because of this reciprocal mission, Christian world mission may once more become acceptable as an authentic expression of Christian faith and not be open to the charge of religious imperialism". Bangkok also touched upon the question of the relationship between dialogue and evangelism. It said, "We will be faithful to our Lord's command to mission and witness, which is part of our title deed and which people of other faiths know as a duty for Christians as their own faith-relationship with the Ultimate gives them a sense of universal significance. A desire to share and a readiness to let others share with us should inspire our witness to Christ rather than a desire to win a theological argument".

Factors in Change and Further Developments

The churches that constitute the fellowship of the World Council come from a plurality of cultural situations, reflect different historical backgrounds and hold a wide variety of confessional beliefs. Therefore different and even conflicting views on dialogue are to be expected within the growing fellowship. Nevertheless, several *factors* have contributed to dialogue being understood in the WCC as a common adventure of the churches and a continuing ecumenical concern. Some of these are:

(a) The involvement of Christians with people of living faiths and ideologies not only in Asia and Africa but also in other continents. The number of people of other faiths in Europe and the Americas has increased in recent years. This calls for new relationships and for a theological reconsideration of former attitudes.

(b) The insights gained in national contexts through the work of Christian Study Centres, particularly since New Delhi (1961).

(c) The gradual recognition that dialogue is not a separate interest but touches other ecumenical concerns as well, such as unity, mission, development, education, human rights, technology and the future of man, and the like. What we do *with* others matters as much as what we seek to do *for* them.

(d) The experience of actual dialogues in the international context, theological reflection on them and mutual sharing of the lessons between Christians and people of other faiths.

Supporting all this is our faith in the living God, in Jesus Christ, as the Lord of history, including contemporary history, and in the Holy Spirit, who is active at all times, leading people into fulness of truth and abundant life. Significant *developments* since Uppsala include the following:

(1) Relations with the *Jewish people* have been a part of the World Council's

programme from the very beginning (and included efforts during World War II to aid Jews in escaping from nazi persecution). Over the years the WCC agency principally concerned for this work has been the Committee on the Church and the Jewish People (CCJP). Recently made an integral part of the Dialogue sub-unit, the CCJP has included among its tasks the re-examination of Christian attitudes towards Judaism. At a 1974 consultation co-sponsored by CCJP the main issue was the relationship between witness, mission and dialogue. "For some years", the participants stated, "it appeared that mission and dialogue would mutually exclude each other—that some would carry on mission and others dialogue. But during this conference it became clear that, even in the Jewish-Christian confrontation, mission and dialogue belong closely together. A Christian witness to Jews or the testimony of Jewish beliefs to Christians is only possible in an atmosphere of dialogue with the willingness to listen, understand and trust, and with the presupposition of solidarity and equality. Christians and Jews must learn together why Jews are distrustful of missionary attempts and why Christians cannot renounce the witness to their faith".

(2) Christian-Muslim dialogues have been going on at both local and international levels. The first invitation to *Muslims* was in 1969, when the Faith and Order Secretariat invited them for joint consultations with Christians. A meeting at Broumana in 1972 was planned by a group of Christians and Muslims. It considered the theme "Human Understanding and Cooperation", in both its theological and practical aspects.* The participants, 46 persons from 20 countries, almost equally derived from the Christian and Muslim communities, declared: "We do not desire to confine our conversation and collaboration to a group of experts. We feel an obligation to help make possible a wider spirit and practice of dialogue in our communities. [In our view] certain irreducible principles should be respected. These are:

"(a) *Frank witness*: We did not ask each other to suppress or conceal his convictions. In dialogue each should bear witness of his motives to his fellows and to God. This frank witness can help to remove complacency, suspicion or unspoken fears.

"(b) *Mutual respect*: . . . This does not involve a stale co-existence of 'live and let live', but a sensitive regard for the partner's scruples and convictions, a sympathy for his difficulties and an admiration for his achievements. . . .

"(c) *Religious freedom*: We should be scrupulous about our protection of religious liberty. This involves not only the rights of any religious minority, but also the rights of each individual. While we accept that both religious traditions have a missionary vocation, proselytism should be avoided. . . ."

By the time of the Fifth Assembly Christian-Muslim dialogues will also have

See <u>Christian-Muslim Dialogue</u>: Papers presented at the Broumana Consultation, edited by S.J. Samartha and J.B. Taylor. Geneva: WCC, 1973.

been held under the auspices of the DFI and the Faith and Order Secretariat in West Africa and South-east Asia. These dialogues should contribute to Assembly thinking about the *common* search for community between ourselves and our neighbours.

(3) Dialogues with adepts of the *Hindu* and *Buddhist* faiths have a long history, particularly in the multi-cultural and multi-religious situations of Asia. The nature of truth, the meaning of spirituality, the struggle for community, the spiritual and cultural resources for development and the foundations of a just peace have been some of the themes of these bilateral meetings.

For example, "one of the favourite topics of discussion with Hindus", Klaus Klostermaier has noted, is "the 'way of salvation'. Often I was asked whether there was a 'Christian Yoga'.‡ The mystical tradition of Christianity is widely unknown among Hindus—but those who know it cherish it and are prepared to 'assume' it. There are several extremely interesting common points in Hindu and Christian mysticism. *The Imitation . of Christ* [by Thomas à Kempis] is a favourite with many Hindus. [Yet] dialogue is as wide as life itself. There are many problems in Hinduism for which we do not have a Christian equivalent—and many of our Christian controversies are unintelligible to a Hindu. Hindu-Christian dialogue is as much a matter of living together as discussion and talk".

Lynn de Silva, in a paper on "Some Issues in the Buddhist-Christian Dialogue", quotes the views of a participant in such discussions: "One of the most important things for us today is to study one another's religions sympathetically and deeply so that we can intelligently discover where we are at one and where we are at odds. A right understanding of our agreements will certainly promote amity and concord, but our differences need not divide us if we rightly and intelligently understand them". In fact, de Silva points out, a dialogue on the subject of "The Self in Buddhism and Christianity" proved to be "one of the most revealing and challenging" in this regard. "It helped to clarify the false notion Christians have that the Buddhist doctrine of Anatta‡ implies a nihilistic view, and the wrong notion Buddhists (and some Christians) have that the Bible teaches a doctrine of the immortality of the soul, an eternalism which Buddhism rejects. It also revealed that the apparent contradiction of the Buddhist and Christian doctrines on man is not so radical as to preclude any possibility of dialogue for which some common ground is necessary"*

It is no coincidence that the impetus for ecumenical recognition of dialogue has come not least from churches living in pluralistic religious situations, such as Asia and Africa, where the results of these meetings have been brought into a wider context.

---

* The papers by Klaus Klostermaier and Lynn de Silva are to be found, along with other noteworthy analyses, in Dialogue between Men of Living Faiths, edited by S.J. Samartha. Geneva: WCC, 1971.

(4) In a consultation at Ajaltoun, Lebanon, in 1970, Hindus, Buddhists, Christians and Muslims came together in *multilateral discussion* for the first time under the auspices of the World Council of Churches. The meeting's starting-point was the sharing of experiences of actual dialogue in which the participants had had personal experience. Throughout the consultation a warm response could be felt on the part of those of other faiths to the initiative taken by the WCC.

The participants noted that "the dialogue did undergo moments of tension, acute consciousness of theological and doctrinal differences, and awareness of ineffectivity and inauthenticity of dialogue carried on in an insulated situation without relevance to the actual contexts from which the participants were drawn". And yet, "out of several informal conversations and encounters among the participants a great feeling of belonging and sharing arose. What mattered most was not just dialogue but a special kind of community that the dialogue seemed to bring about. It was this sense of being drawn into a new community of men of faith that should operate in our particular social contexts. But this sense of being in a new community was not without inner threats and concommitant inadequacies".

A second multilateral dialogue took place four years later in Colombo, Sri Lanka, bringing together people of five different faiths, this time including Jews as well. A great deal of preparatory work had taken place in the mean time (including a number of the bilateral dialogues just referred to). The theme of the gathering was "Towards World Community: Resources and Responsibilities for Living Together". "World Community" was not regarded as "a super-organization" nor as an attempt to shape "one world religion", but rather as a matter of inter-dependence, the quality of mutual relationships and working together for immediate goals.

The *Memorandum** issued by the participants included the following remarks: "We question a utopian approach which oversimplifies the political, economic, cultural, environmental and many other problems involved. . . . We have no illusions that some of us and some of our neighbours believe that our religions or ideologies make us arrogantly self-sufficient; we should beware of the danger of such self-sufficiency. . . . It was also at the local level that we saw some promising signs of fulfilling, in microcosm, the spirit of world community. . . . It might be the special task of religious groups to stress the importance of models of concrete local community as the first reality of world community, but also as the reality which mediates world community. At the local level each and all of us have opportunity to learn to accept and share with people of different convictions in a spirit of mutual respect and reconciliation".

The wider dimension of multilateral debate is necessary partly because of the increasingly pluralistic setting of the Church in the world, partly because the three Semitic faiths (Judaism, Christianity and Islam), despite some mutual involvement, have not really encountered "Eastern spirituality", and partly because a corrective is needed to the tendency to understand God's saving activity in history among people of different cultures in terms which have been shaped and narrowed by the Mediterranean culture.

(5) Another significant change is the emergence of *primal world-views*, including those of African traditional religions, in the forefront of ecumenical dialogue. The implications of this for our understanding of theology and the nature of dialogue have yet to be worked out. The Ibadan consultation, in 1973, dealing with "The Wholeness of Life: Christian Involvement in Mankind's Inner Dialogue with Primal World-Views" was only a beginning in this direction.* It is hoped that local and regional follow-up will take place, not only in Africa, but also in those parts of Asia and Oceania where Christians are influenced by primal world-views.

(6) The ecumenical concern for dialogue takes into account not just "religions" but also "*ideologies*". Ideologies like Marxism and Maoism in the new China, understood both as secular faiths and as tools for social change, raise issues that cut across traditional religious boundaries. The assumptions of science and technology raise questions about the very credibility of faith (and not just that of Christian faith). It has been difficult, however, to find partners for these discussions, even though the issues raised by ideologies have already come on the agendas of several dialogues. The implications of this study go far beyond this particular sub-unit or Unit, and an inter-unit approach is therefore necessary.** Steps have been taken to make this a joint enterprise of the Unit on Faith and Witness with some contribution from other Units as well.

(7) Another new emphasis, controversial but challenging, is the place of "*spirituality*"—in particular, of devotion, prayer and meditation—in dialogue. This issue was either avoided entirely in previous years or touched upon in the most superficial manner. But religion is more than concepts and rituals. The symbols and signs of prayer, meditation and silence have deep meaning for life in communities of faith. Moreover, "the spirituality of the secular" in its thrust for self-transcendence is also part of man's quest for meaning. In every recent dialogue this matter has been present, raising disturbing but searching questions not only for Christians but for people of other faiths as well.

The question is not so much one of definitions or fear of "syncretism"‡. Rather, how do we express the dimensions of our spiritual life (a) in an age of science and technology when quite a few people, including much of the world's youth, are rejecting traditional forms of worship, and (b) at a time when many people, including young people in the West, seem to be turning to forms of Eastern spirituality, such as

* See Dossier Section III, pages 29-38.

** See Dossier Section III, pages 41-8.

Yoga‡, Zen‡, Hare Krishna‡ movements, and the like. In the context of inter-religious dialogue the question also involves trying to understand the religious life of our partners not only through doctrines and academic concepts but in addition through religious symbols, music, art and meditation.

"Spirituality is like a bird", said a Jewish rabbi who took part in the Colombo dialogue. "If you try hard you may catch it; if you try too hard you may choke it". "The more I define the new spirituality", a Western Christian has written, "the more I put the phenomenon into its historical, sociological, psychological and theological (etc.) boxes, then the more I lose touch with 'where it's really at'. To talk about it authentically I should spin a fable, dangle a parable".

In pointing out that many young people in the West are rejecting traditional forms of Christian spirituality and are seeking new forms, Huston Smith has written that the youth are celebrating "the holiness of the 'is' rather than the 'ought', the present rather than the future. For the first time since the Renaissance and the Reformation, Western society is hearing through them the suggestion that perhaps the contemplative life is the equal of the active one". In inter-religious dialogue one common quest could be to seek forms or expressions of the spiritual dimension as a link between the active and the contemplative, the mystical and the historical, the present and the future.

Looking Ahead

It should be obvious that since Uppsala considerable changes have taken place in the area of dialogue. But many churches have yet to reflect these changes in their life and witness. Dialogue is no longer just the hobby of a few in far-away places but an ecumenical concern embracing the whole inhabited earth. It is not a peripheral activity of the World Council, but touches many of its programmes. At its deepest level, it raises questions about the "truth claims" of people of various faiths and ideologies and about their ultimate hopes in a world of science-based technology. It is concerned not just with traditional religions but with living faiths, faith human beings live by today, and with ideologies—their secular promise, historical vision, and tools for revolutionary action. It calls for profound changes in our attitudes to our neighbours of various beliefs and loyalties.

As a result of the experiences of dialogues since Uppsala, and of careful reflection on them, *certain issues* have emerged that should be considered not only at Nairobi but also in the coming years beyond.

(1) There is first the question of *the nature of dialogue* itself. This is not so much a matter of definitions and concepts as of accepting the fact of *living* dialogue, of seeking to understand the mystery of human relationships in community, of commitment to one's faith and openness to that of others. Without the freedom to be open, to be committed and to witness,

genuine dialogue is impossible. But what is the "specificity" of dialogue as distinct from inter-religious meetings?

(2) Then there is the question of the relation between *dialogue*, *mission* and *witness*. This question will be with us for a long time but may have to be formulated differently. Has dialogue blunted the edge of Christian mission or has it produced a climate where Christian witness can be made with more freedom and openness? There are neighbours of other faiths who suspect that dialogue is *a new tool* for mission, and there are Christians who fear that it is a *betrayal* of mission.

Here is a Hindu voice: "Now you want to have dialogue with us. Some wonder, however, at your intentions. Is it not true that all Semitic religions, be they Judaism, Islam or Christianity, are founded on the notion of a chosen people which has received from God directly the mission to convert the whole world to their particular tenets? Do you not realize that such an approach to the religious sphere affects immediately all attempts at real dialogue? You should not be surprised therefore when not a few among us suspect your stretched-out hand and your so sweet invitation to dialogue".

And a Christian voice: "If dialogue is to take the form of true Christian witness, it can never reach the point when the Christian, consciously or unconsciously, has to confess to the other man: 'I am as lost as you are; all we can do is to press forward together in our search for the truth'. The Christian, in his identification with his fellow man, will ever be conscious that he possesses a treasure, and that treasure is Jesus Christ. His basic task will ever be a presentation and introduction of the One who in his unique person and redemptive work is outside the acquaintance of his fellow man".*

Is there an understanding of dialogue which neither betrays the commitment of the Christian nor exploits the confidence of people of other faiths? The views of Archbishop George Appleton may be seen as a counterbalance to those of the previously quoted Christian witness: "If God is the Creator of all, if he has made man in his own image, must we not think of him as coming to all, caring for all, trying to influence all in the direction of truth and goodness? This last question has a sharp challenge to Christians: have we emphasized God so much as Redeemer that we have neglected our belief in him as Creator?"

(3) This leads to a more basic question which can no longer be ignored. Do we still treat the "*truth claims*" in other faiths as we did in a more triumphalistic era—as false, ordinary, discontinuous, distorted, partially true, incomplete, preparatory, and so on, in various polite and impolite permutations and combinations? To what extent have our own ideological assumptions distorted our understanding of the Gospel and Jesus Christ and the manner in which it has been proclaimed? If the common search for community in an interdependent world is a reality, what separates us and

* See Dossier Section III, pages 10-13.

what unites us at the deepest level? How do we grasp the symbols and signs of the sacramental life of other living faiths? Dialogue should provide us with the context to seek fresh answers and to formulate together appropriate questions.

(4) Related to the question of "truth claims" is another question often raised in ecumenical debate: Does dialogue lead to *syncretism*?‡ A group of 23 Christian theologians who met at Zurich in 1970 to evaluate the dialogue at Ajaltoun wrote as follows: "This apprehension should be taken seriously, and the issue of syncretism studied at some depth. But the cry of syncretism should not be raised too lightly. Christian communities in Asia and Africa have often been thrown into such a state of alarm by Western missionaries and theologians about the all-pervasive dangers of 'syncretism' that they have been cut off from living and human relationships with their community and culture. Hence they have been prevented from working at any creative relationship between their Christian commitment and their non-Christian environments which are, strictly, their own environments.

"When the Christian Church becomes organized, it has always to incarnate the Gospel through certain cultural and intellectual forms. In this creative interplay between the elements of revelation and certain select aspects of a given culture, there is the danger that the revelation may be submerged and compromised by these cultural elements. But nothing is to be gained by seeking to avoid this danger. It is, presumably, as unChristian to be trapped in a particular form of a 'Western' culture as it is to succumb overmuch to an 'Eastern' or an 'African' one. We have to discover how to make sure that the revelatory element lives creatively with and transforms the cultural elements while taking from them all that truly enriches. How do we account for the large crop of syncretistic religious sects rising up all over the world? What is the dynamic behind them? And how far are they symptomatic of the churches having failed to take seriously legitimate local aspirations and cultural forms?"

(5) A further question is how far dialogue can be expressed in terms of active *cooperation*? Dialogue is not just a matter of talking, but of living and working together. There are common concerns in society and in the world where Christians can cooperate with people of other faiths and ideologies. Can these be expressed in concrete programmes of action as part of our search for community? What are the provisional goals we can accept without stumbling over possible differences in our understanding of ultimate goals?

(6) A final question concerns the ways in which the Dialogue Working Group is thinking about the *commitment*, *style* and *emphases* of dialogue in the coming years. The Working Group, consisting of 35 people from 21 countries, gave a good deal of attention to this question at its 1974 meeting. Such matters as the specific character of dialogues sponsored by

the World Council, the relationship between dialogue and witness, indigenization in the context of dialogue and issues arising from increasing cooperation between people of different faiths and ideologies must obviously receive attention.

Local and regional dialogues should continue, with contributions from youth and women effectively provided for. The youth of today are more in touch with people of other faiths through travel, exchange of students, teachers and workers, and television programmes than ever before. Ways should be found to bring their contributions into the life and thinking of the churches. The present methods of bilateral dialogues ought to continue, but with less frequent multilateral meetings. More time should be given for careful reflection on the theological implications of dialogues and their consequences on the attitudes of Christians in different countries.

Ways of implementing some of the recommendations that have come out of recent dialogues also must be found, as well as the manner in which the WCC should respond to various initiatives that come with increasing frequency from people of other living faiths. The process of exploring new dimensions in the relationships between Christians and people of other faiths and ideologies is only at the beginning stages. As the Zurich group said: "Dialogue between Christians and men of other commitments, in the sense of a talking together, which is a sharing together concerned with finding a way forward of living together, is an inevitable, urgent and promising manner of discovering how to bring together God's offer of communion in Christ and our diverse ways of common human living".

IV. STUDIES ON CHURCH AND SOCIETY

As an innovator of ecumenical social thought and action the Uppsala Assembly may be considered a landmark in ecumenical history. Stimulated by the findings of the 1966 World Conference on Church and Society (on the theme "Christians in the Technical and Social Revolutions of Our Time"), the Assembly recommended a number of new social programmes: for world economic development, the study of non-violent strategies in effecting social change, the elimination of racism and, perhaps most unexpected of all, an enquiry into "science and the problems of world-wide change".

In the period since Uppsala the sub-unit on Church and Society has been responsible for ecumenical reflection and action on two of these topics: problems of world-wide technological change and the question of violence and nonviolence in effecting social justice.

A. The Future of Humanity in a World of Science-Based Technology

Terra Incognita: The Approach

"A proper theological understanding of the churches' responsibility for man's future may most creatively emerge from the encounter of Christian faith and tradition with various ideologies and with the insights of the social and natural sciences". This assertion outlines the theological approach envisaged in 1969 as the starting point of Church and Society's ecumenical enquiry on the "Future of Man and Society in a World of Science-Based Technology". What was then stated as a possibility has become increasingly urgent and has proved to be a crucial component in the definition of Christian commitment to social responsibility today. A new global awareness of the social and ethical implications of the role of science and technology in shaping human life opened up a broad area of *terra incognita* [unexplored territory] to the ecumenical debate.

An intensified effort to realize more social justice and fuller human dignity in a world conditioned predominantly by science-based technology was indeed long overdue. "Whilst science-based technology and the ability to predict on the basis of it grow rapidly, the ability to use it for agreed social purposes grows much more slowly and the necessary change in social institutions and structures comes slower still. People lack the basic information as well as the ethical criteria for making responsible choices between the new options which technology makes possible". This was the theme of the prospectus prepared by the Working Committee on Church and Society in 1969, outlining the purpose and scope of this new, worldwide ecumenical enquiry.*

The five-year study programme has shown that the impact of science and technology on human development is an issue of rapidly growing relevance to all humanity. The assumption of the 1960's, of a complementarity between the scientific and technological revolution sweeping developed nations, and the social revolution characteristic of Asia, Africa and Latin America, proved misleading. Even in 1969 there was still a considerable measure of optimism that modern man would discover the right uses of modern technology "to enhance his humanity and social solidarity rather than be destroyed by it". While recognizing the hazards, emphasis was still placed on the "unique opportunities [offered by technology] for human development" and for altering the natural and

---

See the Minutes of the WCC Central Committee Meeting, Canterbury, August 1969. Geneva: WCC, 1969. pages 190-8.

social environment. Today, the "limits to growth" debate has exposed the limitations of science and technology. Questions are being raised about the nature of the technological revolution, its exploitative ingredients, its cultural underpinnings of materialism: in effect, its possible threat to the survival of mankind.

It is now fairly generally agreed that the world cannot support for many more decades a steadily rising rate of technological exploitation of natural resources maintained by the industrially developed countries, especially if the needs of the poorer people and of future generations are to be considered.

In addition to the exhaustion of finite resources, rapid industrial development and its accompanying patterns of consumption have brought in their wake a level of pollution and environmental destruction which threatens man's health and well-being in ways never previously foreseen. The prevention of these and other socially undesirable side effects of the new technology can be achieved only through a substantial revision of social goals and behaviour for which people accustomed to modern technological conveniences seem unprepared.

It was the growing awareness of this significant shift in ecumenical thinking, from a rather easy optimism to a sober realism in assessing the future, which provided the starting point for the ecumenical enquiry: "In the light of the Gospel what realistic hopes may we have for human society in the midst of its present crisis and possibilities so that the churches and all men of good will may be moved to turn their hopes into reality?"

Exploration: Finding the Way

To delimit and outline the major issues for the enquiry, an exploratory conference on Technology, Faith and the Future was held in Geneva in June 1970.* It was attended by 100 participants representing a broad cross-section of scientific and technological disciplines as well as theology and the social sciences. It was the first time that the World Council of Churches had obtained the participation of a considerable number of scientists and technologists; and it became evident that they were interested in the discussion of the social and ethical implications of their disciplines and were ready to work with the churches in establishing clearer guidelines for the use of science and technology in society.

In the light of this conference it was decided to focus attention in the study on three themes: Science and Quality of Life; Political and Economic

---

* A report by David M. Gill, entitled From Here to Where? (Geneva: WCC, 1970), presents an evaluation on the basis of background papers and speeches contributed to the conference.

Choices in a Technological Era; Images of the Future. The strategy was to work at these on two levels: through a series of international consultations and working parties focussing on rather specific issues; and a series of regional meetings organized to relate the total enquiry to the problems of particular regions, especially in the countries of Africa, Asia and Latin America.* This enabled and ensured an approach to the main issues of science and technology which drew upon a wide range of perspectives.

(1) *The Ethical Dilemmas of a Scientific Era*. There is increasing concern about the consequences of new scientific and technological discoveries for traditional spiritual and ethical values. This is especially true in the area of the biological sciences. The ecumenical Consultation on Genetics and the Quality of Life (Zurich, June 1973) posed the ethical challenge of scientific advances as follows:

"Churchmen cannot expect precedents from the past to provide answers to questions never asked in the past. On the other hand, new scientific advances do not determine what are worthy human goals. Ethical decisions in uncharted areas require that scientific capabilities be understood and used by persons and communities sensitive to their own deepest convictions about human nature and destiny. There is no sound ethical judgement in these matters independent of scientific knowledge, but science does not itself prescribe the good".**

The uncertainty, the fear of accepting technological possibility too easily as an ethical *fait accompli*, has encouraged new and intensive ethical discussions in this field.

(2) *Science as a Theological Problem*. A Working Party on the Critique of Scientific Rationality (Zurich, June 1973) was organized to evaluate present theologies as tools for a critical analysis of the assumptions of modern science.***

Today technological triumphalism is replaced by technological apocalypticism, the feeling that science-based technology has a momentum which defies any kind of human control or planning and could lead to catastrophe. This mood is rapidly being communicated to the industrially

---

* The findings of the enquiry, as developed in the various conferences and consultations, have been communicated to an increasing number of interested persons through a special bulletin entitled Anticipation (19 numbers in four years). This bulletin contains not only papers and addresses presented to the meetings but documents drawn from the rapidly developing world-wide secular discussion of these themes.

** Report: Genetics and the Quality of Life, Study Encounter 53, Vol. X No. 1, 1974, See also Dossier Section VI, pages 41-43 Prof. Charles Birch has edited the papers contributed to this Consultation in a volume entitled Genetics and the Quality of Life. London: Pergamon Press, 1974.

*** See Anticipation No. 16, March 1974; also Dossier Section VI, pages 53-58.

less developed nations still hoping for their technological fulfilment. The result is growing pessimism about the future and new doubts about the possibility of using science and technology to advance human welfare in an effective way. There is also doubt that any of the known theological and ethical systems have the power to achieve a new understanding of the quality of life and the life styles which might keep life human. Specific issues posed include:

(a) Man's confidence in his right to dominate his natural environment. This domination has produced the problems centering around the general issue of ecology. Today there is an evident need for "new attitudes to nature, the re-evaluation of the human role in the entire creation and of our classical conceptions of human dominance over nature". It is not yet clear what liberation means in this context.

(b) The pressures to organize man's social life into a rationalized system. "Progress" in technology calls for attempts at world-wide centralized control. The result of technology thus becomes "the centralized total system in order to realize its own potentiality, rationality and usefulness".

(c) The acceptance of "technology as historical fate, as something irreversible and unstoppable". Even the requirements for controlling technology add to, rather than diminish, its potential threat to the freedom of man in history. This leads to the apparently unresolvable paradox of a technological culture: to be liberated by becoming more rational (employing more technology) or by becoming more irrational, that is, by accepting dependence on the irrational vitalities of individual autonomy.

The environmental crisis, resulting from man's vast exploitation of man and nature, sharpened the challenge and accelerated the search for ethical criteria for assessing a sufficient quality of life, not only for the present generation everywhere but for future generations as well. It was in the light of this concern that the Working Committee of Church and Society asked Dr. Thomas S. Derr, Professor of Religion at Smith College, USA, to prepare a short but comprehensive study of the issues involved. His book, *Ecology and Human Liberation: A Theological Critique of the Use and Abuse of Our Birthright* (Geneva: WCC, 1973) surveys the several different attitudes and assumptions within the environmental debate and offers a theological perspective based on the biblical tradition.* This book has stimulated an intense discussion, and representatives of the so-called "Process Theology" have, in particular, expressed their fundamental objections to Derr's view regarding their theological rationale for a new attitude of humanity towards nature.**

---

* A second book on similar issues from an Orthodox perspective has been prepared by Father Paul Verghese, India. His study is entitled The Human Presence: Reflections on the Role of Humanity in an Evolving Universe.

** See Anticipation No. 16, March 1974; also Dossier Section VI, pages 35-36.

(3) *Cultural Values and Technologies–Does Goddess Technology Speak ʻwahili?* "The majority of Africans believe that Western technology can be imported lock, stock and barrel for the rapid modernization of their economies, and that total cultural imitation of the West or the East is the fastest and surest way to achieve national greatness....This cultural, political, and ideological subservience to the West or the East creates a barrier to the adoption of distinctive methods and techniques which would lead Africa out of its backwardness, give it a vision of greatness, validate native talents and achievements, and provide the strength of a nationalist ideology for continued modernization". (Dossier Section VI, page 35.)

This assertion by Prof. S.A. Aluko of the University of Ife, Nigeria, in his presentation to the West African Regional Conference,* characterizes the fear of human alienation within a modern technological environment as experienced in many countries of Africa, Asia and Latin America. Prof. Kosuke Koyama has called this the confrontation of the "straight technological mind", with the "curved liturgical mind".** The transfer of resources and technology from industrially developed to developing nations has not only imposed heavy burdens on the recipients in the form of debt obligations, unsatisfactory patterns of production and consumption, drain of resources, and the like, but has also undermined social justice and self-reliance. A new interpretation of "development" has become essential, based on a new understanding of self-reliance in Africa, Asia and Latin America—the effort of these countries to define, interpret and plan development in terms of their own political, social and cultural realities.

(4) *Technology and Ecology in Ecumenical Perspective.* A Consultation on the Human Environment and Responsible Choice, Nemi, Italy, in June 1971, brought together persons of such diverse perspectives on the future as the American writer Theodore Roszak, WCC Central Committee Chairman M.M. Thomas, the microbiologist Bentley Glass, the Latin American urban planner Jorge Hardoy, the Nigerian physicist Ben Nwosu and the Norwegian physicist Jørgen Randers, soon to become known as one of the authors of the Massachusetts Institute of Technology study of "Limits to Growth". This meeting debated the arguements for and against a slowdown in global economic production noting that if the argument in favour "is persuasive, it means that justice will require wealthy societies

One of the three regional meetings held (West African Conference on Science and Technology, Accra, Ghana, March 1972; Conference on the Scientific, Technological and Social Revolutions in Asian Perspective, Kuala Lumpur, Malaysia, April 1973; North American-European Conference on the Technological Future of the Industrialized Nations and the Quality of Life, Pont-à-Mousson, France, May 1973). Report in The Ecumenical Review, Vol. XXIV No. 3, July 1972.

* See K. Koyama, "Theological Reflections on the Bamboo Room and the Oil Room", Anticipation No. 16, March 1974.

to moderate, halt, or even reverse their rates of consumption and pollution in order that other societies may accelerate economic growth. . . . Recent indications that weaker countries, by pooling their efforts, can demand higher prices for their products, as in the case of oil, are small, yet encouraging signs of change in a favourable direction''.*

The 1974 World Conference on Science and Technology for Human Development in Bucharest, Romania,** tried to spell out the impact of natural limits to growth and the pressures of technology on the environment and their consequences for national and international social and economic structures. The 130 scientists, technologists, social activists and theologians present represented a great cross-section of opinion, coming as they did from 44 countries and a wide range of disciplines.

Perhaps the key to the discussions at Bucharest was the bringing together of the representatives of two points of view: those who see the problem of the future only or primarily in terms of achieving greater economic and social justice, and those who see it only or primarily in terms of human survival because of the exhaustion of foreseeable natural resources and the wide-spread destruction of the world's environment due to ever-increasing industrialization. While these two perspectives are not necessarily mutually exclusive they have tended to appear in opposition. The opportunity which the Conference provided for the adherents of different viewpoints to confront each other and hear each other out was perhaps its most signal contribution. Previously their mutual suspicions have frustrated any common efforts by people who, after all, have many of the same concerns and objectives, and who should be allies in the search for solutions.

One cannot say that all conflicts were resolved at Bucharest. Substantial differences of opinion and approach remain. These came out most clearly in the examination of the pressure of population and natural limits to growth on the hopes of man for social justice and material progress. Previous discussions of the energy and resource problems facing the future, notable in an ecumenical consultation at Cardiff in 1972, had clearly affirmed the need to accept a radical new approach to the technical future: "In spite of this uncertainty about the position of resource constraints there is general consensus that we have entered the transitional period during which decisions must be taken and implemented concerning a major redirection of our technology, particularly that relating to resource consumption. The length of the transition period is uncertain, but the main change

---

* Report in Study Encounter 12, Vol. VII No. 3, 1971.

** Selected Preparatory Papers in Anticipation No. 17, May 1974; Selected Plenary Presentations to the Conference in Anticipation No. 18, August 1974; Report in Anticipation No. 19, November 1974.

of direction ought to be accomplished within the next hundred years. Due to the inevitable delays in technological and social adaptation, the initiation of this process should be begun now''.*

The Bucharest Conference went considerably beyond this in developing the concept of a *Sustainable and Just Society*, based on the evident need to see the world's economic possibilities and its material requirements in some kind of equilibrium. The report on this concept recognized that this would mean different things for different parts of the world: "Consideration of the swelling material activity on our fragile, finite planet leads to the conclusion that a point is reached when the benefits of more material production and the material demands of an increasing number of people no longer outweigh the negative effects of this growth on the non-material dimensions of the quality of life. Since many of the negative effects appear only after a lengthy delay, judgement as to the point at which further growth reduces the quality of life depends on the planning horizon employed. Feeling a responsibility at least for our grandchildren, and sensing an incapacity of the physical environment to support for long a load significantly higher than today's, we believe that the rich segments of the world have now reached the critical point where material expansion will reduce the quality of life for some people at some time within the period of concern to us. The remaining, poorer, members of humanity are at a stage where the current benefits of material expansion, except in terms of population, are far larger than the probable costs in terms of reduced quality of life now or in the relevant future. Thus today the world-wide quality of life will be increased by material growth among the poor and by stabilization and possibly contraction among the rich".**

New Vision: A More Humane Technological Society

During recent years the world has had to face several dramatic crises involving its natural and manufactured resources. Emergency programmes were developed to cope with the scarcity of particular resources, and the churches have tried valiantly to involve themselves in these common efforts. Crises, however, are often symptoms rather than the root causes of a malady. This means that the concern for immediate needs requires short-term policies which are an integral part of long-term measures. But long-term concepts ask for a new vision of the kind of society which might be able to meet new and old challenges of common survival. The dominant values and ideologies underlying national and international social structures have to be questioned, and the prospects for human development in each society have to be seen in the light of the society's own genuine

---

*   Anticipation No. 13, December 1972; Dossier Section VI, pages 37-40.

* *   Anticipation No. 19, December 1974, page 12.

cultural creativity; the concern for the material and spiritual well-being of all humanity; and the maintenance of an environment which enables the realization of greater quality of life for present and future generations.

The search for a global human community, in which technology is a means of fulfilment rather then alienation, does not imply that there is a single vision for the achievement of a sustainable, just and participatory society determining further technological development throughout the world. The emphasis for African and Asian countries will, for example, be on combining indigenous with advanced technologies in the light of their cultural values and the demand for more social justice. In Latin America nations, where science and technology are mainly under the control of internal and external military and industrial power groups, conscientization‡ and organization of the struggle for social and economic liberation in national and global terms are the main challenges. The industrially more advanced nations will have to reorient their production and consumption patterns to enable greater justice within global structures and to sustain a worthwhile quality of life for their inhabitants in the indefinite future.

The emphasis on self-reliance does not mean a rejection of global responsibility but is an essential precondition of its realization. Modern technology, however, has pervaded the social life of all countries to some degree, and it can be anticipated that its impact will ever rapidly increase. Its ambiguity as well as the ambiguity of the power it generates will make necessary the creation of new structures of control working in the interest and for the benefit of the great majority of people.

It is the working out of this new vision in its global, regional and local perspectives that the ecumenical movement will have to struggle with in the period after the Fifth Assembly.

B. Violence, Nonviolence and the Struggle for Social Justice
The Challenge to the Churches

How can Christians "become wiser and more courageous in translating their commitment to Jesus Christ into specific social and political engagement for social justice"? This is the fundamental challenge brought to the forefront of our attention by a two-year study programme on *Violence, Nonviolence and the Struggle for Social Justice*. Centered on the examination of the attitude of Christians to the use of violence, this programme took up a vital issue, although one which was hardly new on the agenda of the ecumenical movement.* However in 1970 the first series of grants

* The Working Committee of Church and Society at its meeting in Nemi, Italy, June 1971, outlined the new programme; the report, published in Study Encounter 09, Vol. VII No. 3, 1971, provides a survey of the historical development of ecumenical thought on violence and non-violence.

from the Special Fund of the Programme to Combat Racism turned a dramatic spotlight on the question whether Christians should engage—directly or indirectly—in revolutionary violence aimed at overthrowing a profoundly unjust and oppressive social system. As a result the dilemmas of violence, nonviolence and Christian responsibility aroused a revived public discussion. It was in view of the remarkable confusion of this debate, and also in response to the resolution of the Uppsala Assembly in memory of Martin Luther King (which asked for an exploration of the means by which the World Council could promote studies on nonviolent methods of achieving social justice) that the WCC Central Committee at its 1971 meeting in Addis Ababa requested the Sub-Unit on Church and Society to undertake a two-year programme aimed at

(a) furthering the churches' reflection on the ethical dilemmas posed by violence and nonviolence in the often desperate struggle for justice and peace; and

(b) contributing to the search for strategies of action which will minimize the sum total of violence in conflict situations.

A Redefinition of Violence and a Fresh Look at Nonviolence

The very urgency and controversy of the problem becomes most visible when an attempt is made to take account of real situations and specific areas in which "Christians agonize over questions of violence today". In the final report on the study programme presented to the Central Committee at Geneva in 1973 the attempt was made to give the general reflections some concrete meaning in the description of several specific conflict situations, illustrating the actual experiences and dilemmas of Christians.*
The selection of these illustrations, though in principle incidental to the main thrust of the report, attracted the most attention in the Central Committee debate and in the press—a reaction which demonstrated anew how difficult is is for Christians anywhere in the world to face the beams in one's own eye (rather than the mote in the eye of one's neighbour) and to be concerned foremost with defining and opposing one's own involvement and participation in structures and acts of violence. The multi-faceted nature of violence, often obscured by hidden and unconscious assumptions, demands that Christians become more sensitive to the particular

---

* See <u>The Ecumenical Review</u>, Vol. XXV No. 14, October 1973, pages 430-446, which also contains additional material on the issue of violence; see also Dossier Section V, pages 45-52.

forms of violence which characterize their own social environment. Too often it can be observed that affluent Christians see very clearly the human suffering that may be inflicted by revolutionaries, but fail to see that violence has other faces as well. The churches' thinking on this score must be enlarged to take account of what is variously called silent, invisible, indirect or structural violence, including many forms of "terrorism" not labelled as such because they happen to carry governmental blessing. There is urgent need for the churches themselves to examine their role in supporting—wittingly or unwittingly—existing power structures by legitimizing the political, economic, social and cultural *status quo* and avoiding their proper ministry of reconciliation on the side of the poor and oppressed.*

A consultation held in Cardiff, Wales, in September 1972, which drew together participants with a very diverse range of experiences and viewpoints in regard to their involvement in contemporary struggles for justice and liberation, made the attempt to clarify the various concepts of "violence" and "power", to spell out some of the strategies of nonviolent action and to identify the biblical and theological issues confronting the churches.** The report of this meeting also countered some of the facile assumptions about nonviolence which have been current in the recent debate. Contrary to its popular image, nonviolence is not less controversial than violence; it is not a way of avoiding commitment; and it is not necessarily bloodless. There appears to be a wide range of possibilities for action, little known and even less practised, about which the churches, however, need to discard some highly romantic notions. That is why the final report on the enquiry, commended by the Central Committee for study, comment and action states: "We are convinced that far too little attention has been given by the Church and by resistance movements to the methods and techniques of nonviolence, in the struggle for a just society. . ..Nonviolent action represents relatively unexplored territory: initiatives being taken by various groups and individuals to help the exploration happen deserve the strongest possible support from the WCC and the churches".

The Continuing Debate

Since the release of the report in October 1973, a considerable number of comments and reaction has been received. Four main attitudes emerge in the responses:

---

* See Hohn H. Yoder's report on a "Working Party on Jesus and Power", in The Ecumenical Review, Vol. XXV No. 4, October 1973, pages 447-454.

** Mimeographed report. Geneva: WCC, 1972; see also A Survey of Reactions to the Report of the Cardiff Consultation, mimeographed. Geneva: WCC, 1973.

(a) The statement has been especially favourably received by the "Historic Peace Churches" (Society of Friends, Church of the Brethren, and Mennonites) who welcome the major thrust of the document, while suggesting refinements on detailed points.

(b) There has been a negative reaction from those who believe that the choice between violence and nonviolence does not offer realistic options and that the true option is rather the establishing of peace and justice. They believe the means to achieve them will be determined not by the oppressed but by the oppressor. Some would say that there is even a biblical basis for a theological justification of the "counter-violence" of the oppressed.

(c) Another group feels that the terms "structural violence" and "power" are not yet sufficiently well defined and need further clarification. Since these are the most common and yet most complex forms of violence they need further spelling out in social, political and ethical terms.

(d) There are those who believe that the report does not provide sufficient recognition of a positive and creative role of law in the organization of society.

The desperate quest for justice and peace in our time, however, is a fundamental challenge to all Christians, regardless of whether they are committed in principle to nonviolence or whether they are prepared to endorse Christian participation in revolutionary violence as a last resort. Though there is no clear cut distinction between these two groups (and in the choice of one's particular stance) a mutually challenging dialogue can prove 'helpful and needs to take place on the widest scale. Both groups have to be willing to face crucial questions from one another, but their encounter, set in a genuinely ecumenical perspective, may help their churches to escape from their various parochialisms.

V. FUTURE PROSPECTS FOR FAITH AND WITNESS

From the reports of the sub-units concerned with Faith and Witness, what implications for the future can be drawn? A number of major areas continues to call for attention, and certain possibilities are indicated in the paragraphs that follow. The working out of these possibilities must, however, depend on the whole shape of the programme as it emerges from the Nairobi Assembly.

(1) *Searching for new expressions of the apostolic faith*. One of the tasks of the Unit on Faith and Witness is to help the churches in their efforts to give fresh expression to their faith in Christ. We are in a situation of pluralism, and thus two aspects of this endeavour have to be combined: a concern for a contemporary expression in a given social and cultural context, *and* the concern for a faithful preservation and presentation of the

rich heritage of apostolic truth. An ongoing process of theological reflection along these lines is not only the responsibility of the Unit itself, but should also penetrate all the various activities of the World Council of Churches.

(2) *Commitment to evangelism* within the WCC and the member churches calls for the announcing of the good news in Jesus Christ, by word and deed, to every individual in every part of the world, inviting all persons into Christian discipleship. The urgency of this task should always be present in the life of the churches: it is a clear command of our Lord. It is also called for by the present human situation in which multitudes everywhere are yearning deeply for meaning, struggling for justice, searching for spiritual values. Perhaps without recognizing it they are looking for God. This commitment needs to be fulfilled in new situations: the challenge of world religions, primal world views, science and technology, new life styles, oppressive systems. The churches are present in practically every nation. More than ever we have the possibility of proclamation in word and deed. With their life rooted deep in the Gospel, churches and Christians are called to struggle at the side of God for the liberation of all human beings, to suffer with them, and in this sharing, to give account of their hope in Jesus Christ. We need to discover ways of addressing men and women so that the offer and demands of the Gospel can clearly be heard and understood.

(3) *Spiritual life* for the WCC, as for groups of Christians in the member churches, involves the search for ways of group and personal self-discipline which enable people to live the life of the Spirit in the midst of the daily struggle for deeper fellowship in the churches, for the integrity of witness and for advancing justice and righteousness in society. Particularly important are the dialectics between our fundamental relationship to God, on the one hand, and our relations with fellow human beings as well as with the whole of creation, the elements of nature, and the things which we make and use, on the other hand. How may we recognize the resources of the Spirit in the community of faith, and how do we draw upon them for our sustenance and nourishment and for the creation of a new life style?

(4) *Courage for dialogue*. In what ways can Christians communicate and cooperate with their neighbours of other convictions in the local and world communities? In commitment both to witness and to dialogue how do we give an account of the hope that is in us "with modesty and respect"? The implications of these questions for ways of theological reflection and for our understanding of the Church in the new situations of today need to be explored further.

(5) *Vision for society*. We live in a world of contradictions: excitement about technological possibilities and revolutionary changes, on the one

120

and, and anxiety about abuses and growing injustice, on the other. Mankind has to decide how to control its future and how to overcome its internal inequalities. Hope in Jesus Christ leads to concern for models of the coming society: there are no specific Christian solutions, but rather the right knowledge of alternatives and the will to pursue them. We need action to change individual life styles and institutional patterns of power; this calls for the continuation of work in common among theologians, scientists and politicians. This is a promising possibility of new cooperation if we can move from over-specialization to mutual, fruitful illumination.

(6) *The unity of the Church* is both gift and task. It is the gift of our Lord Jesus Christ, founder of the one, holy and apostolic Church. Yet it is also a permanent task for all Christians who must seek to overcome division: division into separate churches and division in our understanding and approach to vital questions which thus hinder unity. Among these vital questions is the need of a new and mature relationship between the churches, making it possible for them to share in Christ's mission on the basis of mutual responsibility. There is also a growing need to deal more effectively with institutional questions and the impact upon those questions of sociological structures related to particular cultural backgrounds or imported from other cultures. Our Lord prayed that "they may all be one". For this we must strive until that time when Christ shall consummate our perfect unity in him, in the kingdom of God. Therefore every Christian has an obligation to work for this unity in faith and in fundamental order. The unity of the Church is thus both the first task of the WCC and also that end to which all our ecumenical work converges. Thus it must permeate the whole programme and structure of the World Council.

The Unit on Faith and Witness recognizes that the inter-relatedness of its sub-units has implications for the ecumenical communication both to the churches and to other Units in the WCC. And we must ask the larger question: how can our experience within the World Council of Churches be communicated to the churches as a whole?

3

justice and service

Historical Background

From its very foundation the ecumenical movement has had a deep concern for justice, peace and social welfare. The Life and Work Movement, one of the forerunners of the modern ecumenical movement, was a manifestation of this concern. And when the World Council was formed, the heritage and concerns of the Life and Work Movement became a central part of its life. What are known today as the Commission on Inter-Church Aid, Refugee and World Service (CICARWS) and the Commission of Churches on International Affairs (CCIA) both began in the very early days of the Council.

The first article of the Constitution defines the WCC as a "fellowship of churches ... which seek to fulfil together their common calling". The third article spells out the meaning of the common calling which it relates to the mandate of the WCC: "to express the common concerns of the churches in the service of human need, the breaking down of barriers between men, and the formation of brotherhood, justice and peace . . . the renewal of the churches in unity, mission and service". So the concern for justice and service has always been seen as one of the essential functions of the WCC.

This concern was further strengthened and deepened at the Fourth Assembly at Uppsala. The reports of the Sections and committees and the Message of the Assembly itself reveal the new mandate given to the Council by the churches to increase its efforts on behalf of human welfare and world peace and to take new initiatives in the promotion of racial justice and world development. The challenge presented to the churches by the twin spectres of racism and underdevelopment preoccupied the Assembly and has had a profound impact on the subsequent work of the WCC.

The Central Committee has since taken various steps to give programmatic shape to these concerns. In 1969, a Programme to Combat Racism (PCR) was constituted, followed in 1970 by the establishment of the Commission on the Churches' Participation in Development (CCPD). At the same time, the Structure Committee was giving consideration to how the study and action programme related to justice and service could be expressed in one programme unit of the Council. After much difficult discussion, the new programme unit was born in 1971, and the new programmes were linked together with CICARWS and CCIA in the Programme Unit on Justice and Service.

122

Programme Thrusts

Inevitably then, the World Council's involvement in the field of justice and service has increased considerably in the post-Uppsala period. The impact of the various programmes at the local, national, regional and world levels has been unprecedented in the history of the ecumenical movement. It is perhaps a result of these activities and the significant coverage they have received in the mass media that the WCC is better known in the Member Churches. A great debate has been started which has been of great value for the ecumenical movement, and while there has been severe criticism of the WCC's engagement in social action in some quarters, there has also been a great deal of appreciation from others, including governments, intergovernmental bodies, secular movements and other religious organizations.

The individual reports from the four sub-units testify to the ways in which the WCC's contribution to justice, peace and human welfare has been intensified. But a number of overall trends can be noted:

• Financial contributions to service programmes and development assistance have trebled over the past six years;

• The programmes are more global in their nature than ever before. A number of countries which previously received no assistance whatsoever, such as the countries of the Sahelian‡ zone in West Africa, are now being aided by WCC programmes;

• The number of Member Churches, especially those from the Third World and the socialist countries, who contribute to service and development programmes have increased significantly;

• The work of CCPD has enabled a comprehensive approach to development questions, including study and research, education, technical services and documentation as well as financial assistance;

• The establishment of the PCR demonstrated the WCC's concern to move beyond words and declarations to actions aimed at combatting racism;

• CCIA has been able to make an effective contribution to resolving international conflict, in which the most successful was the part played in aiding reconciliation in the Sudan.

The most significant changes in the WCC's involvement in justice and service activities, however, have taken place at the level of reflection on the issues, the style of work and the process of decision-making.

The concern for justice has become the touchstone for the work of the whole unit. Traditional service programmes such as emergency aid, refugee resettlement and social welfare projects have been increasingly assessed in terms of their contribution or relationship to social, economic and political justice. This is not to undermine the role of service, which has its own validity, but it becomes increasingly clear that service can only be rendered effectively when it is related to the question of justice. Its contribution must be assessed in the light of overall needs. In the same way, peace efforts have to be related to the concern for justice. For example, there can be no lasting peace in the Middle East which does not take seriously the just claims of all parties to the conflict. Justice has also been a key concept in the work of CCPD and PCR. Development is understood as a process with three inter-related goals: social justice, self-reliance and economic growth. However important the last two are, they are ultimately subordinate to justice. Racial justice has been the goal of the PCR, and this has involved a strong attack on institutional and structural racism. The overall concern for justice has made the Council more aware than ever before of the political dimensions of its work.

Equally important is the fact that each problem is understood from an ecumenical perspective which gives consideration to the theological implications and the significance for the churches. No one would pretend that this process is in any way complete. There is still much to be done to relate theological understanding to action programmes in a way which is understood, or at least appreciated, in the churches. The Unit is still struggling to give better expression to the way it does theology and draws out today's theological understanding of the biblical words "justice" and *diakonia* ["service:"]‡. This will undoubtedly be one of the greatest challenges in the period after the Nairobi Assembly.

But if that is one of the weaker points of the work of the past few years, the way in which the *style of work* has changed to cope with the new challenges is one of the strengths. Reflection and action have become two aspects of one and the same effort, and financial assistance is increasingly seen as the expression of solidarity with, and the means of empowering, the powerless. In all of this, service or the promotion of justice is not complete within itself but is a means of educating, renewing and even uniting the churches.

So each sub-unit has come to see itself not as *the* agency that is responsible for service or justice concerns but as an enabler, stimulator and catalyst for churches and church-related agencies in various parts of the world. The sub-units see themselves as part of a network of churches and groups engaged in a mutual conversation but also a mutual struggle for liberation, justice and peace. But these concerns are not limited to the churches, and therefore the Unit has been deeply involved with people of good will outside the churches and with groups and movements committed to the same goals. This has meant collaboration with liberation movements and action groups, joint work with Muslims and others in countries where there are no churches, and is also reflected in the fact that the CCIA has shifted its main emphasis away from working with UN agencies to direct efforts among the parties engaged in conflict.

At the level of *decision-making*, the commissions of the various sub-units have become more global in character. There is a much greater involvement of church people from the Third World and the communities directly involved in the programme work. Oppressed people and those directly involved in the struggle for liberation and human dignity have also been given a share in shaping WCC programmes through consultations. At the same time, the centre of decision-making, particularly in the project system of Inter-Church Aid and the technical services provided by CCPD, has been shifted into the regions. This also has a financial impact as attempts are being made to enable the agencies and churches who receive funds through the WCC to have greater control over the money that is allocated to them, within a given understanding of how the money is to be used. So, for example, the Special Fund of the PCR and the Ecumenical Development Fund of CCPD transfer resources to groups without designating the money for a specific purpose, though there is a general agreement on how it will be used. CICARWS has introduced a category system within the project system which enables the churches to ensure that their priority projects are covered.

Unit Structure

The aim of the Unit structure introduced in 1971 was not simply to regroup "traditional activities, but the deliberate placing of functions in mutual tension". At the same time, the Structure Committee said it was making provision for coordination, mutual support and correction. Two of the key words were "coordination" and "simplification". "The committee envisages a process in which changes can be gradually implemented, rather than a rigid structure to be instituted instantaneously. . . . On the other hand, the intention is that the unity of the new Programme Units should, over a period of time, become a reality".

That is what is currently happening within the Unit. As has already been seen, there have been several very noticeable trends resulting from the creation of the new Programme Unit, but this has been achieved without any rigid Unit structure or administration. Each sub-unit continues to operate more or less independently within its own special area of competence. Each commission meets to determine policy, but reports to the Central Committee through a Unit Committee made up of representatives of the Central Committee together with five representatives from each of the four sub-units. The directors of the four sub-units meet regularly to coordinate activities, and the staff of the Unit meets at least twice a year to review common concerns. The Unit has also published a magazine in English and French covering the work of the entire Unit.

The main practical result of the Unit structure has been a coordinated approach to certain particular geographical situations or concerns, where the interests and resources of more than one sub-unit were required. So, for instance, in situations such as Nigeria during and after the civil war, in Sudan, Vietnam, Chile and the Middle East, CICARWS and CCIA have worked closely together in developing and implementing programmes which were related to justice and service concerns. This meant, for example, that when the coup in Chile threatened the safety of many foreign refugees and Chileans, CCIA went to work on the political aspects of the crisis and was liaison with agencies such as the United Nations High Commissioner for Refugees, while CICARWS started to assist the churches in Chile in the practical arrangements for getting refugees out of the country and raising the necessary funds to cover the operation. Throughout the crisis an inter-Unit task force oversaw the work responsibilities, and this continued into the second phase of the programme concerned with the violation of human rights inside Chile.

Similarly, in the drought situations of the Sahel‡ and Ethiopia, which have required both immediate emergency aid and also a commitment to longer-term development programming, CICARWS and CCPD have been in close collaboration. Another important point of coordination has been around programmes of assistance to people in the liberated areas of Mozambique and the other Portuguese territories in Africa. PCR, CICARWS and CCPD have all joined forces and pooled knowledge and resources. Attempts have also been made to evolve a common approach and policy with regard to church assistance in Southern Africa.

Currently, there are two desks which, because of the nature of their work, have been made responsible to the whole Unit rather than just to one of the sub-units. The Secretariat for Migration had traditionally been within the structure of CICARWS, but in fact its concerns and work load relate to all four of the sub-units, so it has been under the supervision of a Unit task force. In the same way, the newly-established Secretariat on Human Rights and Refugees in Latin America, created in 1974 as a follow-up to the events in Chile, was made responsible to the whole Unit.

The development crisis and its implications for the work of the World Council are leading the sub-units to collaborate even more closely in order to devise a common approach in both studies and action programmes in response to this important concern. CICARWS is looking at the present food crisis. CCIA is making its contribution by studying the economic threats to peace. PCR concentrates on the racial struggle as part of the world-wide attack on colonialism and neo-colonialism, while CCPD looks specifically at the development issues involved. This is certainly one way in which the different sub-units give mutual support to one another as they attack a particular problem.

The experience of working together and the results achieved through better coordination of activities reveal the potential that exists for even greater coordination and the beginnings of a unified administration, but so far little has been done to implement this. One advance, however, is that a combination of the sub-unit budgets is now presented to the churches for their support. This enables them to see more clearly exactly what the work done by the Unit as a whole costs.

Certain questions will therefore have to be faced by the Assembly as it thinks about the future of justice and service activity within the WCC:

(1) Should such a Unit continue to exist, and if so, should it continue as a federation of independent commissions, as at present, or become a more integrated programme unit as envisaged by the Structure Committee?

(2) What changes are required in the structures and programmes of CICARWS and CCPD, both of which have a strong development content, to avoid overlap of work or confusion within the churches?

(3) Inevitably the current world situation and the pressures of the Uppsala Assembly have meant that there has been a great deal of concentration on justice concerns. But what are the responsibilities of the churches in service during the last quarter of the 20th century? How do we understand Inter-Church Aid?

Major consultations have taken place or are planned which will address themselves in a preliminary way to some of these questions. Their findings will be reported to the Assembly. It is also clear that the Nairobi Assembly will be faced with a desperate world situation which will call for a renewed and strong involvement of the churches. What is the unique role of the World Council of Churches in all of this, and how can it be implemented effectively?

I. COMMISSION OF THE CHURCHES ON INTERNATIONAL AFFAIRS

In a recent publication* giving the record of its activities during the years 1970/73 the Commission of the Churches on International Affairs (CCIA) described itself as follows:

"This Commission is charged to serve the nations by making a Christian witness on behalf of peace with justice and freedom. In the United Nations, at diplomatic conferences and other appropriate occasions it advances judgements and proposals, drawn from the best thinking of the world Christian community, on the key points of dispute, whether disarmament, national rivalries, patterns of economic domination. By calling the churches' attention to the factors causing international tension and to situations where basic human rights are violated, and by being available to represent the churches' concern in areas of conflict, it seeks to stimulate Christians everywhere to work for the healing of the nations".

The idea of such an ecumenical agency, when plans for the CCIA were agreed upon by the International Missionary Council and the Provisional Committee of the World Council of Churches, and were fleshed out at the Conference of Church Leaders on International Affairs which met at

---

* The Churches in International Affairs: Reports 1970-1973. Geneva: WCC, 1974.

Cambridge in 1946, was basically a new one. Even today there are many persons who find it disturbing, or at least strange, for the churches to see involvement in international affairs as a basic part of their task of proclaiming the Gospel of Jesus Christ.

Characteristically the ecumenical movement—and the World Council of Churches as an organ of that movement—has tended to treat the various international issues coming before it in relative isolation one from another, attempting to provide solutions which could be achieved by adjusting, sometimes very seriously, the existing framework of the world-wide economic, political and social relations. This approach, broad in concept and demanding of action, lies behind the Aims of the CCIA contained in its new Constitution adopted by the Uppsala Assembly in 1968.

The World Council of Churches, throughout the years before Uppsala, effectively described and even applied a certain degree of critical analysis to the problems confronting the world. Without being triumphalistic it may be said that the WCC raised and communicated some of these issues earlier and more forcefully than most of the secular media or other bodies based in the industrialized world. What was clearly not foreseen was that all of these issues would converge, as indeed they have in the recent past, into a single, inter-related and inseparable complex of crises. The ecumenical movement was not alone in its surprise at this sudden, dramatic development.

Nevertheless, the commissioners and staff of the CCIA did not find themselves altogether unequipped to face these events as they occurred. At a meeting shortly after the Uppsala Assembly the Commission resolved upon a new programme intended to provide for the continuation of its long-standing duties but at the same time initiating supplementary work to be done by studies in depth on important issues of international relations and by consultations which might provide more data and give a fuller background to CCIA actions as well as to the information sent out from it to the Member Churches.

All actions undertaken by the CCIA during the period since Uppsala were performed in the light of this new programme. A few of the most important accomplishments may serve as indications of the whole range of work.

The Indochina War. Together with the Indochina Secretary for CICARWS, the Commission staff followed Indochina affairs very closely since 1969. Numerous conversations were held both in Paris and in Geneva with the four delegations to the Vietnam Paris peace talks. The staff performed research and provided guidance to the Member Churches and to interested WCC committees as the basis for important and influential WCC actions.

The Middle East Conflict. The Middle East conflict has provided some opportunities for direct engagement. Important steps were taken to broaden the WCC's possibilities to be of service in this area. While maintaining close contacts with Israel and its religious and political leaders, discussions were also held with the Palestinian leadership and with Arab statesmen. The CCIA organized, for example, an official visit by the WCC General Secretary to President Boumedienne of Algeria, a cordial meeting which prepared the way for new future relations.

The Sudan. The role which the CCIA was able to play in aiding the parties to this country's seventeen-year-long conflict to negotiate their differences and establish peace was significant. Although the WCC has rightly and properly been hesitant to claim too much for itself in relation to these activities, this was a very important engagement for the churches, and one from which important lessons are to be learned.

Human Rights. Human Rights have continued to be a central CCIA concern, and a major consultation on the subject was held at St. Pölten, Austria, in October 1974. It is important, however, to note the self-critical approach taken by the Commission as it recognized what little progress was being made in the implementation of human rights standards all over the world.

Disarmament. Disarmament received constant attention, and a new area of concern emerged—European security and cooperation—which was a topic of serious conversation in two successive CCIA Executive Committee meetings.

Relations with the United Nations. The Commission has continued to play a leadership role in the non-governmental organization (NGO) community. One CCIA Executive Secretary is now Vice-President of the Conference of NGO's in Consultative Status with ECOSOC and Chairman of the Geneva Bureau. Another chairs an NGO *ad hoc* committee in New York and was a member of the management board of the population tribune held in conjunction with the 1974 UN Population Conference in Bucharest.

The convergence of these various concerns became more and more clear as the years progressed. And it is in the light of the new situation facing the world which has arisen since Uppsala that reflection on the involvement of the CCIA and other ecumenical attempts to counter injustice among and within the nations must take place.

On the following pages is given a report prepared by the staff of the CCIA which seeks to analyse the new situation in the world today and to suggest the appropriate ways and means for the fellowship of churches in the ecumenical movement to respond. Not all Central Committee members would agree with everything that is said. Agreement within the fellowship becomes harder to achieve as the situation grows more critical. But the issues lifted up in this paper demand serious attention by the Member Churches at the Nairobi Assembly and in the years beyond.

*   *   *

The intention of this report is to justify neither what the Commission of the Churches on International Affairs has sought to do, nor its continued existence in one or another form. Rather, it is to understand ourselves better in the light of present reality, and to draw some provisional conclusions from it which might aid Christians and churches constructively and efficiently to meet the qualitatively new challenges which will certainly shape history in the future. It seeks to inter-relate "text" and "context" in a dynamic and creative way. Let us, therefore, see the present world "context" as it was so forcefully sketched out at the April 1974 special UN Assembly on Raw Materials and Development.

The World Today

Objective Conditions. The objective conditions of the poor segment of the world today have not been substantially improved since Uppsala. On the contrary: authentic peace is as remote as ever.

● Clubs of a few privileged states continue to enjoy discretionary powers in the handling of major international problems.

● Very little progress has been made in dismantling military bases, withdrawing troops from foreign lands, prohibiting nuclear testing or destroying nuclear weapons.

● The gradual shift away from "Cold War" tensions has not been accompanied by a corresponding improvement in the conditions of the Third World. Rather, the foci of political tension and armed conflict have been transferred to Asia, the Middle East, Africa and Latin America, which have become the zones where most of the contradictions of our contemporary world are most apparent and destructive.

Economic development, despite the international concern shown in two UN-declared Development Decades, has produced no real progress for most poor nations. That economy is a means to achieve social and cultural progress for every citizen is often proclaimed, but the achievements have been mainly rhetorical. This failure is primarily due to the lack of political will in the wealthy countries, to their ignorance of the real concerns of the developing countries, and to the inadequacies of international economic cooperation.

The world economy, its trade and monetary systems, continue to be controlled by a minority composed of the highly developed countries and a very few "developing" ones, like Brazil. They maintain virtual hegemony over raw materials markets and a practical monopoly over manufactures, capital and services.

The international monetary system today functions in such a way as to compromise the expansion of world commerce and especially thwarts the Third World countries' attempts to overcome their underdevelopment.

● Unrestrained by any significant national or international control, the multi-national corporations manipulate, more efficiently than ever, the multiple mechanisms whereby the wealth of the poor countries is transferred away from them, and fix most prices for the underdeveloped world's products. The unrestricted economic and political power of these corporations over certain countries has been demonstrated dramatically in Chile, where they played a central role in overthrowing the democratically elected government.

• Under the sole heading of profits declared by corporations, the capital, U.S. $23 billion [thousand million], that flowed out of the developing countries during the second half of the First Development Decade (1960-1970), was one-and-one-half times the total foreign aid grants that the countries where these companies are based made available to the underdeveloped world.

• The indebtedness of underdeveloped countries to industrialized ones now amounts to approximately U.S. $80 billion [thousand million]. They are forced to borrow continually and thus chronically aggravate their balance-of-payments position.

• Unemployment, migrant workers and the ''brain drain'' are problems which continue to plague the poor countries. The chronic immobility thus brought upon the underdeveloped countries has condemned them to see their human resources continually bled and exploited. In many industrialized countries migrant workers make up the bulk of the sub-proletariat.‡ There also the technical and scientific personnel of the developing countries are attracted and enticed by the opportunities for promotion and progress of which they are deprived by the chronic immobility in their own countries.

• Between July 1972 and July 1973, the price of wheat doubled, and it nearly redoubled during the second half of 1973. The price of those fertilizers most commonly used in the developed countries almost doubled between June 1973 and September 1973, as a direct result of the way the industrialized countries exercised their control over nine-tenths of world fertilizer production. That means that for the majority of the developing countries which import grains, primarily wheat and rice, the additional cost of these products will have caused an additional drain of more than U.S. $7 billion [thousand million] in 1974 over 1971 expenditures. Drought is killing human beings by the thousands in Africa. This region could have managed with one-twentieth the amount of wheat that many developed countries feed their cattle each year. Over the last five years the price of steel has tripled, the price of cement quadrupled, that of wood increased two-and-one-half times, and that of tractors doubled. All of these figures, due to the recent petroleum and related crises, are certain to be more dramatic in the 1974 statistics when they are authoritatively compiled.

Population continues to escalate rapidly throughout the world. However this, like the food problem, must be seen in the light of the whole complex of "crises" listed here.

Colonialism and *apartheid* are still alarming factors. The international community as a whole has hardly gone beyond verbal condemnations.

Human rights violations, for all of the reasons listed above, have massively increased. Especially alarming is the almost systematic incidence of certain violations like torture.

Some Profound Changes. In the light of the above, the unity of mankind may appear to be further off than ever. But strangely enough, abrupt changes of late may have begun to prove the contrary. They have contributed to an increasingly universal awareness that the present economic and political interdependence of nations must be made a positive, rather than the negative force it is today.

For this, thanks are largely due to the United Nations. The UN is often criticized for its inefficiency, but it cannot, in its present form, be more effective than its member states would have it be. But there is one unique service which the UN does provide, the vital importance of which cannot be sufficiently emphasized: The UN supplies the only universal platform for putting before the world public opinion the different concerns and points of view of almost *all* the members of the world community of nations.

This became especially clear during the UN Special Session to which reference was made earlier. As the United Kingdom delegate said following that meeting: "Things will never be the same again".

In UN Secretary-General Kurt Waldheim's opening address, he stressed the following:

• The questions before the General Assembly relate directly to the future peace of the world and encompass problems which affect the lives of virtually every human being on earth.

• The fundamental question of the kind of world economic system and social order we wish to establish and live under demands rational and agreed choices which will be decisive in determining the quality and condition of mankind's future life on this planet.

• It has become a commonplace to say that nations of the world are interdependent and that their interdependence will inevitably and rapidly increase. However, economic, social and political forces have been building up for many years which now affect the stability and growth capacity of the world economy and also have the most fundamental political implications.

• Most of the elements of the present situation are not new. In fact, most of them have been considered by the international community for many years. What is new is the sudden, dramatic urgency of the situation and the acute acceleration of the historical process which has brought us face to face with a global emergency.

● That is why interdependence must become a positive, and not a negative, force, as it is at present. Such a positive interdependence will have to take into account not only the interests and needs of *all* nations but also the imperative inter-relationship of the several parts of the problem: poverty, population, food, the conservation and just apportionment of natural resources, the preservation of the environment, and the problem of trade and monetary systems. Each of those problems has a direct bearing on the peace and stability of the world. No one can insulate himself from their effects. And, if these problems individually were not bad enough—he concluded—we must recognize that since they interconnect and interact they have a multiplier effect on one another and tend to create new difficulties.

"Text" and "Context"

While it is true to say that justice, reconciliation and peace have been, still are, and should continue to be the "international affairs" concerns of the World Council, this has to be seen in the *context* just described. We are not speaking here of any "contextual ethic", but rather stressing that our word and actions must be historically rooted in the present-day world, with its real problems. From this context we are able to perceive more clearly some previous ecumenical and CCIA assumptions which may have been hidden from us at one time, and to formulate new, very different ones out of our experience since Uppsala.

Early WCC, and especially CCIA, assumptions, consciously or unconsciously, did not often escape the parameters‡ established by and for the rich, powerful and privileged of this world. The need for change was often seen in terms of "middle axioms", that is, through the negotiating of principles or guide-lines in the middle ground between two opposing points of view. Contacts and dialogues with high-standing, well-known, well-established diplomats, politicians and experts prevailed. We took for granted, often, that only by convincing these people and changing their mentality—inasmuch as they were those who possessed formal power —could any significant change in the world be effected. Logically, therefore, the United Nations became one of the central places for WCC international affairs work.

The East-West conflict of the "Cold War" period provided the main context for priorities-setting in international affairs. The main concerns were peace (principally between East and West), disarmament and, especially later on, nuclear disarmament. This particular juxtaposition of powers dominated earlier analyses and actions, and when concern for injustice in economic relations was expressed somewhat later, it was most often expressed in the terms dictated by the dominant East-West relationship.

Perhaps it was with the 1966 Church and Society Conference (on the theme "Christians in the Technical and Social Revolutions of Our Time") and its consequences for the Uppsala Assembly that the ecumenical movement first began to analyse injustice in the world from the points of view of the "poor", the "underprivileged" and the "oppressed", paying more special attention to economic factors. This shifting of the "poles of injustice", more and more consciously taking place in the WCC, caused us to become increasingly aware that *all* our actions, *all* our analyses, *all* our descriptions of the world situation, were based on certain presuppositions upon which our "universals" were based. CCIA's experiences have forced us to challenge the idea that we can conceive of specifically Christian universals, and to suspect that absolute objectivity and neutrality in political, economic and social matters is probably impossible. The CCIA's basic assumptions and partners in dialogue began to become more diversified. More and more those "who are not yet, but will be, or should be" were drawn into our sphere of action. This signified no abandonment of the UN as an essential base of operations (though perhaps now it is less exclusively relied upon). One can see many areas in which the UN and the WCC have undergone parallel developments. Both have become increasingly representative of the world's real composition—nationally, culturally and racially—over the years.

Some of these shifts in the CCIA's approach can be seen in its work on *Human Rights*. This was a central CCIA concern from its very beginnings and continues to be so. But today, the human rights issue is seen very differently, both qualitatively and quantitatively. The Universal Declaration on Human Rights was proclaimed in 1948 as a "standard of achievement for all peoples and all nations". It is not the Gospel, and Christians do not have to base their actions primarily on it. But its challenges to the churches and to Christians are not unlike those contained in the Bible. It demands concrete action to safeguard human life and dignity. As never before, human survival depends upon the realization of human rights.

Today, it is not so much the nuclear "overkill" capacity which poses the most immediate danger to humanity but "conventional" welfare and the new features of oppression throughout the world which modern technology has made exceptionally cruel. There are dozens of areas today where actual or potential conflicts threaten to explode into major international, perhaps even, finally, into nuclear confrontations. Almost without exception, those are places where the human rights of masses of human beings are being grossly violated.

Sometimes, people deprived of every other recourse have taken up arms to defend their rights and dignity. They have seen how many other millions have already lost the struggle for human survival. They have experienced starvation, disease and poverty in lands rich in human and natural resources. Unless urgent steps are taken, famine will soon overtake still greater portions of humanity.

But there are other ways to die, as millions discover daily. Torture is one. It is more widespread than ever, and is spreading like an epidemic. Assassination is another. Political opponents of certain regimes are being clubbed and shot to death in the streets of the world in ever greater numbers. One can also "die to society", by being locked away in its prisons. An increasing number of inmates has committed no physical crime but are condemned for "thought" crimes, for having dared to speak out against self-appointed authorities in power as a result of mass brutality. And it is possible to kill a human spirit, to rob a person not just of physical well-being and freedom, but of dignity and hope.

Through the Human Rights and other programmes of the WCC/CCIA, the churches have begun to reflect upon their own unique responsibility to participate in the *implementation* of human rights. Many times the churches have been tempted to judge other societies more quickly than their own, and to see the problems of others through the lenses of their own histories, theologies and world-views. Experience has shown that this approach has often been ineffective in promoting real implementation of human rights either at home or abroad. A failure to understand the true nature of another's problems and how they can be overcome has often led to naive actions which have even worsened the situation of those churches and individuals who have sought to help.

Concentration has shifted, therefore, away from a more partial approach to human rights where religious freedom was sometimes given exclusive or exceptional attention. This remains a priority concern, but is now seen in the context of other recognized rights and worked at much more in terms of the particular historical situation in which it is endangered. We have moved away from a quite exclusively individualist approach to human rights and have begun to speak of "people's rights" —without losing sight of the value of each of God's creatures living in society. And we have begun to see how effective ecumemical action for the implementation of human rights depends upon international solidarity with Christians and others who are seeking ways shaped to their own particular circumstances to promote and defend the rights and dignity of their fellow human beings.

But any attempt to place our entire analysis of the present structures of injustice under any single, overall label would be to confound the issue and to provide "alibis". Today, we must remind ourselves constantly of the inter-relationships mentioned earlier. Only if we take into account the interests and needs of all nations and the inter-related parts of the present crises can we move towards the positive interdependence of which Secretary-General Waldheim has spoken. Each of those elements has a direct bearing on peace and stability in the world. Nobody can insulate himself from their effects.

Some Conclusions for an Ecumenical Methodology in International Affairs

The Temptations of Jonah.

Jonah was very unhappy about this, and became angry. So he prayed, "Lord, didn't I say, before I left home, that this is just what you would do? That's why I did my best to run away to Spain! I knew that you are a loving and merciful God, that you are always patient, always kind, and always ready to change your mind and not punish. Now then, Lord, let me die. I am better off dead than alive". (Jonah 4:1-3, *Today's English Version*)

One temptation in today's world is to withdraw from the unpleasant realities we see about us, to give up the hope that Nineveh might repent and not be destroyed.

Some think, unrealistically, that they can still "go it alone"; others desire to avoid "unpopularity", to be defeatist; or to give in to a pervasive feeling of despair, saying, "What is the use?" Especially in the "rich world" this multiple "withdrawal" syndrome has become more apparent since Uppsala, even in some Christian circles. Some have seen in this phenomenon a crisis of spirit or of the faith. WCC General Secretary Philip Potter calls it a "crisis of faithfulness", seeing in this trend to return to (withdraw to) the inner spirit, to individualism, or to involvement only with small, intense groups, and at the same time in the trend to withdraw from institutional, structural and political questions, a serious crisis in spirituality, taken in its most profound sense.

Another temptation becoming more and more prevalent is to produce apocalyptic visions which leave no real hope for repentance and salvation. Indeed, we stand under God's judgement just as surely as did Nineveh, and there are just as few signs for us to justify our being optimistic. God has however promised to save us even from ourselves. Yet we are often tempted, like Jonah, even to hope for the worst!

136

Today, none of us has any need "to go" to Nineveh. We all live in Nineveh—if not downtown, at least in the suburbs.

"Solutions". Our experience since Uppsala has shown how elusive are the "ultimate" solutions. Yet we have not given up our attempt to do what we can, and to discover what, today (and each new day), Christians can contribute, specifically and uniquely, in matters political.

We often tended, before Uppsala, to take existing power relations for granted, allowing them to become, in fact, our "ultimate" in terms of possibilities for justice. Within this restricted frame of reference it was thus possible to propose "ultimate solutions". It was possible to search for —even sometimes to think we had found—the specific Christian definition of what is "just" for the world, and to define the acceptable and universal "Christian political position" or set of "Christian principles" to guide ecumenical actions in the realm of international affairs.

Seven years of experience in an interdependent, yet conflictive, divided and polarized world—in which Christians and churches are often bound to their own particular national or confessional history—have shown not only that ultimate political, economic or social solutions are elusive, but that even by seeking them we often lose our way.

We have found that the specificity or uniqueness of any Christian contribution can only be found in the basic conviction that there is a "hope beyond hope". We have had to try to discover when and how Christians can act, where others either cannot do so as well or cannot at all.

Our search for this type of specificity or uniqueness has given both practical and relevant results. Increasingly, governments, political movements and other bodies—many of them previously wary or ignorant of the WCC—seek our advice or assistance. Sometimes they seriously overestimate our capacities, but they do look increasingly to the WCC as a trusted partner in dialogue. Indications are that this is happening not because we have a strictly "humanitarian" or "neutral" position, but because they perceive in us signs of a hope which goes beyond apparently real historical possibilities, because they find us willing to listen and to try honestly to understand their positions and dilemmas—even, sometimes, if they find us in disagreement with their views. Perhaps most important is that many of those who seek us out today are from sectors of the world society with whom the WCC has had little or no previous contact, and many of whom are not Christian.

Dialogue as a Precondition. We have learned Paulo Freire's lesson in practice: the precondition for meaningful dialogue is the ability and willingness to learn from another, and not to offer him "instant solutions" drawn from general principles, Christian or otherwise.

Dialogue, however, is not an end in itself. All dialogue begins on the basis of the partners' presuppositions and value judgements; and the clearer one is about them, the better. Dialogue is always a *means* to ends of mutual understanding, reconciliation, justice and peace; and there are occasions when the preconditions for dialogue do not exist, where one has to wait, actively, constructively and intelligently.

Our experience with the mediation which ultimately brought about peace in the Sudan is an illustration of this. Often we were asked why the WCC, while flatly condemning the White racist regimes in Africa did not equally condemn the Khartoum government for its alleged racism, opting instead for "dialogue" with its leaders. Our position in this regard was not accidental.

The White regimes of South Africa or Southern Rhodesia [Zimbabwe] have never (or at least not until very recently) demonstrated their willingness to enter into an open conversation. They constantly reject the basic equality and humanity of Black Africans and thus refuse to accept them as equals in dialogue. The opposite was the case on both sides of the Sudan conflict. Unless those in political power are willing to build bridges and demonstrate respect for the opponent, no amount of outside assistance can help.

The WCC has often been criticized for not strongly condemning certain parties in other conflicts from the outset, and for having contacts with certain "unusual" governments or parties (previously considered "weak", agitators", "terrorists", because they were not direct participants in the major polar relationship), for being, therefore, "selective". But in the Sudan, in Indochina, in the Middle East, and elsewhere, our experience since Uppsala has shown that this new openness to the former "outsiders" has, on the contrary, given the churches unique opportunities to act as agents of reconciliation and peace.

The assumptions behind the accusations made against the World Council seem to be, first, that "Christian actions" can, and must, be absolutely "neutral" and "humanitarian"; and secondly, that Christians are immune from "violence" and must remain untainted by condemning it whenever it occurs. Unfortunately, the latter argument generally refuses to recognize systemic violence, and is only aware of the "defensive violence" of the objects of the former.

Again, our pragmatic experience shows that, often, the statements, positions, contacts and actions which have been considered "biassed" in some quarters have proved to be the very conditions required for the most fruitful and creative ecumenical attempts at reconciliation and peacemaking.

General Secretary Eugene Carson Blake's acceptance of President Boumedienne's invitation to visit Algeria, WCC positions on the Nigerian civil war, the 1969 Canterbury Central Committee statement on the Middle

East—which speaks of "injustice having been done to the Palestinians", several statements on Indochina—especially Dr. Blake's letter on the bombing of the dikes in North Vietnam, must all be seen as having been preconditions for positive, concrete actions. And these are but a few examples.

The WCC has also been accused of becoming increasingly critical of the industrialized Western world, and for being "soft" on the European Socialist countries. Certainly in a sinful world no nation is completely free of guilt for injustice. But especially in the light of the UN Special Assembly referred to earlier one must agree that the most massive injustice in the world is clearly located along this North-South axis and that that is where the most urgent ecumenical attention is needed. Our commitment to "peoples' participation" and the imperative necessity to find qualitatively new solutions to old, still crying problems, require that we listen and respond as never before to the voices of those struggling to overcome the poverty, structural violence and injustice of which they are the main objects.

II. COMMISSION ON THE CHURCHES' PARTICIPATION IN DEVELOPMENT

Historical Background

Development was a major theme of the Fourth Assembly at Uppsala. Speakers in the plenary sessions called attention to the plight of the poor, who form more than half of the human family, and challenged the churches to launch a war on mass poverty and economic and social injustice. One of the Sections, entirely devoted to the topic "World Economic and Social Development", made an analysis of the situation and stated: "We live in a world where men exploit men. . . .The political and economic structures groan under the burden of grave injustice". It urged Christians everywhere "to be on the forefront of the battle" and "to participate in the struggle of millions of people for greater social justice and for world development". At the same time the report warned that "to be complacent in the face of the world's need to be guilty of practical heresy". The seriousness and urgency with which the Assembly considered the development concern was also made clear in its Message, which declared that "The ever-widening gap between the rich and the poor. . . is the crucial point of decision today".

The Assembly did more than make declarations to the world at large. It made specific recommendations to the churches everywhere, in rich countries and poor ones. It spoke of the educational and prophetic tasks, as well as the service functions of the churches. Furthermore, the Assembly instructed the World Council of Churches to assist the member churches in participating effectively in the development process. For this purpose the Assembly urged "that in the restructuring of the WCC a concerted approach to economic and social development be made a priority consideration. . .in order to launch a new expanded development service".

To determine how the WCC could carry out this mandate a world consultation was held at Montreux in 1970, where further clarity was given to the ecumenical perception of the development task. The consultation spoke of development as aimed at three interrelated objectives: justice, self-reliance, and economic growth. The task of the churches was seen primarily as participation with the poor and the oppressed in their struggle for development. It also involved efforts to change socio-economic and political structures which continue to enslave, impoverish and dehumanize the poor population. The task of the WCC was to assist the churches in their concern for reflection, development education, political action as well as provision of technical and financial assistance to development programmes.

Viewed from such a perspective the efforts of the WCC's existing departments were found inadequate. For one thing, no single department was concentrating its attention on the development issue. The partial involvement of several departments made it difficult to evolve an overall strategy and a concerted effort. As the development concern required a comprehensive approach, assignment of reflection to one department, political efforts to another, financial support to a third, and so on, weakened rather than strengthened the overall concern. It was felt that if monetary assistance was not placed in the context of reflection, political action and development education, it could at best be a partial response and at worst anti-developmental.

For these and other reasons, the Consultation recommended and subsequently the Executive Committee approved the establishment of a new Commission on the Churches' Participation in Development (CCPD). The establishment of such a Commission would give expression to the urgency and significance with which the Assembly treated the development challenge and make it possible to approach the development concern in a comprehensive way.

Ecumenical Reflection

One of the tasks assigned to CCPD was to assist member churches in their involvement in the development process by helping them carry out

140

their own studies and thinking, by engaging them in ecumenical processes of reflection and by gathering and disseminating the emerging insights. In a great many local situations, action-oriented study groups concerned with development have come into being during the last four years.

Inevitably, there are differences of views among church groups. At one extreme, there are those who still consider development as a process aimed solely at the economic growth of the poor nations. At the other extreme, there are those who consider development as "integral human development" and thereby include all processes which contribute to the improvement of the quality of life everywhere. However, the reports from the churches indicate that the perspectives which emerged at Montreux seem to meet with the widest acceptance.

The major ecumenical debate seems to be over the differences in emphasis which should be accorded to the three dimensions of the development objective identified by Montreux. Those who emphasize justice often concentrate their attention upon structural changes at national and international levels. To some of these people, attempts to improve the economic conditions of the poor communities on the local level are self-defeating as long as unjust and exploitative structures continue to prevail. Some of those who emphasize self-reliance go to the extent of advocating complete isolation from the rich and powerful.

There are also differences of opinion among churches with regard to the theological basis for action on development. Those who consider development mainly as improvement of the economic misery of the poor think of it as a modern version of traditional Christian charity. Some of those who consider development as integrated human development which includes evangelism find the theological rationale in the mission of the church. The major theological debate seems to be among those who see development as a quest for justice. What is justice from a Christian perspective? How does that differ from ideological concepts? What is the role of the church in bringing about justice? How far can the churches, as corporate bodies, enter into the realm of power and politics? Can a Christian use violence as a means of fighting injustice? These questions, which the churches have wrestled with through centuries, continue to be raised with new urgency and meaning. In spite of the diversity of answers and practical responses to these issues, there is a growing ecumenical appreciation of the following theological insights:

● The recognition of the growing importance of international structures and interdependence among nations has led to a deeper appreciation of the fundamental unity of mankind and the mutual responsibility of the family of nations. The biblical view of the common origin, predicament and destiny of the whole of humanity acquires new meaning and relevance. "The vision that beckons the churches to move forward in the concern for development is the vision of the one human family all of whom have opportunity to live truly human lives".*

● The prophetic role of the church in denouncing injustice and exploitation and in announcing liberation in Christ through words, deeds and life styles is necessary and possible.

● The recognition of the ambiguity of power, human values and hopes leads on the one hand to an appreciation of secular insights without absolutizing them and on the other hand to greater reliance on the resources of faith in the living Christ as the guide for decision-making.

● An understanding of justice comes from perception of the righteousness of God revealed in Jesus Christ. It is to be discerned in complete identification with the poor and the oppressed and through participation with them in their struggle, as God in Christ has done by divesting himself of all power, taking the nature of a slave, accepting, suffering unto death on a cross.

Specific Studies

Besides reflecting on the overall objectives and processes of development, the Commission also undertook a number of specific studies.

An enquiry on international trade examined an area which is often overlooked in secular debates: how far the present system meets the real needs of poor people and the quest for self-reliance among poor nations. The findings of the study which called for radical changes in the thinking and structural patterns of international trade were published at the time of the Third UNCTAD conference in Santiago, Chile, and proved to be a significant contribution to an ongoing debate.**

Under the title "Poverty 2000" a research programme was carried out to assess the magnitude and acuteness of poverty at the end of this century. It involved studies in selected countries, such as Egypt, Tunisia, Ivory Coast, Ghana, Uganda, Zambia, Madagascar, Tanzania, Malaysia, and Sri Lanka. Two developed countries were included for comparative purposes. The data collected was projected on a global level and to the year 2000. The study points out with scientific evidence the appalling conditions that await the coming generations in most of the poor countries if present trends continue. The study was conducted over a period of three years on a contractual basis by the Overseas Development Group of the University of East Anglia.

---

* A quotation from Fetters of Injustice, the report of the Montreux consultation on development. Geneva: WCC, 1970.

** See Marion Gallis: Trade for Justice: Myth or Mandate? Geneva: WCC, 1972.

Another study was undertaken to explore the most effective ways of utilizing part of the investment capital held by many churches for development purposes. The study concluded with a proposal to establish an Ecumenical Development Cooperative Society to administer investment resources from the churches, mainly in the form of loans on concessional terms for development efforts among the poorest sectors of societies.

Underdevelopment is essentially a state of dependency and domination. Conversely, the quest for development is the struggle to break the fetters of domination and exploitation and to bring about self-reliance. At the same time, no community or nation can be an island; all live in an interdependent world. Besides, in the Universal Church and in the ecumenical movement, as Christians we have the vision of a community that transcends class, colour and nationality. How can this vision of a true community within the Church and the world at large be realized when there are groups and nations which dominate others? Is a true partnership possible or desirable between two unequal partners? These questions have been examined through a study entitled "Domination and Dependence".

Aid is considered by many as a necessary factor in the development process. However, there are a few who question the value of aid, as it tends to perpetuate dependency. Therefore, they make a case against all forms of aid and call for a moratorium. In between these two extremes there are those who hold the view that it is not aid as such that stands in the way of self-reliance and therefore genuine development, but the manner in which it is given, received and used. In other words, the question is essentially the "quality of aid". Under what circumstances can aid be a help to development and when and how does it act as a hindrance? This question is another topic for ongoing study.

Development, rightly understood, is a people's movement. People, the poor masses, should be the active agents and immediate beneficiaries in the development process. Due to lack of recognition of or concern about this fact, many poor countries are failing in their efforts. How can such a state of affairs be changed? The answer to this crucial question can be sought not by academic study, but by examining the experience of people's organizations around the world who are making such attempts. This is currently being done.

In most poor countries about 80% of the people live in rural areas. If the development process has to be people-oriented, then the peasants in the rural areas must be given top priority. However, in many countries, the rural sector is a neglected sector. How can the churches and other organizations get involved in rural development? With this purpose in view, a handbook on rural development has been published.

The purpose of all these study programmes has been (a) to involve a wide spectrum of persons and groups in deeper analysis of the issues, (b) to formulate emerging ecumenical insights, and (c) to make use of such insights for educational and training purposes.

Development Education

The Uppsala Assembly and the Montreux Consultation rightly stressed the role of the churches in development education. If economic structures and behaviour within and among nations have to be changed, then public opinion needs to be built up towards increasing the political will of the people. In this respect, churches have a unique role to play.

Churches in the rich countries have attempted to perform this task in various ways. One method is to make use of the existing educational processes within the churches, such as Sunday Schools, church-related educational institutions, theological colleges, and lay training centres. On the parish level, a number of congregations have introduced the development concern in the order of Sunday worship, preaching, Bible study groups, youth groups, and men's and women's organizations.

Certain denominations and councils of churches have taken initiatives in promoting nationwide educational compaigns. A typical method adopted by some churches is by setting apart a week or ten days, or even a month, as a period for concerted campaign. During that period regular Bible study groups are organized throughout the nation. Special orders of service are used for Sunday worship. Action programmes are introduced to inform the communities and influence the decision-makers on the development issue. Third World leaders are invited to participate in the campaign. Secular mass media are also used to communicate the issues to the public at large. The effects of such efforts are not confined to the duration of the campaign. The long preparatory process engages a large number of leaders at the local level in thinking, planning and organizing. Various other groups are engaged to produce materials for study, orders of service, posters, and audio-visual materials. These continue to be used even after the week or month of the actual campaign.

Sometimes certain specific occasions are used for educational campaigns, for example a Sunday during the week of a major UN conference. Specific action programmes around a particular issue have also proved to be an effective means of education. The campaign against the import, sale and use of Angolan coffee in the Netherlands is a good illustration. The role of CCPD in such national efforts has been primarily to assist in the planning and conducting of such campaigns, to make the experiences known to others and to share materials produced. Attempts have also been made to bring together representatives of churches engaged in similar ventures to share ideas and internationalize their efforts. As there are a number of secular groups and agencies in every country committed to the ause of development, church groups in many instances cooperate with them in undertaking educational efforts. CCPD not only encourages churches to make such cooperative efforts, but also keeps in touch with many secular groups and assists them when required.

Education for development is needed as much in the poor countries as in he rich countries, though its emphasis and methodology may have some differences. The existing social, economic and political structures are often created and controlled by a small minority of the rich and are operated mainly for their benefit, often in collusion with power interests in the rich countries. In order to effect any changes in the prevailing structures, the poor majority have to exercise organized power. But the poor people may not be aware of the oppressive situation in which they live, the need for structural changes and their own potential to effect changes. Such a situation calls for a process of conscientization,‡ a process aimed at self-awareness, leading to organized efforts on local and national levels. Many churches in the poor countries recognize that they have a role to play in this regard. For one thing the majority of the churches' constituency belongs to the poor communities. Therefore, attempts to conscientize local congregations of the poor communities can be an effective contribution. Such efforts can be more effective if the entire local community, and not only the Christians, is brought into the process. A few churches in the Third World have taken initiatives in this direction. CCPD has stimulated such initiatives and provided appropriate assistance.

In order to stimulate such local initiatives at the grass roots level, certain churches and Christian Councils have pioneered in training "animators" or "initiators". Persons who have expressed interest and leadership in such community actions are brought together for training at a national centre. The courses vary from two weeks to six months. Then they are sent back to their own communities and their efforts are given encouragement and continued support by national church agencies. Certain churches are making use of existing church institutions and different instruments and media of formal and informal communications, for a conscientization process aimed at the membership of the churches, the public at large and those in key positions of power.

The role of CCPD with regard to such local and national initiatives has been primarily to provide support in the form of ideas, sharing of experiences and financial help.

Documentation and Publications

To provide churches and church-related groups with the thinking and experiences of groups elsewhere, CCPD has established a documentation service. Publications from various parts of the world are collected, classified and shared with those interested. Dossiers on topics such as the churches and development, development education, appropriate technology, low cost housing and people's participation have been compiled. Groups related to CCPD are kept informed about each other's work through the medium of an occasional newsletter. The findings of the specific studies undertaken by CCPD have also been published in the form of books or booklets. The regular periodicals of the WCC have also been used to communicate to the churches and the public at large the ecumenical insights and experiences in the development field.

Technical Services

Development efforts, to be effective, require technical competence in planning and execution. Some churches often overlook this requirement and rely solely on goodwill, enthusiasm and financial outlay. Many who recognize the importance of technical competence do not have access to appropriate expertise. For these reasons, the Uppsala Assembly called for the establishment of an Advisory Committee on Technical Services (ACTS). The Central Committee established such a committee and appointed a team of technically qualified staff to carry out this task. ACTS was later integrated with CCPD to simplify structural arrangements and to provide better coordination of development efforts.

The primary objective of the technical services provided by CCPD is to respond to requests received from churches or church-related agencies for technical assistance at any stage of their development efforts: (a) preplanning surveys, (b) feasibility studies for projects, (c) evaluation of projects in the process of implementation or when they are completed, (d) evaluation of projects and programmes carried out by a church or council over a given period of years. Such services are rendered by CCPD staff, or by consultants or institutions competent in the field under the supervision of CCPD.

Recently the direct staff involvement in surveys and evaluation has been reduced to a minimum. Instead, the staff provides links between the requesting agency and appropriate technical institutions. For this purpose a list of experts and institutions, particularly in the Third World, has been drawn up and is constantly kept up to date. One reason for this shift of emphasis is to encourage churches in the Third World to make better use of experts or institutions in their own countries or regions, instead of continuing to look to the West for technical advice.

The technical services staff of CCPD has also engaged in promoting certain specialized concerns, such as appropriate technology, low cost housing, handicrafts and rural development, where the churches could play a meaningful role. In the field of appropriate technology an attempt has been made to make available data and technical drawings of simple tools and equipment which may be locally manufactured. In the field of handicrafts, CCPD has acted as a catalyst to improve the quality of products and marketing of goods in the Western world.

The objective of CCPD in this area is not merely to provide technical assistance in the usual sense. A programme or project which is technically feasible will not necessarily serve the quest for justice, self-reliance and people's participation. It is relatively easy to find technology that is "growth" oriented; it is extremely difficult to secure appropriate technology which is geared to growth, justice and self-reliance simultaneously. It is in this difficult but badly neglected field that CCPD strives to make its contribution to the churches and to the development process.

Financial Assistance

When the Executive Committee established CCPD in 1970, it authorized the Commission to administer the Ecumenical Development Fund (EDF) recommended by the Montreux Consultation. This was intended as a new means of mobilizing resources, by appealing to the churches to set aside two per cent of their regular income for development purposes, and as a new method of channelling funds, whereby the power of decision-making regarding the actual use of funds was vested in the receiving agency.

The two per cent appeal had its origin in the Uppsala Assembly. The Montreux Consultation reiterated the appeal in view of the immense need, first for additional resources for development efforts and, second, for encouraging congregations and churches to make the development concern a priority in their normal work and financial expenditure. It was hoped that the Fund would help to motivate people on the basis of justice rather than charity. The Central Committee has twice repeated this appeal. But despite repeated calls and efforts by CCPD staff, very few Member Churches have made a positive response. The most notable examples of those who have responded positively are all the Member Churches in Germany and the Netherlands, the Presbyterian and Methodist Churches in New Zealand, and the Society of Friends in a few countries. The Evangelical Church of the River Plate, Argentina, the Presbyterian Church in West Cameroon and the Ethiopian Orthodox Church are among those churches which have agreed to support the appeal in principle.

As the EDF has to seek its resources mainly from the two per cent appeal, and as the number of churches which responded to the appeal were few, the amount of money secured has been far below expectation. In the three-year period of its operation, 1972/74, EDF secured a total of about U.S. $7.5 million.

The Commission has decided that the limited resources of EDF should be used strategically not only because of the limitation of funds, but because the staff would be able to focus its attention in making new experiments and evolving development programmes according to the principles and insights of the Montreux Consultation. Therefore, the major share of resources has been transferred to four selected counterpart groups in Ethiopia, Cameroon, Indonesia and the Caribbean. The rest has been designated for providing assistance to agencies and movements engaged in the development struggle who are willing to enter into a network relationship. Lately an attempt has been made to bring the consortium approach to the support of the four counterpart groups. A meeting of representatives from the counterpart groups and a large number of aid-giving agencies and mission boards was held with this end in view. It is hoped that this approach will have taken definite shape in 1975.

Network Strategy

The strategy which lies behind all the programmes is two-fold: to assist Member Churches to become more informed and better involved in the development process and to establish a network relationship among church-related groups and people's movements committed to development efforts. So far CCPD has identified about fifty such groups around the world with whom a supportive relationship has been established. It is hoped that in the coming period the network relationship among these groups will be further strengthened. CCPD acts as one of the groups in the network and offers its resources—insights, technical know-how, communication facilities and financial assistance—for their support.

Within the network CCPD maintains an intense relationship with four groups: the Development Centre of the Council of Churches in Indonesia, the Development Commission of the Ethiopian Orthodox Church, the Development Commission of the Federation of Evangelical Churches in Cameroon, and Christian Action for Development in the Caribbean of the Caribbean Conference of Churches. The growth and efforts of these four groups are closely linked to the thinking and growth of CCPD. (In 1974, a decision was taken to add the Commission on Justice and Peace of the National Council of Churches of India and the Commission on Development of the Federation of Evangelical Churches in Uruguay. And the Working Group on Church and Development of the National Council of Churches in the Netherlands also maintains a counterpart relationship with CCPD.)

● *Indonesia*. The Development Centre of the Council of Churches in Indonesia was established in 1971. During the past three years its programmes have included the following: (a) Organization of about 12 consultations in different parts of the country as a means of awakening the

churches to the development issue. (b) Establishment and continued supervision of three regional centres in Salatiga (Central Java), Kupang (Timor)
and Medan (Sumatra). Each centre concentrates its work in three model
villages, one for agriculture, one for animal husbandry and one for fishery.
(c) A training course for "motivators" or animators for development. The
course lasts for five months. One group of 25 people has already completed the course, and a second group is being trained. Those who complete the course are assigned to different parts of the country and are given
support and supervision by the Development Centre. (d) Three income-
earning projects—an agricultural farm, a poultry farm and a fishery
—designed to help the Centre to achieve financial self-sufficiency by
1975.

• *Ethiopia*. The Development Commission of the Ethiopian Orthodox
Church was inaugurated in 1972. Its main strategy is to enable the large
number of priests to become "animators" for social change and development efforts in their local communities. With this in view, in 1973 a group
of 100 selected priests was given a six-month training course. This assisted
them with ideas and technical know-how and, in a few cases, modest
financial support. Another group of 100 priests is now undergoing similar
training. The Commission has also undertaken three studies, one on low-
cost housing in Addis Ababa, one on church administration and one on the
proper use of church resources. A cotton farm project is being developed
in northern Ethiopia as an income-earning effort for future work.

• *Cameroon*. The Development Commission of the Federation of
Evangelical Churches in Cameroon came into being in 1971. Prior to this,
there existed a committee on rural development which initiated and supervised a few farm schools and other rural services. This committee was
transformed into the Development Commission, with a new orientation and
a wider mandate, including mass media and interdenominational projects.

The primary task of the Commission is to provide technical services to
the churches in Cameroon in planning and implementing development
programmes. The highlights of these efforts are two comprehensive regional development programmes, one in Ambam and the other in Babimbi.
In Ambam the programme began with community educational efforts.
Consequently the people in the region identified their own priorities. The
Development Commission assisted in turning their needs into a project
aimed at a comprehensive effort to improve living conditions in which the
people in the region would continue to be the active agents of implementation. In Babimbi a different approach was followed due to the particular
situation of that region. It began with a survey of the region, its needs and
potentialities. Out of the survey a specialist formulated an integrated
programme for the development of the rural community. The participation
of the people is being sought in the process of carrying out the programme.

Leadership training is another task of the Commission. Training in farming and rural development is being provided by farm schools and rural assistance centres. The Commission also hopes to establish a training centre for technicians, educators and managers of development projects and programmes.

● *Caribbean*. The Christian Action for Development in the Caribbean (CADEC) was formed as a result of an ecumenical conference held at Port of Spain, Trinidad, in October 1971. The conference was sponsored by SODEPAX and CADEC, which then functioned as a development agency solely for the Eastern Caribbean. CADEC's constituency was widened to include the entire region and all churches, including the Roman Catholic Church. It enlarged the scope and range of its activities, and sharpened its development objectives in line with the Montreux principles. In November 1973, when the Caribbean Conference of Churches came into being, CADEC became part of its structure.

The two major thrusts of the CADEC programme are development education and the operation of a Caribbean Development Fund. Several educational efforts at the local, national and regional levels have been made during this period. Consultations have been held in different islands to build up awareness among Christian leaders and to formulate development programmes. Conscientization‡ programmes have also been carried out among several communities. A monthly newspaper, *Caribbean Contact*, has been published and is widely circulated.

The Development Fund operates to provide loans and grants to development projects. The main sources of the Fund are churches in Western countries, foundations and ecumenical bodies. A small but growing proportion of the Fund has come from the region itself, through a Caribbean Community Appeal.

The First Few Lessons

CCPD has been in operation barely four years. Its assignment is a long-term concern. Therefore it is not possible to assess the effectiveness of the Commission from short-term efforts and achievements. However, a few lessons learned are worth noting:

● Without any doubt it can be stated that the establishment of CCPD has manifested the seriousness with which the Uppsala Assembly treated the development concern and has promoted new thinking, initiatives and efforts among the churches to participate in the development process.

● In establishing CCPD, the Executive Committee felt that the development concern should be approached in a comprehensive way. Experience has shown that this was the right approach. To separate any of the elements from another would distort perception of the objectives and the

150

dynamics of the development process. For example, if financial aid to development projects is isolated from other aspects, it will present a wrong conception of the development concern and even prove to be anti-developmental in practice. Here the principles behind the establishment of the Ecumenical Development Fund have proved to be extremely significant, in spite of the practical difficulties involved.

• The churches in the Third World can make a significant contribution by identifying themselves with the struggle of the poor and the oppressed and by providing them with necessary moral and material support.

• Experience has confirmed the conviction that the area in which the churches have the greatest potential contribution to make is in the field of development education.

• One of the unique roles of the WCC is to maintain a network relationship among groups and movements, within and outside churches, engaged in the struggle for justice and development, and to facilitate sharing of ideas, experiences and resources among them.

• Another contribution that the WCC can render to the churches is in the area of "ideas and insights". Providing opportunities for those who are acting and reflecting at the local level to come together in ecumenical forums will facilitate not only the sharing of insights and experiences but will also heighten their perception to an international and ecumenical level. Specific studies undertaken from an ecumenical perspective involving a great many people around the world also have a contribution to make in this regard.

• One of the fields to which CCPD did not give adequate attention is in the realm of theological reflection. This needs to be rectified. The need is not so much to produce new theological formulas, but to bring about changes in conscience, attitudes and values and to provide the spiritual resources for those who are in the actual struggle for justice and liberation.

Beyond Nairobi

When the delegates of the Member Churches met at Uppsala, they were rightly confronted with the challenge posed by the two-thirds of the world's population who live in poverty, oppression and deprivation. Many of the churches and the World Council of Churches have taken the first few steps in response. However, it is impossible to be sanguine about what has been achieved; it is a mere drop in a sea of need. The challenge of development remains in all its overwhelming proportions.

In fact, the plight of the poor societies is even worse today than in 1968. In spite of all the efforts made by peoples and nations, the actual number of people below the absolute poverty line has increased considerably. The pace of development has in no way caught up with demographic growth.

As the President of the World Bank stated recently: "One-third to one-half of [these] two billion [thousand million] human beings suffer from hunger or malnutrition; 20-25 % of the children in poor countries die before their fifth birthday; about 800 million are illiterate". Food in many countries is in short supply. Widespread famine has occurred in such regions as the Sahel‡ and Northern Ethiopia. Grain reserves have shrunk to a dangerously low level. Prospects for increasing food production to reach the level of growing demand and increasing population have become doubtful, while the cost of food has more than doubled during 1973/74. Consequently, even in countries which do not have an actual food shortage, the poor are finding their meagre resources inadequate to buy the minimum amount of food to ensure their survival.

What is happening on the food front is one more twist to the vicious spiral of underdevelopment confronting many poor countries. For the first time in 25 years, the rate of economic growth in some countries is falling behind the rate of increase in population. The poor nations' share in world trade is decreasing. In spite of all the appeals made in recent years, the net flow of aid in real terms from the rich countries is also decreasing. Recent world trends such as the oil crisis, inflation and monetary fluctuations have played havoc in the poor countries.

It is in the context of a deepening development crisis that the Fifth Assembly will meet in 1975. The delegates will not require addresses or statistics to convince them of the gravity of the situation. They will be able to see it in the eyes of the poor around them, in the plight of the masses in the villages, in the misery of the slums of Nairobi.

One thing is clear. The development challenge requires far more drastic steps and remedies than those envisaged at Uppsala. A little more aid or a little better trade will not suffice. The situation has reached crisis proportions. The prospects for the future are so bleak that only a concerted effort to bring about a new world social and economic order will do.

III. PROGRAMME TO COMBAT RACISM

The Historical Context

When the delegates met at the Uppsala Assembly there existed no Programme to Combat Racism. This is not to say that the ecumenical movement or the WCC had ignored the issue of racism; nor is it a simple coincidence that the PCR was prompted by the Uppsala Assembly. The decisions taken at Uppsala and by subsequent meetings of the Central and Executive Committees of the WCC came almost at the tail end of the process of decolonization in Asia, Africa and the Caribbean and must be seen as a reflection of and a reaction to the aspirations of the majority of the peoples of the world to get rid of the yoke of foreign domination (even if only to be replaced by neo-colonial domination in most instances).

The history of the ecumenical movement records many statements, both by individuals and groups, denouncing racism as being incompatible with the Christian doctrine of man and with the nature of the Church of Christ. These statements reflect moral indignation and deep resentment concerning the racial dimensions of conflicts in various parts of the world.* After the New Delhi Assembly the WCC set up a Secretariat on Racial and Ethnic Relations. This was a first attempt to act together as churches in the field of race relations.

Though in some instances moral exhortations were backed up by ecumenical programmes in support of the needs of the victims of racial injustice, the distance between word and deed lengthened. The repeated failure of churches to participate in the struggle for racial justice became painfully clear. Yet it was these same churches and missions which had, by their preaching of the Gospel, helped the racially oppressed peoples to discover that God is the liberating God, that Christ died and rose again for *all* men and women, and that he gave himself for the liberation of all people without distinction.

In their statements the churches insisted that "any form of segregation based on race, colour or ethnic origin is contrary to the Gospel", but at the same time they refused to accept the necessary implications of this position, acting instead according to an ethic that sustained the dominant Western power interests which were not prepared to accept any radical change in the existing power relationships.

It was not until the Uppsala Assembly in 1968 and the International Consultation on Racism held at Notting Hill in 1969 that the urgency for the churches to undertake a vigorous action programme through the World Council of churches was recognized. The meeting of the Central Committee which took place in Canterbury soon afterwards translated this demand into action.

---

* Clear examples are J.H. Oldham's book Christianity and the Race Problem in 1924, the statements by the 1928 meeting of the International Missionary Council in Jerusalem, the 1937 Oxford Conference on the Church, State and Community, the Amsterdam (1948) and Evanston (1954) Assemblies of the World Council of Churches, the report by Dr. Visser 't Hooft in his Memoirs on his visit to South Africa in 1950 and the 1960 Cottesloe and 1964 Mindolo Consultations.

The Central Committee meeting in Canterbury had the choice between continuing the existing minimum concern and the setting up of a programme which would attempt to express the churches' solidarity with the struggle for liberation of the racially oppressed. It chose the latter.

It became clear that racism is "not confined to certain countries or continents", but that "it is a *world problem*. White racism is not its only form". It is recognized that in some areas there are other forms of racism, and ethnocentrism. "It is the coincidence, however, of an accumulation of wealth and power in the hands of the white peoples, following upon their historical and economic progress during the past 400 years, which is the reason for a focus on the various forms of *White* racism in the different parts of the world. People of different colour suffer from this racism in all continen s. . . .While many formerly colonial people have become independent, they still suffer from the aftermath of colonialism".

The Programme to Combat Racism* was created to develop and implement these functions in a process of "coordinated action by all departments and divisions" of the WCC. Until the re-structuring of the WCC in 1971, the PCR was lodged as a direct responsibility of the General Secretariat and was mandated to "prepare, execute, stimulate and coordinate the programmes outlined" by the Committee and to "gather information and provide necessary technical expertise for the operations as a whole". To advise and guide the Secretariat, the PCR Commission was set up as well as a Staff Coordinating Group drawn from the different divisions and departments of the WCC to coordinate their involvement in the overall programme.

At Canterbury the Central Committee envisaged the PCR as "a five-year programme of the World Council of Churches". By its meeting in West Berlin, 1974, the Central Committee saw the clear need "to continue the Programme to Combat Racism as an ongoing programme of the WCC". During its initial mandate the PCR had become an integral part of the Programme Unit on Justice and Service, and the Central Committee therefore accepted the proposal put before it that its location be continued and normalized so that the PCR, in common with all other sub-units, become an ongoing part of the total WCC programme, and, together with all other programmes, be reviewed by the Assembly in 1975.

Programme Policy

If the Canterbury Central Committee had a choice, the Programme to Combat Racism had *no* choice in the policy it was to pursue. That policy

---

* For an assessment of the first five years of the Programme to Combat Racism, see Elisabeth Adler: A Small Beginning. Geneva: WCC, 1974.

was outlined in Canterbury. Any discussion about policies and programmes in support of the racially oppressed must start with the assumption that the liberation of oppressed peoples is an act which can only be validly undertaken by the oppressed. No well-meaning outsiders can achieve this for them. Leaders of the oppressed have made it abundantly clear in their statements that the outsider's role can only be a supportive one. Thus the question posed to the churches is how they can positively support the liberation struggle. On the basis of this assumption PCR's main task is to isolate the root causes of racism in order to discover ways of effectively combatting them.

At the same time, the very nature of a Programme to Combat Racism undertaken by the churches means that it is involved in a process of liberation of the oppressors. In fact, the liberation of the oppressors is closely related to the liberation of the oppressed. Oppressors in many ways are restricted human beings who need to be liberated from blindness, guilt and fear and liberated *for* a shared life in community, in justice, mutual respect and trust, to be free to become authentic persons, able to fulfil their capacities as human beings.

The PCR since its coming into operation in January 1970 has developed a series of programmes and policy actions and guidelines in fulfilment of the Canterbury mandate. This mandate stipulated the following major emphases for the PCR:

● White racism in its many organized ways is by far the most dangerous form of present racial conflicts.

● It is institutional racism as reflected in the social, economic and political power structures which must be challenged; moreover, it is the power structures which use racism to empower themselves which must be challenged.

● Combatting racism must entail a redistribution of social, economic, political and cultural power from the powerful to the powerless.

● No single strategy to combat racism is universally appropriate.

● The need to analyse and correct the Church's complicity in benefitting from and furthering White racism. This is an absolute priority if the churches want to make any contribution to the solution of the problem of society.

Programme Activities

(a) *General*. In line with these emphases, the more significant developments in the PCR may be summarized as follows:

Through its *Special Fund* it has supported various groups and organizations of the racially oppressed and organizations supporting victims of racial injustice through the world, laying special emphasis in the struggle for liberation in Southern Africa. To date it has distributed $1,050,000 (including government support, which has not been considered as part of the $ 1 million to be raised by the churches) to various groups throughout the world, the grants being used for humanitarian purposes consonant with the aims and policies of the WCC. The Central Committee in Utrecht received a full report on the experience with the Fund and unanimously, decided to extend the Fund from $500,000 to $1 million. Two years later, at its meeting in West Berlin, when it made the PCR a permanent feature of the work of the World Council, the Central Committee resolved "to continue to make grants from the Special Fund, with a minimum target of $ 300,000 to be raised and distributed each year".

One of the important functions that PCR has performed has been in providing opportunities for *contact, consultation, and dialogue with the leaders of the oppressed*. In many places responsible church leaders are involved in dialogue with the leaders of these liberation movements. PCR has facilitated this dialogue, convinced that this is an integral part of a programme for racial justice. This is all the more significant since many of the liberation movement leaders are of Christian background.

An annual *Programme Project List* (administered separately from the Special Fund) was developed to serve the purpose of supporting local, national and regional churches and groups as well as projects initiated by the PCR, in solidarity with the racially oppressed.

PCR has investigated and exposed the nature of the exploration of Indians in Latin America* and developed programmes designed to *support the struggle of the indigenous peoples* not only in Latin America but also in the United States, Canada, Australia and New Zealand. Various follow-up actions and supportive policies have been developed in several of these regions.

Research has been done and *documents* published *espousing the causes of racially oppressed groups*, especially in areas where these groups have not had access to present their own cases through the conventional avenues. The publications have aroused action initiatives by interested groups in the affluent world and contributed to eradicating the illiteracy among peoples in the affluent world about the nature and causes of racial oppression. The mobile exhibition on "Man and Racism" is available in different languages as audio-visual aid to help in this education process.

A programme has been developed to call upon the member churches of the WCC to use all their influence to *bring pressure upon corporations*

---

*   This major study was published as The Situation of the Indian in South America: Contribution to the Study of Inter-Ethnic Conflict with Regard to the non-Andean Indians. Geneva: WCC, 1972. It has also been published in Spanish by Tierra Nueva, Montevideo.

nvesting in Southern Africa to withdraw,* recognizing that such corporations are responsible in giving economic, political and moral support to undergird apartheid and colonialism.

The Central Committee decided at Utrecht in 1972 that the WCC should *disinvest from corporations directly involved* in investments or trade *with Southern Africa*. As an international body and ecumenical Christian voice in the world, the WCC has made a symbolic action that has given a moral lead. Member churches, Christian agencies and individual Christians were urged to use all their influence as stockholders in such corporations to press for a withdrawal of the corporations from Southern Africa. In order to assist member churches, lists of corporations investing in Southern Africa were published.

An *examination of international banking*** was a further consequence of the decision taken at Utrecht. A list was compiled of banks in various countries which are currently participating in loans to the South African government and its agencies. And in 1974 the Central Committee instructed the Finance Department of the WCC to communicate with certain of these banks "to solicit assurances that they will stop granting such loans" and gave authorization, "if satisfactory results are not forthcoming, to ensure that no WCC funds are deposited with those banks".

Finally the 1973 and 1974 meetings of the Commission on the PCR additional programme developments were approved, namely:

● A programme to investigate and work towards the elimination of racial and ethnic tensions in Asia in furtherance of the small beginning made by the PCR in developing programmes in Asia. They now include a seminar on *Caste, Class and Regionalism in India* and also a major study of the role of foreign investments in Malaysia and the extent to which the existence of such links underline the racial and ethnic tensions in that country. This programme will be carried out in close cooperation with the Christian Conference of Asia (CCA).

● In collaboration with the Education Office of the WCC, a project to

---

*   See Time to Withdraw. Geneva: WCC, 1973. This pamphlet gives the rationale for the WCC's approach to the investment issue. Also worth close attention is the Second List revised) of Corporations directly involved in Southern Africa. It too is available from the WCC.

**. In July 1973 the Corporate Information Centre of the National Council of Churches in the USA published The Frankfurt Documents: Secret Bank Loans to the South African Government. This publication has disclosed that a multinational banking firm, the European American Banking Corporation (EABC) has raised money in the USA, Europe and Canada to provide secret loans totalling over $210 million to the South African government and its agencies since late 1970. The basic document on the whole subject is Business as Usual: International Banking in South Africa, an "Anti-Report" published by Counter Information Services, London 1974, for the Programme to Combat Racism.

develop an action-oriented study programme to *investigate the extent of racism in textbooks used in church-related schools* to counter the existing theories and myths imposed by the dominant structures.

(b) *In cooperation with other WCC programmes*. One of the PCR's original mandates was "examination of the programmes, budgets and structures of the World Council of Churches with a view to increasing support of efforts for racial justice". In light of this the following developments have taken place in other WCC sub-units:

Faith and Order. The work of section III of the Louvain meeting of the Faith and Order Commission in August 1971, on "The Unity of the Church and the Struggle against Racism" (see *Faith and Order, Louvain 1971, Study Reports and Documents*) dealing with the tension between racial identity and the unity of mankind, the significance of Black Theology, the positive values of conflict and tensions, and the need to discuss the Sacraments as well as Church Order and Discipline in the context of racial conflict.

CWME. Three Consultations of Mission Boards involved in Zimbabwe, Mozambique, South Africa and Namibia were held to discuss Missionary responsibilities; and an investigation into the existence of racism in Mission materials has begun.

CICARWS. A project for material aid to liberation movements in Southern Africa was adopted and is being carried out; and a programme to support the needs of conscientious objectors, draft dodgers and deserters in Europe from the Portuguese army has been carried out.

CCPD. Support was given for the development fund of the Mozambique Institute (of FRELIMO) operating in the liberated areas of Mozambique.

CCIA. Discussions are regularly taking place with the UN, OAU, ILO and UNESCO and with NGO's to explain and obtain further support for the work of the Commission of the PCR.

Migration Desk has taken main responsibility in carrying out the Central Committee resolution requesting all member churches to mount campaigns to discourage White migration to Southern Africa. A consultation on this issue was held.

Office of Education has developed a study of racist literature, as already mentioned.

Finance Department has compiled the lists of foreign companies investing in South Africa, Namibia, Zimbabwe, Angola, Mozambique and Guinea-Bissau, and has implemented the Central Committee resolution on investments.

Church and Society has completed a major study on "Violence, Nonviolence and the Struggle for Social Justice".

Communication Department has made a concerted effort to publicize both the Special Fund and the Programme through the channels of the secular and religious press.

These initiatives and cooperation between the various departments of the WCC need to be further strengthened in the fulfilment of the Canterbury Mandate.

(c) *Regional developments*. The development of a world-wide programme has made it necessary to regionalize some of the activities of the PCR, particularly in supporting regional organizations like the *AACC's Programme to Combat Racism and Tribalism*. The relationship with AACC has so far been limited to developing a programme for exchange between theologians from the USA and Africa, and it is hoped that participants from other parts of the world will be included at later stages. An encouraging new development is the acceptance on the part of the *Christian Conference of Asia* (CCA) of the need to start a special programme to deal with racism and ethnic tensions in Asia. This was decided at the 1973 CCA Assembly in Singapore in response to a request made by the Commission of the PCR. *UNELAM* in Latin America has taken the initiative to follow up certain recommendations from the Barbados Symposium.

(d) *National developments*. Various committees at the national level have been formed in response to the PCR programme by national church bodies or groups, particularly in the United Kingdom, the Netherlands, West Germany, the USA. These committees are providing important means of communication with the local situation. Some have initiated study and action programmes and fund-raising campaigns.

Some Issues Raised in the Race Debate

While the PCR is a new body in the World Council of Churches, it expresses a concern which has been part of the WCC from the very beginning of its existence. The WCC is in the process of becoming a *World Council*. The new role of Churches of Asia, Africa and Latin America in the WCC coincides with a re-awakening of the peoples of the three continents. The WCC has started to take seriously the aspirations of the majority of the peoples of the world to get rid of the yoke of foreign domination. The PCR is an important expression of this new development in the WCC.

In historical terms, it is important to remember that the basis for the PCR action so far, though criticized by a minority in the West, remains within the spectrum of the minimum demands made by racially oppressed and colonized people in their struggle for liberation. The PCR has come under attack from a number of churches, or certain sections within churches, but the question which has to be asked consistently is whether

159

the WCC is willing to serve that part of its constituency whose aspirations are being expressed through the PCR—the racially oppressed.

The PCR has no choice between merely demanding standards of minimum treatment or identifying the causes of racism and combatting them. The latter course was the only one possible. It was the right decision if only for the reason that the oppressors wrongly claim that human rights can be donated by the powerful to the powerless.

The present PCR policy is given validity by a long process of social and theological thinking within the WCC and its Member Churches. The 1966 Church and Society Conference, for instance, shifted WCC thinking from a concept of integration to one of a radical change of economic and political structures in society. Persons and groups should not be forced to adapt to structures, but vice versa. The 1973 Bangkok Conference on Salvation Today clearly re-emphasized the biblical insight that the churches' concern for individual salvation must be complemented with a concern for the salvation of peoples. That conference also brought sharply into focus the relation between salvation and liberation and its implications for cultural and racial identity.

The PCR's actions have exposed not only the existence of racism but also the structures which are geared to its maintenance, such as:

● *Economic structures*: Many churches in the West are big investors and thus indirectly partners in oppressive economic and military complexes, as for instance in Southern Africa. These issues require further action-oriented research. PCR is not the only WCC sub-unit concerned with these wider issues of economic and social justice, and possibilities of more coordination within the WCC (and particularly within the Programme Unit) need to be carefully studied.

● *Legal structures*: The enactment of laws which perpetuate racial discrimination and through the enforcement of such laws by the legal machinery of the state including the courts of law and the police. Both the process of enactment and enforcement can institutionalize racism either at the individual or structural level.

● *Political structures*: The process by which racial minorities or majorities are deprived of representation rights, the right of meeting, the right of free expression, trade union rights, and other basic requirements of democratic participation.

In the final analysis the question is one of power. Theological reflection by the Church on power as related to liberation and justice and its translation into action require urgent attention. The mandate given to PCR by the Canterbury Central Committee lays special stress on the relation between combatting racism and liberation from the oppressive structures of power distribution in the world. Since the 1975 Assembly has as its theme "Jesus Christ Frees and Unites", it is imperative that a basic discussion take place in *all* the Sections, highlighting the racial aspects of the struggle for liberation.

The development of PCR research initiatives and programmes have to some extent been moment to moment. This has partly been the result of the pressure caused by having to respond to a controversial programme, but it was accentuated by the fact that only three executive staff members were given the responsibility for handling a world-wide programme. The task is even more difficult now since it has become necessary to take into account new developments in the area of racism.

It is also necessary for the PCR to avoid a crisis-oriented approach and for this reason it should develop more regular relations with the churches and racially oppressed groups so as to keep in touch with developments in their thinking. The supportive function of the PCR—in consonance with the general purposes of the WCC—is extremely important.

As the World Council of Churches continues to work on "the Unity of the Church and the Unity of Mankind", the Programme to Combat Racism has made a significant contribution by raising crucial issues related to this goal. In its early attacks on racism, it has combined the elements of reconciliation and prophetic action, and helped the churches see that reconciliation can only take place in a climate concerned about liberation. In John Deschner's phrase, the PCR has tried to demonstrate "that racism is, in ecumenical terminology, a faith and order question of the first magnitude". Lukas Vischer has developed this further in suggesting that the PCR pre-supposes "the vision of a world community in which not only all races but also all nations have their adequate share; an 'international responsible society' in which each part is enabled to be itself and to develop its own identity. The struggle against racism must be understood as a contribution towards this goal. If this is made manifest, PCR will be shown to be part of a much larger struggle. The accusation of selectivity can be rejected by pointing to the need of concreteness. The concentration on one evil is not an arbitrary choice but a contribution to this larger goal. Furthermore, the talk about redistribution of power loses its abstract nature. Power is related to a positive goal. It is subordinated to the goal of reaching a viable world community. Redistribution of power means empowering to become partners in one world society"

The Mandate given to PCR at Canterbury includes among other things: (a) "examination of all the means available for promoting political actions towards the bringing about of racial justice, including economic sanctions" and, (b) the recognition that "there can be no justice in our world without a transfer of economic resources to undergird the redistribution of political power and to make cultural self-determination meaningful". Clearly the work of PCR in the last five years has hardly begun to reveal the many facets of the problem: yet some clear lines are already indicated:

- The relationship between structures of racial oppression and the economic structures of the world today.

● The relation of the Faith and Order study on "The Unity of the Church and the Unity of Mankind" to the PCR study on Racism. The theological work on racism has barely started.

● Practical options available to people who want to disengage themselves from supporting racism by direct or indirect participation in economic and political structures that foster racial oppression.

● The ethical considerations raised by methods used by Christians and others to combat racism.

The PCR has now been made a permanent part of the work of the WCC. The Assembly, therefore, must contemplate the challenge of the future in a larger ecumenical context. The basic question is how the whole of the WCC—which means 271 Member Churches, not simply the Geneva-based organization which serves them—can be helped to greater understanding, deeper commitment and more courageous action in the struggle for racial justice. What is at stake is not just the future of a programme, but the integrity of the Church's life and the credibility of our witness to Christ as Lord of all.

IV. COMMISSION ON INTER-CHURCH AID, REFUGEE AND WORLD SERVICE

A Time of Challenge and Change

In hearing the cry "of those who long for peace; of the hungry and exploited who demand bread and justice; of the victims of discrimination who claim human dignity; and the increasing millions who seek the meaning of life", the churches represented at the Uppsala Assembly set in train a pattern of events which has had profound effects on the life and work of the World Council of Churches. Few sections of the Council have had to go through such a fundamental re-thinking as the Commission on Inter-Church Aid, Refugee and World Services (CICARWS). Old traditions of service have been analysed and appraised, and new patterns have emerged to fit the demands and challenges coming from within the ecumenical movement and, just as importantly, from those the Commission is charged to assist.

These new insights, and especially the new structure introduced in 1971, were not easy for CICARWS to absorb. The discussions were long and often painful. To place justice concerns alongside traditional forms of service is in fact a very considerable upheaval. But the process has been aided by the fact that the Commission itself is now more widely representative of the whole fellowship of the WCC. For the first time more than half the Commissioners are drawn from the Third World—the traditionally receiving churches.

This has meant, for example, that the project system, which currently tries to find support for some 650 projects dealing with education, agriculture and medical work—as well as projects more generally involving the life of the churches—put forward by churches in more than 90 countries (now including those in North America) has been the subject of a thoroughgoing process of change designed to give more responsibility and control to regional groups as well as reflect locally determined priorities more faithfully. The process is far from complete, and radical questions are being raised as to whether the project system is in fact the right way of expressing fellowship between the churches. Just as important are the theological questions that have been raised within the ecumenical movement on the kind of fellowship that the WCC should be seeking.

At the same time there has been acute awareness of some of the political sensitivities involved in trying to channel resources from all over the world into programmes of relief, rehabilitation and development. The tragedy of the conflict in Nigeria put this problem in a sharp and dramatic form at the time of the Uppsala Assembly. Groups of Christians found different answers to the same question of how to act compassionately in a country torn apart by civil war. All that has happened since then has gone to underscore the importance of the question as the churches, through CICARWS, have tried to respond to disasters, both natural and man-made, in Bangladesh, Sudan, Indochina, Burundi, the Middle East and Chile. No startling answer has come, but it can be said that more churches and agencies are more aware of the political implications of their work than ever before, and there have been some remarkable accomplishments in working together in situations of great difficulty.

Another effect of the Uppsala Assembly has been the amount of money that has subsequently become available for development and inter-church aid within some, at least, of the churches. One feature of the past six years has been a dramatic increase in the amount of money channelled through CICARWS—from US $10.7 million in 1968 to $26 million in 1973. This has resulted, in part, from the impact of the Assembly, in part from the increasing amount of money governments are prepared to give through the churches and in part from the increased attention given by the mass media to disaster situations in different parts of the world.

This has been something of a mixed blessing. More money has meant bigger programmes (such as the $ 13 million that were spent on relief and rehabilitation in Bangladesh). But success of this kind has its own dangers. First, the churches become in a sense captives of media attention. One country attracts the world's headlines and concern. Money comes that must be spent in that place. And the pressing, equally urgent but sometimes invisible needs of a hundred other situations (such as the psychological impact of oppression of people in Southern Africa) have to be ignored. That does not make for real justice, nor does it encourage those who give to consider long-term development needs. Too much emphasis is put on a disaster that strikes in a day rather than the long and painful tragedy that saps strength, energy and life every day of the year in countless places around the world.

A second problem is the effect on the local church. The pressure is on the "donor" churches and the WCC to create large programmes often in situations in which the local churches are too small and weak to cope with the demands of massive international aid and attention. Churches in the West perhaps expect too much from their sister churches in the East or South: expectations which they themselves would find very difficult to fulfil in similar circumstances. There is a real need to go deeper into what the power of money does in this situation and how the churches can balance their desire to serve with the needs of the local Christian community in a way which takes the identity of the local churches seriously. Parallel with the increase in available resources has been the enlargement of the various agencies attached to the traditional "donor" churches. Inevitably there has been a heightened desire to spend money in support of "development" and a slight reluctance to consider all the obligations of inter-church aid, understood in the sense of how the churches may best help the churches. Especially in discussions of the project system, questions have been posed about the mandate of the agencies and whether the *churches* in Europe and North America in particular are sufficiently involved in the whole consideration of Inter-Church Aid concerns.

CICARWS has to serve the totality of the constituency of the World Council. The larger churches and their agencies are in daily contact with the Commission, but it must at the same time seek ways and means of being in close contact and conversation with the smaller churches that have not established service agencies but who nevertheless feel challenged to take part in the Church's ministry of service.

An increasingly important role is being played by the Orthodox churches in the life of the Commission. They continue to receive assistance for various church-related projects in different countries, especially in Eastern Europe. But more significantly they are trying to find the means to share some of their resources with others. Notable contributions have been made by the Orthodox churches in Greece and Russia to material aid programmes in Bangladesh and North Vietnam.

These are some of the issues which will have to be considered in the period before, during and after the Fifth Assembly. The Commission's contribution to what has been accomplished in the Sudan may serve to illustrate some of the more general points just made about the binding together of justice and service as well as some of the financial issues.

The long civil war between the Arab North and the African South in the Sudan had been of real concern to the churches. The All Africa Conference of Churches had tried on many different occasions to bring some measure of peace and reconciliation, but with little success. Thousands of refugees made their way to neighbouring countries, while Christians in different parts of the world were beginning to find ways of aiding the victims of the long drawn-out guerrilla war. The tension was, in a certain sense, between justice and service: the justice of peace, which could take into account the claims of the South to a better deal, and the desire to serve those who were the victims of war by relying on the channels of the rebel forces to reach people in the bush areas. Inevitably such an action would have been interpreted by the North as "interference" and would possibly have lessened the chances of achieving peace.

Together, CICARWS and CCIA tried to make a contribution to peacemaking which might in the long term also give a chance to serve the whole nation. (What they were able to do in company with the All Africa Conference of Churches was in fact also dependent on the contribution of the WCC's Programme to Combat Racism to liberation movements in Africa. The grants that had been made helped to establish the credibility of the WCC and the AACC in the minds of both northern government leaders and the leadership of the southern movement.) The Member Churches and their agencies agreed to respect this basic decision to work for peace even though it meant delaying service to the suffering. The story of what happened through the long-drawn peace talks during most of 1971 and early 1972 has been told in other places.* What was important for the WCC was that it had caught a glimpse of what could be achieved by trying to hold justice and service in creative tension.

The contribution made towards peace provided a solid foundation for church efforts in support of rehabilitation and development. Led by an African Christian with great powers of leadership and a keen vision, churches around the world and churches in the Sudan planned together to make a substantial contribution towards securing the peace by supporting

---

* See Kodwo Ankrah: "In Pursuit of Peace in the Sudan". Study Encounter Vol. VIII No. 2, 1972 (SE/25).

the efforts of the Sudanese to rebuild their country. Their plans and preferences have been central to the whole reconstruction programme. The only disappointment has been that it has been impossible to raise the kinds of funds that were available for Bangladesh. The forgotten war looked at times in danger of becoming a forgotten relief and rehabilitation programme. So far, less than US $5 million has been raised for work in Sudan, which reflects the lack of coverage given to the country and its problems by the mass media in comparison to other places.

Inevitably what is written here is no more than a highlighting of certain trends in the life of the Commission between assemblies. It does not adequately reflect the tremendous contribution of thousands of people in rich and poor churches all around the world who have given themselves in the work of inter-church aid and service, nor the support and interest of the members of the Commission who have come faithfully to meetings and given helpful advice to the staff who have lived the excitements and the tensions of the work day by day. It is difficult for them to be objective about the events that they have been so close to. But they are, perhaps, more conscious of the challenges that have been presented, the substantial changes that have taken place and above all the fact that what has been done is, of course, quite insignificant in comparison to what needs to be done.

The Commission at Work

Inter-Church Aid works in four main clusters of activity. The first group, mainly the area secretaries responsible for relationships with the various regions, is centered around the project system. In the second area of activity is all of the work that goes into coordinating church response to disaster and the longer-term rehabilitation programmes. The traditional concern of the WCC for refugees is represented in the work of the Refugee Service, the third of the work clusters. Direct services to individuals and churches are the concern of the fourth cluster.

(1) *The Project System*. From the very beginning, the project system has been at the heart of the Commission's work in helping the churches to reach out across national and denominational boundaries to support Christian service throughout the world. A programme that started in Europe has become a truly world-wide network of relationships that channels assistance to more than 650 projects in 90 countries through a total transfer in any one year of around US $10 million. The emphasis has always been on *service*, projects which enable the churches to serve in their own society, and on the *ecumenical* nature of the enterprise, either projects which churches carry out together or where the giving church aids the work of a

church from a different tradition. While support through the project system has normally been limited to three years, it has also been the sign of a continuing commitment to the churches in a particular country by their sister churches throughout the world.

The Uppsala Assembly called for an analysis of what had been achieved through the project system as a means for determining guidelines for the future. At the same time, the emphasis of the Uppsala Assembly on development meant that the Commission and the churches wanted to find ways of integrating development concerns directly into the project system. A registration desk was established within the Commission to make a detailed analysis of the pattern of support channelled through the Commission as well as establish a system of registering all projects seeking support from church sources. Registration is well under way and includes details of the askings to most Protestant and Roman Catholic agencies so that a full picture is available on what is being asked of whom. The analysis revealed some disturbing trends: first, that a few countries in each continent were receiving the lion's share of the resources coming from outside, and, second, that decisions on funding being taken by agencies were in fact determining what would be done without any real reference to the desires or the priorities of the asking churches.

Parallel with this discovery was the advice offered by the Consultation on Ecumenical Assistance to Development Projects held at Montreux in 1970. The consultation expressed strong support for self-reliance as one of the keys to WCC development policy. It made some searching criticisms of the project system, which it described as basically a "donor's system" not reflecting any real trust between giver and receiver. The consultation's desire to underline development as a WCC concern by creating a new instrument for development policy was a strong challenge to the Commission, though it was understood that CICARWS and the newly established Commission on the Churches' Participation in Development would cooperate closely on all levels of activity from fund-raising to programme. One of the first results was an experiment with a limited number of Special Development Projects in Africa, Asia, Latin America and Europe designed to demonstrate the Commission's commitment to development and find a way of channelling increased support to it through the project system, which had always listed a considerable number of projects contributing to development. But the more fundamental emphasis was put on bringing about a reshaping of the project system to make it a more adequate means of transferring resources between the giving and receiving churches.

No adequate terminology exists to describe the relationship that exists between the churches. The traditional terms "donor" and "receiver" have been under strong attack. Unfortunately no new words have been coined to reflect the fundamental fact that everyone who shares in the project system both gives and receives. The money that often forms the currency of the exchange is less important than the conversations that should take place at each end of the relationship, but also between two *partners*. The Commission's concern has been to stress that unless there is a real partnership of dialogue as well as financial assistance there is no true exchange, and the whole enterprise is a charade.

So the accent has been put on two basic issues. The first has been to make sure that the projects coming from each region are examined by a representative group drawn from that region, together with a few representatives from funding agencies. It is the regional groups which make the final recommendation to the Commission as to which projects should be accepted for listing in' the Project List presented to the churches by CICARWS and the Commission on World Mission and Evangelism. This process makes for a far more responsible and authentic decision-making process than for the Commission itself to approve each project from each region, as happened in the past.

To undergird the responsibility of the regional groups, CICARWS has established a category system by which the local churches list their priorities. CICARWS has undertaken to secure 90% coverage of the first category projects totalling $3.5 million, as a recognition of the priority concerns of the local churches. Projects not given priority are placed in Category II, and support for them is sought in the normal way. Regional projects or specific pieces of WCC work, such as support for Urban Industrial Mission or the Refugee service, are generally placed within Category III.

So far these innovations have worked successfully and have been respected by both giving and receiving churches. The category system began in 1971, and the pattern of support has managed to keep up with the 90% target. But the Commission is convinced that these changes are not the whole answer to the problem. The search goes on to find new ways of expressing the fellowship between the churches. Several sessions of the Commission have been devoted to the future of the project system. One of the ideas proposed is that churches be encouraged to present five-year plans which set out what they would like to achieve in their mission and service activity. Contributing churches would then be invited to give general financial support to a whole programme outline rather than identify individual projects for support.

Consultations have been held in all of the regions as these changes have developed, and the actions taken reflect the agreements of the churches. The different regions have established distinctive regional contributions to the whole process. In Africa, for example, the churches have emphasized the need to be self-reliant and find ways for the African.churches to mobilize their own resources. In the Middle East there has been a new ecumenical development. The historic Orthodox churches are now much more ready to work with the Protestant churches in the region. In Europe, churches in the socialist countries are rethinking the whole pattern of assistance coming to them from outside in order to see whether it meets their real needs or the challenge of their situation. They are also giving consideration to how they can participate more fully in sharing in the aid and assistance programmes.

Another issue imposing itself in the discussion is the question of bilateral as opposed to multilateral assistance to projects. The money being channelled ecumenically has always been a small percentage of the money channelled directly between churches and agencies. CICARWS has in the past emphasized its commitment to a multilateral approach. Would it now in fact be better for the Commission to bow out of the process of the transfer of resources and rather concentrate on stimulating and inspiring the churches in their search for fellowship? A major consultation has taken place to focus further thought on these issues which will need to be brought for policy decision at the Assembly.

Since Uppsala, the *Ecumenical Church Loan Fund* (ECLOF) has expanded the number of national revolving loan funds to 25 in five continents, its capital to $2.4 million and total loans to 1,700. This makes possible loans at low interest (3%-5% per year) to church endorsed projects which cannot get or afford credit from other sources. The fund is growing faster, and loans are now larger, but the 100% repayment record has been maintained largely through an emphasis on thorough planning and follow-up. NCC's which screen projects are increasingly encouraging a loan element, but progress here is slow. ECLOF now supports development projects, such as irrigation in Burma, workers' cooperatives in Malaysia (rubber) and Trinidad (footwear) as well as many office blocks or agricultural businesses in India and elsewhere to provide continuing support for local church work.

An essential but often difficult and sensitive role has been played by the different area secretaries in encouraging the churches in their region to play a full part in the discussions on the present pattern of Inter-Church Aid and its future. For the first time in the history of the Commission all the area desks are on a strictly geographical basis, and each is served by someone from the region. In their regular travelling and consultations, the area secretaries are increasingly representing the whole of WCC relationships to the churches. One of their concerns in the reshaping of the relationships between the churches has been to find better ways of presenting the WCC to the churches and the churches to the WCC. This, together with changes in the project system, would mean a certain freedom from narrow bureaucratic and technical responsibilities to individual projects and an opening up towards a more wide-ranging, stimulating and pastoral relationship with the churches.

(2) *Disaster Response and Rehabilitation Programmes. Bangladesh, Nigeria, Sudan, the Sahel.* There has been a dramatic growth in both the number and the size of emergency appeals issued by the Commission in support of relief and rehabilitation work in time of disaster. The number of appeals has grown each year from an average of 12 at the time of the Uppsala Assembly to an average of 20 in the years 1972/74, while the amount received in any one year has varied from $5.8 million in 1973 to $10 million in 1972. Throughout the period under review, the Commission has been kept fully stretched by a terrible sequence of tragedies beginning with the conflict in Nigeria, the earthquake in Peru, the floods in the then East Pakistan followed by war and the birth pangs of Bangladesh, the challenges of peace in the Sudan, a dramatic earthquake in Nicaragua, the serious drought that has swept across Africa from the Sahel‡ and, of course, war ravaged Indochina.

These major disasters, coupled with scores of smaller but nonetheless serious problems, have been a heavy burden on people and churches in many parts of the world. While the causes and the effects of these tragedies have been horrific, one encouragement has been the dedicated and outstanding work carried out by the local churches, whose members have given themselves without stinting in their service to their fellow citizens. Local Christians in many places have taken the initiative and responsibility for directing massive church programmes. Their contribution has reflected the desire of the Commission to support local responsibility for rehabilitation efforts and has played an important part in building up the confidence of both "poor" and "rich" churches.

An essential emphasis in all of this has been in making sure that church involvement at the time of emergency keeps long-term development in mind. In Bangladesh, for example, the churches were not just content to find food and clothing. In consultation with the government and local leaders, the churches became involved in assisting basic recovery and development by helping to build up the transportation system in a country that had lost many inland cargo ships, by providing "miracle rice" seeds, a pilot project for "green revolution" agriculture, by restoring two basic industries, hand-loom weaving and fishery, and by giving women the chance to take their place in society. The local churches have now taken complete responsibility for the programme and have included Muslim and Hindu participation in their committee to better represent the whole society. A similar effort has been made in other emergency situations, especially in the Sahel. With practically no churches in this area, there was little knowledge within the ecumenical movement of its special situation.

New patterns of work and collaboration with a UN agency were built up which overcame the initial ignorance and made a meaningful WCC contribution to long-term development possible. Another new emphasis has been the encouragement given to development education efforts in European countries as a means of support for the programmes in the Sahel. This is an experiment which it is hoped can be applied in other situations as a means of making the long-term nature of many of the problems clear to those who contribute to the appeals.

A full-time emergency officer was appointed in 1971. Much of his time has been spent in travelling to different emergency situations as well as acting as a communications centre linking churches and agencies throughout the world. Area task forces have assisted and advised on particular problems. Emergencies have also been the means by which many traditionally receiving churches have become giving churches as they have sought to express their solidarity with disaster victims in other parts of the world. A great deal of study and attention, together with agencies such as the Red Cross, the UN Disaster Office and Roman Catholic agencies, has been given to identify disaster-prone areas, build up stocks of relief supplies and generally be better prepared for emergencies.

Indochina. Indochina does not fall within the duties of the emergencies and rehabilitation desk. However, the Commission is responsible within the World Council for the WCC instrument to provide aid and assistance to the whole war-affected area of North and South Vietnam, Laos and Cambodia. The Board of the Fund for Reconstruction and Reconciliation was established by the Central Committee in 1972 to express the totality of WCC concerns for this area, which had previously been met by CCIA statements in support of peace initiatives and the regular assistance to relief and assistance programmes in Vietnam carried out by the Asian and American churches and by local organizations. When the cease-fire agreement was signed, the WCC decided that it would like to give regular and substantial assistance to the whole region and give support to what was being done by local groups and governments to rebuild and develop their countries. Unfortunately, the peace until lately has been less than overwhelming. Nevertheless an initial appeal for $5 million was fairly successful, and some programmes have been under way, such as a $2 million hospital rebuilding scheme in North Vietnam and a few isolated medical and agricultural programmes in South Vietnam. Here again the emphasis has been on listening to and supporting the plans and expectations of local people. The Board of the Fund has five people from Indochina, five from the rest of Asia and five from the rest of the world; it also represents the involvements and insights of CICARWS, CCPD and CCIA.

(3) *Refugees*. Change has also been a feature of the refugee work of the Commission. Unfortunately it is not possible to report a diminishing in the

number of refugees in our world. In fact, the reverse is the case. But there has been a new emphasis in the focus of the work. For the first twenty years of the Council's life, major attention was put on the refugee situation in Europe. The aftermath of the Second World War and then the exodus from Poland, the German Democratic Republic, Hungary and Czechoslovakia meant basically a solidly European reception and resettlement operation with offices throughout the continent as well as in the Middle East. But in the period under review, greater concentration has been given to the new refugee problems in *Africa*, where despite the ending of the Sudanese conflict there are still some 900,000 refugees from *apart-heid*, colonialism and various inter-African conflicts; in *Latin America*, where political oppression is creating many refugee problems such as the mass exodus from Chile following the military coup in 1973; in the *Middle East*, where the question of the Palestinians continues to burn away at the centre of a political tinderbox; in *Asia*, where wars and other conflicts have reaped their own particular harvest of refugees; and upon the new kinds of refugees in Europe and North America who have refused to fight in their countries' wars. Europe has also begun to receive refugees from other continents, particularly Latin Americans and the East African Asians forced to leave Uganda.

All of that has meant a new challenge to the staff of the refugee service and a demand to re-think traditional policies. A continuous review of the structure and priorities of the refugee service has taken place. European offices have been reduced to a skeleton staff, and increasing efforts are being made to help the local churches to take greater responsibility. Refugee secretaries for Africa and Asia have kept in touch with the situation in those continents and have helped the local churches in their service to refugees. But the resettlement work has been based in Geneva.

In 1969, as the result of a CICARWS-sponsored consultation, the churches of the *Middle East*, Protestant and Orthodox, decided to take greater responsibility for the on-going work with Palestinian refugees. The Near East Ecumenical Committee for Palestinian Refugees was established, and it took charge of determining the priorities of the different area programmes. Their concern has been to alert the churches of the world to the basic injustice done to the Palestinians while at the same time trying to give the means to the refugees to become self-sufficient through vocational training plans and elementary development work. The annual budget of approximately $1 million has been difficult to raise, as many people have become weary of supporting a dispossessed people for 25 years. The churches in the Middle East and the Commission itself have continually re-emphasized their commitment to the programme and at the same time have made fresh efforts to try to secure peace so that a long-term and just solution to the problem could be found.

What has happened in the Middle East is a reflection of the decentralization that has begun in the refugee work. The Refugee Service staff is there to help, advise and assist in the raising of funds, but the fundamental policy decisions and programme responsibility in the major programme areas are increasingly taken by the local churches. *African refugees* have always been the concern of the African churches, and in each country touched by the refugee problem the local churches have their own refugee officer who relates to the refugee office of the All Africa Conference of Churches. The resettlement schemes, the scholarships and other assistance to refugees, are aimed at trying to make the refugees self-supporting, and there has been collaboration with African governments in finding jobs for highly skilled refugees. Training programmes have been held by the African churches, and the Africa Refugee Secretary of the Refugee Service, himself a former AACC refugee worker, has acted as a consultant and support agent to the local programmes while trying to raise approximately $1 million each year from the churches around the world.

The most recent large-scale refugee situation involving church response was the product of the military coup in *Chile*. Within hours of the coup in September 1973, it was clear that many foreigners who had originally taken refuge in Chile were going to be made homeless again by a military government determined to move against "leftists". The Chilean churches immediately began to organize themselves to help the foreigners leave Chile. Under the protection of the United Nations and with help from churches around the world, a difficult and sensitive refugee operation began to move more than 5,000 refugees out of Chile and away to new countries of asylum in Europe and other parts of Latin America. The situation in Chile provided yet another example of the serious problem in that continent where human rights concerns and political oppression have combined to create many thousands of refugees who are finding it difficult to remain with the continent as country after country is taken over by the military. More than $1 million have been sent to churches in Chile and other parts of Latin America as they sought to assist the refugees from Chile.

As the pattern of refugee work has changed, there has been an increasing controversy over programmes that were formerly accepted as 'humanitarian''. This has been particularly strong with regard to the question of support for American draft-age immigrants in Canada and Sweden who resisted service in the American armed forces because of their opposition to the war in Vietnam and more recently over a programme of support to uprooted people from Portugal who have also decided not to fight in their country's colonial wars in Africa. In both cases, the Commission's support has been for the humanitarian programmes of the churches in the different places where these people, who do not meet the agreed international definition of "refugee", are. The Council's decision has been based on a consideration that they are people of conscience, suffering because of the stand that they have taken, and in this way are just like any other kind of refugee. The commitment is primarily humanitarian though it is obviously linked to the fact that the Council has repeatedly called for peace and self-determination in Vietnam and has defended the rights of the people of Angola, Mozambique and Guinea-Bissau to independence. Part of the problem no doubt relates to the shock that many people feel when confronted by events that challenge them directly. It is always easier to feel sympathy for the refugee fleeing from another political system, much more difficult to take seriously the claims of someone who rejects your own society and its policies. It is by facing these kinds of questions openly and honestly that the churches and the Commission grow in maturity and in the fellowship which the Council represents.

(4) *Direct Services*. The fourth and last cluster of the Commission's work has to do with direct services to people and churches. There has been much discussion during this period about the proper location of the *Health, Literature and Casa Locarno*‡ programmes. These programmes are largely concentrated in Europe, which gives them an anomalous position as part of the programme of a world-wide body. They are now supported through an asking on the Project List rather than through the central budget of the Commission. In addition, a survey of the Health Programme is to be carried out over the next two years which will look again at the need for a programme which was set up in response to needs which are very different from those of today. There has been the beginning of a discussion with the Conference of European Churches about the possibility that it might take over administrative responsibility for at least part of this programme, but these discussions are not yet concluded. The importance of this kind of programme for the churches is not questioned; the questions being raised concern its proper location within the fellowship of the churches.

One change that came about as a result of the new structure has been to relocate the *Scholarships Office* within the Programme Unit on Education and Renewal. A special review of the Scholarships programme in 1969 recommended that much greater attention be given to widening the fields of study undertaken by scholarship students, particularly in fields related to development. The newly-created Office of Education was involved in taking this discussion further through an intensive examination of the objects and the achievements of the Scholarships programme. It seemed logical and natural, therefore, that while the programme would continue to be funded from the Service Programme of CICARWS and the Project List, it was important to have day-to-day contact with educationalists inside the third of the new WCC Programme Units. The Scholarships programme continues to provide assistance to some 230 students each year. It is worth underlining that this programme, while representing only a very small part of the total work of scholarships of the churches, has always had a considerable problem in providing an adequate number of scholarships in comparison to the demands made on the programme.

Another programme which involves help to individuals is the *Social Service* Portfolio. Originally known as the Diakonia‡ Desk, the change in name came at the end of a period of intensive study into the task and objectives of this particular concern. The new name is meant to broaden the responsibilities of the Desk and emphasizes the part all Christians have to play in the work of social service. The secretary keeps in touch with developments relating to the social services, and the work of churches and Christians in this field. A preliminary point of concentration has been on working with churches in different parts of Africa on how they understand the task of the Church in relation to diakonal and social service work and so enlarge the ecumenical understanding of the issues involved. Close contact is kept with other sub-units of the WCC concerned in this work of caring for people, including the Family Ministries Desk in the Programme Unit on Education and Renewal and the Faith and Order Secretariat of the Programme Unit on Faith and Witness.

As part of a general programme review, the *Personnel Desk's* responsibilities for *Teams* in the Mediterranean were reduced and re-aligned in 1973. The two teams in Greece were discontinued, while in Italy and Cyprus they continue to function under oversight of national committees. The resources required are being raised in an integrated fashion through the project system on the strength of national and regional screening. *Recruiting* continues in response to specific personnel requests from churches and their institutions as well as for skilled workers to serve in emergency and development programmes. Some 100 personnel requests are being processed a year. Slightly more than half are being filled through a network of national correspondents and recruitment agencies. In the last year, special efforts were made to secure personnel for the Sudan and Niger—with mixed results.

Increasingly, the movement of people and the relationships between "sending" and "receiving" churches are set within the context of the *Ecumenical Sharing of Personnel*, a programme jointly sponsored and supported by CICARWS and the Commission on World Mission and Evangelism (compare Chapter Two, pages 88-89). Issuing from the Uppsala Assembly, defined by several meetings of the ESP committee, debated at the Salvation Today conference in Bangkok, Ecumenical Sharing of Personnel attempts to break away from traditional West-East, denominational and bilateral patterns of personnel movement. National and regional initiatives in the Third World; movement of people in and among all continents, including some to the First World for "people in mission everywhere"; multiple ecumenical patterns of exchange and greater flexibility between persons and money are some of the elements in the design and emerging reality of ESP. They challenge "mission" and "service" agencies alike and present an agenda item for the Nairobi Assembly.

Strictly speaking, the secretary for *Material Aid* does not fit within the direct service concern, as his help tends to be given mainly to on-going projects or emergency situations. Each year the value of the shipments made by church agencies related to CICARWS amounts to approximately $35 million. About 10% of that total is handled, initiated or coordinated by the Material Aid Secretary. The hybrid nature of his work makes it difficult to give him any one responsibility. Emergencies call for the fast movement of relief materials, medicines and so on. The Material Aid Secretary is available to coordinate this flow of resources on behalf of the churches and build up a data bank of knowledge about where the best materials can be obtained quickly and cheaply. Projects too often require pieces of equipment or supplies from different places Here again the Secretary's task is to identify the best piece of equipment for doing the job and make sure it reaches the people who need it efficiently and safely. Much more emphasis is being put on local purchases which are both cheaper and also more beneficial to local industries.

A major concern of the Material Aid Desk over the last four years has been finding and shipping annually some $340,000 worth of educational, medical and agricultural supplies to the liberation movements in Southern Africa. The liberation movements have made specific requests to the WCC for various kinds of supplies such as books, pens, medicines, seeds and so on for use in their humanitarian and development programmes in the liberated areas. The Material Aid Secretary has coordinated this programme and arranged for regular shipments to Africa.

The *Migration Secretariat* was the first desk to be made responsible to the entire Programme Unit on Justice and Service. The Secretary has kept in close touch with different church groups around the world as he emphasized the churches' concern for this important modern phenomenon which involves elements of development, racism, service and political awareness on the part of the churches. The Secretariat keeps in close contact with the Churches' Committee on Migrant Workers, the body of a number of European churches. It has concentrated its attention on issues in Latin America, Africa and Asia. Important new work is going on in each of the continents as the churches seek to aid people who have migrated for economic and political reasons. The Secretariat has also begun a major investigation into how the churches can stop the flow of White migration from Europe to Southern Africa, which is one of the principal supporters of *apartheid*. *Migration Today* is published once a year in three languages.

The Future

Much depends on the Nairobi Assembly of the World Council of Churches. The ecumenical movement as a whole, and each of the programme elements of the WCC, is at a crossroad. The choices confronting the churches have far-reaching consequences. If commitment to the ecumenical movement remains serious, the churches must rigorously examine the need for separate programmes which duplicate and sometimes even frustrate ecumenical action. If the movement is to have relevance to the issues confronting people throughout the world, it must also have adequate support and reflect within its own structures and programmes the concerns it is trying to promote.

The specific issues involving Inter-Church Aid have been raised throughout the previous pages. To summarize them, they are:

● the future of the project system understood in the sense of how the churches manifest their fellowship and solidarity and share their resources—financial, spiritual and human—with one another;

● and, second, the appropriate style for emergency response which safeguards the concern for the suffering as well as the integrity of the local churches in such a way that immediate needs and long-term plans can be met. Under these issues are questions such as:

● how can the "rich" churches and their counterparts in the poor countries avoid being corrupted by their money and the power that this brings?

● how can the "poor" churches be enabled to live out creatively the mission of the Church as they understand it?

All of these concerns feed in ultimately to *the whole question of the Programme Unit on Justice and Service*. Up to now, the separate sub-units have continued to retain their individual identities to a substantial degree. This has obviously been, and will continue to be, important, but *to what degree should they lose a part at least of their identities in the Unit structure? What would this mean for CICARWS?* More discussions will continue on this question before the Assembly. It will certainly be on the Agenda of the Assembly itself.

The future is open. Only one thing is absolutely clear. The churches cannot escape from their obligation to render service and to be with the oppressed in their struggle for justice. In that sense there must always be something like a CICARWS within a Programme Unit on Justice and Service. Therefore the preparation for the Assembly, the discussion which takes place there and the decisions and commitments which flow from it will be crucial to any meaningful continuation in a tradition that is as old as the Gospel and as modern as those things which have been accomplished through the Commission on Inter-Church Aid, Refugee and World Service of the World Council of Churches.

4
education and renewal

The Background

The Programme Unit on Education and Renewal is a special creature, very different from the other Units of the World Council of Churches. This difference is partly due to the nature of its work, but is also the result of its history, which has been one of wide-spread change, trial and error, yet always openness to new ideas and insights.

Its predecessor, known as the Division of Ecumenical Action (DEA), was born at Evanston in 1954, when the Second Assembly said: "We are confident that the Central Committee will view the scheme as somewhat *provisional and experimental*, and as subject to revision in the light of its workings". The Third Assembly at New Delhi in 1961 continued the work of the somewhat diverse and distinctive elements of the Division, namely the

---

THE RECORD

The following list is only a partial record of the many activities of the Programme Unit on Education and Renewal which took place during the years 1968/74. But it gives a glimpse of the wide variety of work undertaken.

1968
1. *Report of Joint Study Commission on Education (WCC/WCCE)* surveys world education, recommends greater church involvement in general and church education.
2. EYS in concert with the Latin American Union of Ecumenical Youth (ULAJE) co-sponsored a *year-long development project in Guropi, Brazil*, with 14 trained and skilled volunteers working in the rural sector, all of whom, except one, came from the Southern hemisphere. (Youth) See RISK *"Good Will or Evil Goods"*

Laity Department; the Department of Cooperation between Men and Women in Church, Family and Society; the Youth Department; and the Ecumenical Institute. At Uppsala in 1968 the Fourth Assembly added the Office of Education and at the same time provided for the integration of the committees of these Departments into one Divisional Committee. Finally, following the process of restructuring, the Central Committee at Addis Ababa in 1971 added the Department of Communication, the Scholarship Office and the Secretariat on Relations with National Councils, and dropped the *Institut de Bossey*, to form what was then called the Programme Unit on Education and Communication. The metamorphosis was almost complete.

And the "provisional and experimental" scheme had taken on a provocative new form. Here was a staff team directed to work together in stirring up the people of God "for ecumenical understanding, active engagement in renewing the life of the churches, and participation in God's work in a changing world". It was a team relating directly to youth, men and women, the laity, in every part of the churches' life and beyond the ecclesiastical boundaries.

A decisive element in the process of change was the World Council of Christian Education (WCCE), which traced its ecumenical history even further back in time than the Faith and Order and Life and Work Movements.

―――――――――――――― THE RECORD ――――――――――――――

1969
3. *Consultation on Man-Woman Dialogue, Geneva*. Exploration of nature and causes of discrimination against women in contemporary society; of identity of man and woman; the sharp division of roles in technological society; the prejudices created and perpetuated. (Cooperation Men/Women)
4. *Consultation on "Ministry in Meeting" in Heerlen, Holland* with students of theology held at a Roman Catholic seminary. Participants were involved in simple group encounters and investigations in their way to Heerlen. This led to further contacts with radical student groups in Europe. (Youth)
5. *Seventh Orthodox/Protestant Study Encounter for Younger Theologians*. Theme "Man's Image of Man" and as an exercise in using literary models for study. (Youth)
6. *Consultation on Relations between WSCF and WCC on Middle East* Youth and Student Office. This led to relationships helpful in the uniting of this work with the later established Near East Council of Churches. (Youth)

It began with Sunday school conventions in the nineteenth century and was organized formally at Rome in 1907 as the World Sunday School Association. Successive Assemblies, held every four years, met in all parts of the world: Toronto, Tokyo, Belfast, Nairobi and Lima. During the 1960's the WCCE moved its headquarters to Geneva and increasingly shared in many activities with the World Council of Churches, chiefly in youth work and education. Joint appointments of youth staff were made, and the WCCC shared in sponsoring major youth meetings in collarboration with the WCC, the World Student Christian Federation (WSCF), the World Alliance of Young Men's Christian Association (YMCA) and the World Young Women's Christian Association (YWCA), In 1964 a WCC/WCCE Joint Study Commission on Education was established which presented its report to the Uppsala Assembly in 1968 The Office of Education was established on the basis of that report, as well as the accompanying survey of church engagement in general and religious educaiton in many parts of the world. The basic task of this effort was to bring the churches' attention to education in the widest sense. In 1968 a joint negotiating committee went to work and, in 1971, at its Assembly in Lima, Peru, the WCCE voted to integrate with the WCC. Thus, a fine tradition and lengthy experience of work with children, youth and adults in education was added to the Division's already wide constituency, as the new Unit on Education and Communication took shape.

THE RECORD

7. *World Consultation on Leisure-Tourism, Tutzing, Federal Republic of Germany*. (Laity) See report on *Leisure-Tourism, Threat and Promise*.

8. *World Scholarship Consultation, Canterbury*. Moves toward new guidelines for WCC Scholarship Programme. (Scholarships, then in CICARWS)

9. *European Conference on Laymen Abroad, Holland*. Part of follow-up to 1967 world consultation. (Laity)

1970

10. *World Youth Meeting in Piriapolis, Uruguay, on "Development - A Search for a New World"*, with participation of Roman Catholic Youth movements. The necessity of self-determination and social involvement of the churches were issues of priority. (Youth) See *Piriapolis Report*.

11. Three successive *Consultations on Rural, Industrial and Urban Development in Papua, New Guinea*. Recommendations from these meetings have since found their way into government legislation and

Structural Problems and a Changing Constituency

During the period which followed, an effort was made by the considera-
ly enlarged and further diversified staff to try to go beyond a mere
malgam of the former departments or a simple confederation of interests.
This effort, among other things, tried to mark out the constituency with
which the Unit ought to try to work. Clearly it was a wide one—made
wider by the addition of more church-related organizations as well as the
institutions of the mass media with which the former Department of
Communications had to keep up contacts. To this, also, was added the full
mandate of contacts with National Councils and Christian Councils as well
as Regional Councils of Churches. The total effect, especially considering
the newly added relations for which the enlarged Office of Education was
responsible, was complex and challenging.

And yet the new Unit was plunged into a difficult time. It was a time for
participation, when all were encouraged to share their views as to how this
enormously increased Unit should work. It was a time when the difference
had to be faced between the programme-oriented former departments of the
WEA and the media-conscious, sophisticated interests of the Department of
Communication.

Clearly the new frictions which emerged needed some adjustment in the

---

THE RECORD

have led to a significant consultation on education. (Youth,
SODEPAX and Melanesian Council of Churches). See *SODEPANG
Report*

2. *Consultation on the Ordination of Women*, Cartigny, Switzerland.
An urgent review of recruitment practices within the structures of the
WCC was asked, as well as scrutiny of the Member Churches for
barriers against women in theological education. (Women's Desk)

3. *Consultation on "The World Educational Crisis and the Church's
Contribution"*, Bergen, Netherlands. Analyzed churches' role in
education. (Education) See Report "Seeing Education Whole" and
RISK *"School or Scandal"*.

4. *World Consultation on Family Life Education*, Geneva. Explores
broader scope of family ministries. (Family Ministries)

5. *Second Course for Leaders of Lay Training*, Europe. Course for
directors of lay centres from Africa, Asia and Latin America. (Laity)

6. *Christian Family Life Seminars* held in the Pacific, Asia and Africa.
(Family Ministries)

structure of the Unit, and so, in 1973, the Department of Communication was removed and related to the General Secretariat, and the *Programme Unit on Education and Renewal* emerged. In its current form the Programme Unit, with its greatly reduced staff, includes these elements: the *Sub-Unit on Education*, involving General and Christian Education, Family Ministries, Laity and Adult Education, and Scholarships; the *Sub-Unit on Renewal*, to which are linked the Women's Desk, Coordination of Youth Work and, in particular, Ecumenical Youth Service (EYS) and World Youth Projects (WYP), and the magazine RISK.

Aim and Functions

Arising out of this process of change came a refined official Aim and a new listing of Functions. At the 1973 meeting of the Central Committee the following Aim and Functions were approved:

Aim. To assist churches, Councils of Churches and renewal movements through processes of education and communication to enable persons, communities and institutions to participate as fully as possible in the changes that faith in God in Christ calls for in them, in the renewal of the churches, and in the transformation of society.

Functions.

1. To develop ways by which persons, groups and movements engaged

---

THE RECORD

1971

17. *Eighth Protestant/Orthodox/Roman Catholic Theological Encounter*, Crete. Theme "Ways of Life, Ways of Death" was used for an issue of RISK, of the same title. (Youth)

18. *Pan-African Seminar on "Youth and Voluntary Service in Africa 66"*, Kitwe, Zambia. Youth movements in Africa have been following its recommendations and have been exchanging volunteers across the continent for short-term experiences. (Youth)

19. *Seminar on Nutrition*, Bothas Hall, South Africa, with 40 participants from 12 women's organizations. Seminar looked at three basic causes for malnutrition: poverty, ignorance and disease. Concrete recommendations were made for the women's organizations, welfare agencies, churches and governments. (Women's Desk)

20. *North America Educational Consultation*, Greenwich, Connecticut. For US and Canadian church educators. (Education) See Report, *The Education Crisis and the Church*.

in renewal may be mutually involved and supported for the benefit of the whole people of God.

2. To study practices and theories of education, communication and processes of social change in the light of Christian experience, theological thinking and other relevant disciplines.

3. To develop programmes for, and stimulate informal processes of, Christian nurture of children, youth and adults, relevant to life in contemporary society.

4. To develop working relationships, mutual aid and interchange of information among the churches, their councils, agencies and movements, which deepen their involvement in the determination, implementation and appraisal of ecumenical strategy.

5. To improve the processes of communication by which the relationships with and among the constituencies of churches and movements in their diverse life and experience can contribute to one another, to the ecumenical movement and to the life of the World Council of Churches.

An Open Style

Throughout all of these changes and realignments, the basic orientation of the Unit has been towards people. And it seemed more and more, as

---

THE RECORD

21. *Latin American Educational Consultation*, Lima. For church and other educators. (Education). See "Education, Liberation and the Churches". (*Study Encounter* No. 38)

22. *WCCE World Assembly*, Lima, Peru. Final Assembly of World Council of Christian Education on theme "New Perspectives for Christian Education": voted to integrate with WCC (WCCE, Education). See "Encuentro: New Perspectives for Christian Education", (double issue of WCCE *World Christian Education Magazine*), "Encuentros: A New Ecumenical Learning Experience". (*Study Encounter No. 24*)

23. *Women's Leadership Training Seminars* in Africa during 1971 and 1972 in Lomé, Togo; Monrovia, Liberia; and Kampala, Uganda. Over 100 women from 23 countries took part. (Women's Desk and AACC)

24. *Conference on "The Image of Women in the Mass Media"*, Vienna, Austria. About 100 Protestant, Roman Catholic and Orthodox women, mainly from Europe, attended this meeting. (Women's Ecumenical Liaison Group, Women's Desk, Renewal)

developments occurred, that a particular kind of people was meant. Words such as "the dispossessed", "the powerless", "the silent", "the unrepresented" were used to describe the particular constituency. Jargon, such as "multipliers", "conscientization", "mini-consultation", "cuadros", "marginal church" became familiar in the Unit's work and documents. Programmes were designed which tried to build on the aspirations of people who were mostly cut off from the more familiar patterns of ecumenical engagements. An important tool in this work was shared with the Unit by Paulo Freire as it became more and more involved in finding ways to awaken the consciousness of people to situations in which their own silence and submissiveness contributed to their continued bondage. And "liberation" became a more and more significant theme of the work, whether it was with women, renewal movements, children, schools, lay people, church administrators or those seeking to stimulate awareness about development. But, throughout all these modest efforts, people remained the basic factor.

The style of work in the Unit necessarily remained provisional for three reasons. First, experiments were being made with new methods of work. At Uppsala the Division of Ecumenical Action was asked to "explore new means of creating ecumenical involvement in addition to consultations and conferences". One attempt do do this was to change the consultation

---

THE RECORD

1972

25. *Consultation with Portuguese military deserters* on developing aid programme. This led to a recommendation agreed to by Central Committee, August, 1973. (Renewal and Refugee Desk, CICARWS)

26. *Consultation on Renewal Movements*, Eyelshoven, Holland. Exploration of new contacts. (Renewal)

27. *Consultation on "Women's Role in Peace Education"*, Cyprus. Topics included: neo-colonialism, cultural imperialism, racism, trade, violence. (Women's Desk)

28. *World Consultation on Lay Centres*, Crete. (Laity in cooperation with regional associates) See RISK, "The New Fishermen".

29. *First African sub-regional consultation on "The Role of the Church in the Future of African Education"*, Sierra Leone. (Education and All Africa Conference of Churches, AACC)

technique to suit unlearned but deeply educated people, sometimes illiterate but very articulate. The small meeting of persons sharing their own experiences but not bound to a stereotyped agenda was developed and elaborated. The principal intention was to find ways and means of letting people tell their own stories and, together, to discover how to move on from the understandings such experiences reveal. Naturally, the aim was to conduct these meetings in an international and ecumenical environment. Another attempt to experiment was in the use of the encounter method in setting up a meeting, in which people shared together a fresh and intensive common experience before meeting to reflect on it. A small experiment of this sort in Holland in 1969 was followed by a wider use of this method in Papua New Guinea and, later, a massive use of "encuentros"‡ for the WCCE World Assembly at Lima, in 1971, culminating in the experience of the World Assembly on the Family, *Familia '74*, and the application of this technique in preparation for the Nairobi Assembly.

Secondly, the Unit remained provisional in view of the fact that it had the courage to pursue work in one or another direction, either independently or in collaboration with other colleagues in the WCC or in Regional and National Councils of Churches, often to find, at an appropriate moment, that it had gone far enough, and that the time had come for a programme more attuned to conventional methods of ecumenical en-

---

THE RECORD

30. *A series of South Pacific Encounters and plenary conferences* in Port Vila, New Hebrides, on Churches' involvement in Development in the South Pacific. Follow-up in PCC Spades Secretariat. (Renewal) See SPADES Report.

1973

31. *Theological Symposium on "Black Theology and Latin American Theology of Liberation"* for 65 European theologians, students of theology and religious media representatives, a symposium that has found a wide-ranging audience and interest. (Youth) See RISK, "Incommunication", also translated into French, Spanish and Italian.

32. *Renewal Consultation*, Hothorpe Hall, U.K. A meeting with European and North American persons involved in Renewal and Charismatic movements. (Renewal)

deavour to take over. One example of such a provisional initiative is the Unit's struggle to deal with the problem of languages in cross-cultural exchange. It was soon recognized as being more than a simple question of interpretation and translation; the development of the Language Policy Task Force (described later on in this chapter) was the result.

Thirdly, the provisional character of the Unit's work is worth celebrating precisely because it relates to people—and people's needs and desires change. To be tied to a particular line of continuing and developing programme in one direction or another may simply mean that one is not adaptable or responsive to newly emerging needs. Since 1968 how many fresh cries for liberation have sprung up, echoing from voice to voice; and how many fresh impulses of the Holy Spirit have shown his abundant grace for many, moving in marvellous ways!

Who would have foreseen, in 1968, that the time was near for a Symposium on "Black Theology and Latin American Theology for Liberation"? Who would have foreseen the need for a world consultation on questions related to women's liberation in quite such sharp focus as the Berlin meeting in 1974 on "Sexism in the 1970's"? Who would have predicted that within five years of Uppsala a totally new, strange word with complicated meaning would have become a focus for attempts to reconstruct and revolutionize education all over the world, and that a staff

---

THE RECORD

33. *Ninth Orthodox/Protestant/Roman Catholic Theological Encounter* on "Man in Community". (Renewal)

34. *First meeting of World Collaboration Committee for Christian Lay Centres, Academies and Movements for Social Concern*, India, for coordinated programme planning. (Laity)

35. *World Consultation on Family Life Education*, Malta. Proposed priorities of national case studies on changing family patterns, emphasis on educational aspects of· family planning, training family counsellors. (Family Ministries)

36. *International Conference of Education*, sponsored by International Bureau of Education (UNESCO), Geneva. Theme "Education, training and employment". Office of Education, YMCA, YWCA, WSCF cooperated in preparing a reference paper: *Ongoing Social Education*.

member of the WCC would be identified with the term "conscientization"?‡ Who would have foreseen the puzzlement and excitement about life styles and the family which emerged at the previously mentioned assembly on the family? Who would have prepared for the newly spreading charismatic‡ movement, touching greater and greater numbers in many of the historic churches? Who would have foretold of the growing disenchantment with traditional systems of education to such an extent that some governments look to innovation to help free the school system of so much that is now regarded as unsatisfactory? Who would have anticipated the amazing eruption of the Jesus Movement after the turbulent period of the late 1960's, with the parallel emergence of so many independent, ecumenical and eccentric communities of the young? (One must recognize, however, that while a dramatic change may lately be discerned among the youth of the West, as witness a renewed spiritual searching on their part, young people of the Third World continue to grow conscious of their role in society, faced with problems of development, class structures and neo-colonialism.)

No matter how any of the above questions was posed during the turmoil of the past seven years, the provisional character of the Unit allowed for some kind of response to be made; such a style of preparedness has had its satisfactions in spite of seeming, at times, to present a very inconclusive case when asked about specific programmes.

THE RECORD

37. *European Conference on "The Future Contribution of the Sunday School and Kindergottesdienst to Church Education in Europe",* Glion, Switzerland. (Education, Lutheran World Federation) See report *"Learning Community"*: book by John Sutcliffe published by National Christian Education Council, Great Britain, 1974.

38. *World Seminar on "Education and Theology in the Context of the Struggle for Liberation",* Bossey, Switzerland. Studies educational and theological implications of liberation activities. (Education)

39. *The Participation in Change Programme* reported on many small consultations and contacts with working groups for change, in four *Study Encounter* articles. "Participation in Change Programme" (SE No. 5); "Salvation and the Struggle of the Poor" (SE No. 39); "Let My People Go" (SE No. 40); "Straws in the Wind of the Spirit" (SE No. 43).

The slogan "people and provisionality" may perhaps be at one and the same time too arrogant and too modest for the Programme Unit on Education and Renewal during the years 1968-1975. But it is a phrase which perhaps best explains what has been done, and how and why.

MAJOR INITIATIVES

Education

Educational Strategies

In 1969 the new Office of Education began immediately to implement one of the strong recommendations of the Joint Study Commission by exploring ways to encourage among churches and nations a wide-spread re-appraisal of educational strategies. A first world consultation on "The World Educational Crisis and the Churches' Contribution" (see "The Record", No. 13) was convened at Bergen, Holland, in 1970.

Representatives from a dozen countries in all continents urged the WCC

THE RECORD

1974

40. *Bossey Course on "Non-Violence and New Community"* Follow-up on study of Violence and Non-Violence. (Renewal)

41. *Conference for Overseas Students studying in Europe* on "Preparing for Service in their Home Countries", Zeist, Holland. Students from Africa, Asia and Latin America discussed the problems related to their studies in Europe, as well as the implications of brain-washing and brain-drain, etc. (Youth, Scholarships)

42. *World-wide Ecumenical Consultation on "Sexism in the 1970's"*, West Berlin. 150 women from 54 countries participated. The consultation topics were: "world-wide manifestations of sexism in society today", "what liberation from sexism could mean for the whole human family".The consultation sought to discover ways and means of overcoming sexism. (Women's Desk)

43. *All African Consultation on "The Role of the Church in the Future of African Education"*, Limuru, Kenya. Final review consultation

---

to provide help to churches caught in changing situations with regard to their educational activity. In many countries of Africa and Asia government systems of education were taking over church schools, thus forcing the churches to re-think their roles in relation to public education and to ask what new strategies they should adopt as the old functions disappeared. In many countries rising secularism and pluralism cast the teaching of religion in schools, and indeed the total process of socialization‡ and nurture within the particular Christian community of the Church, into new and threatening uncertainties about how to build up the people of God. In other places acute social, political and economic problems forced Christian educators to re-appraise their work in the broader context of social justice, and to enquire how the churches could make a contribution to education for the liberation of the oppressed.

The effect of the Bergen Consultation and its report, *Seeing Education Whole*, was felt during the next four years as participants sought to implement its findings in many countries and churches, and because the Office of Education worked with local committees to arrange regional consultations in North America, Latin America and in Africa, as well as national meetings in many countries and on all continents. This has resulted in wide-spread discussion and action regarding changing strategies

---

THE RECORD

on series of consultations on the theme. (Education and AACC) See report by AACC.

44. *Familia '74, World Congress on the Family*, Tanzania, with 260 persons exploring the meaning of family today in setting of the Ujamaa‡ society. (Family, Renewal Ministries and International Confederation of Christian Family Movements)

45. *All-European Consultation on "Pastoral Care for Those Confronted with Abortion"*, Monbachtal, Federal Republic of Germany. (Family Ministries and Portfolio on Social Services, CICARWS)

46. *World Consultation on "New Trends in Laity Formation"*, Assisi, Italy. (Laity and Roman Catholic Council on the Laity)

47. *Latin American Consultation on "Education for Liberation and Community"*, Colombia, in preparation for the Fifth Assembly. (Education and CELADEC)

and programmes of education in many churches and countries. In Africa, for example, a series of five regional consultations was sponsored jointly with the AACC, culminating in February 1974 with an All Africa Conference in Limuru (see "The Record", no. 43) which sent a report on "The Role of the Church in the Future of African Education" to the AACC Assembly in Lusaka.

In Europe, in addition to many varied staff involvements with education groups, there was in 1973 a more specialized effort sponsored jointly by the Department of Studies of the Lutheran World Federation and the Office of Education, concentrating this time on "The Sunday School Contribution to Church Education in Europe" (see "The Record", no. 37). Eighty people involved in educational programmes of churches in 19 countries prepared a report that has been widely distributed. A more popular book has been published by the National Christian Education Council in England. This conference has been followed up by a 1974 meeting sponsored by the European Conference on Christian Education.

In a more massive effort at the Assembly of the World Council of Christian Education in Lima, 1971 (see "The Record", no. 22), over 380 delegates explored new perspectives in Christian education. In travelling to Lima small groups of delegates spent a week in *encuentros*‡ in 17 Latin American cities where they engaged in intensive observation and discussion of church involvement in education. WCC staff were fully involved with the WCCE in planning and conducting the *encuentros* and the Assembly itself.

Scholarships

In 1971, the W-C Scholarships Office was transferred from Inter-Church Aid to the Staff Working Group on Education. Before this took place, the 1969 Canterbury Consultation of Scholarships (see "The Record", no. 8) sought to evaluate the programme in order to meet the directives from Uppsala by providing for more non-theological studies, short study periods as against long academic courses, and encouraging studies within the applicants' own cultural regions where applicable. Consequently, the offer of free places in theological seminaries no longer met the new needs. As a result it has become increasingly necessary to look for other financial resources to pay for the new study programmes, and in the future it will be necessary to secure an increased basic budget rather than depend too heavily on responses to project askings.

Laity

In the area of laity closer relationships have been established with various lay training centres, evangelical academies and other residential or mobile centres for social concern. A strong emphasis has been placed on regionalization, beginning with an Asian Consultation held in 1969, when representatives of various centres formed an Association of Christian Institutes for Social Concern in Asia which arranges regional courses for staff members, exchange of staff, consultations for people to share experiences and to develop new models, exchange of information, and so on. There has been a similar development in Africa where the Association ot Christian Lay Centres in Africa serves in similar ways more than 20 centres, most of which have been established during the last decade. The WCC Laity staff cooperated with these Associations and the older Ecumenical Association of Directors of Academies and Lay Centres in Europe, in holding a world consultation at the Orthodox Academy in Crete in April 1972 (see "The Record", no. 28). That event is reported in the RISK special issue *The New Fishermen* Vol. 8 No. 4, January 1973. A World Collaboration Committee, representative of the three regional associations and of the WCC is planning a world Course for Leaders of Lay Training (CLLT) to be held January to March 1976. Most people from Africa and Asia who attended similar CLLT's in Europe in 1968 and 1970 are still deeply involved in the work of centres in their own countries. Such programmes on world and regional levels provide for continuous reappraisal and modification of centres and their activities.

Leisure-Tourism

Following the encouragement of the Uppsala Assembly that the WCC do studies in "Changing Concepts of Work and Leisure" the Laity staff of the DEA arranged a world consultation on Leisure Tourism at Tutzing, Federal Republic of Germany, in the third quarter of 1969 (see "The Record", no. 7). The report, *Leisure–Tourism,Threat and Promise*, has enjoyed wide circulation. There have been follow-up conferences in many areas, including the Caribbean, the Pacific, East Africa, Korea, Japan and Sri Lanka. The topic appeared again as a major concern at the Crete consultation mentioned above, and there has been further work in several countries represented there, such as Trinidad, Canada and Japan. Substantial WCC contacts have been made in 32 countries in all, and yet there has been no staff time available for further follow-up. The effects on people of the rapidly growing tourism industry deserve more attention by WCC staff and committees in the near future.

Family Ministries

Through the work of the Family Minsitries office, specialized training programmes have developed leaders in family counselling in the Pacific, Africa, Asia, the USA, Australia and New Zealand. Most family life seminars are now conducted by leaders from the areas themselves, as the programmes have gradually moved more and more into the cultural setting and resources of particular areas. This has naturally resulted in some tension over the various Western accreditation schemes.

191

A valuable aspect of that tension is the analysis of different communal forms in various cultures, and the relationship of family and sexual problems to the style of family structure and life.

From many of those involved in this widespread programme came proposals for reappraisal. A major consultation held in Malta in 1973 (see "The Record", no. 35) noted the privatistic‡ tendencies in much family counselling and spoke of family power: of how families can be strengthened to provide more support for the challenges Christians should bring to problems in society.

Education Renewal Fund

Strong initiatives for reappraisal of the Church's role in education were provided by the Education Renewal Fund (ERF), established and sponsored jointly by the WCCE and the WCC during the period of integration 1970-1973. It encouraged many churches and councils in their ecumenical efforts towards educational renewal and reform. More than a dozen curriculum projects, many of them initiated through the support of the WCCE before integration, engaged church leaders in rethinking the meaning of faith and the processes of education. For many of the churches the new programmes provided the first systematic lesson aids for teachers and the first organized training for those teaching religious courses in day schools or churches. For others the ventures gave opportunity to up-date their theological understanding and teaching in the light of modern society and its demands upon the churches. WCC staff involvement in many of these curriculum projects supplemented the financial support provided through the ERF. Many other projects, more than 70 altogether, in youth work, adult education and research programmes were supported by the ERF, through which many church mission and governmental agencies contributed more than U.S. $1 million before the end of the ERF mandate in 1973.

Conscientization‡

Essentially related to adult education, conscientization attacks the problem of apathy, the state of human beings who have been so conditioned by their relationships in society that they internalize failure and accept their situations without hoping to change them. As a result, the Gospel message of abundant life seems to become a sham. Conscientization offers a way for the Christian vision of human life and society to be put into practice by working towards an awareness of human possibilities for changing one's situation. The consciousness-raising becomes the criterion for evaluating all kinds of educational practices. Does a particular educational activity liberate a person to be more fully human, more able to share in what affects his or her life, or does it leave the person less human, passively accepting what others determine for his or her life? Furthermore, conscientization poses radical political and ideological questions about education,

192

which cannot be neutral with regard to the political and economic systems of a society. From the first consultation held by the Office of Education in Bergen (see "The Record", no. 13), the prophetic challenge of conscientization has been a factor in the WCC's work in education, and indeed the prophetic challenge of this emphasis has become central to the work of the Unit on Education and Renewal as well as of programmes in other Units of the WCC. Not only churches but many universities and government departments have become excited about this new educational emphasis. For example, in 1971 and 1972 there were seminars arranged by the University of Dar es Salaam and the Ministry of Education in Tanzania; in 1973, in Argentina with the Ministry of Education and in a series of workshops with oppressed groups in the United States; in 1974, in Australia, New Zealand, Papua New Guinea and Fiji with church, university, government and minority groups, and in the Caribbean.

During the period, too, the Office conducted a study on "The Ecumenical Task in Education—A Test for the European Churches". The report, circulated far beyond Europe, stresses the point that "education is not something neutral but a political responsibility . . . especially for the fulfilment of society's educational tasks".

In 1973 the sub-unit collaborated with the YMCA, the YWCA and the WSCF in preparing a reference paper for the International Conference on Education in Geneva (see "The Record", no. 36), sponsored by the International Bureau of Education (a UNESCO agency), on the theme "education, training and employment, with particular reference to secondary education". The WCC paper challenged societies to analyse the causes of the problems, not just the symptoms. It called on Non-governmental Organizations, including the churches, to "raise the levels of consciousness of groups and persons wherever possible" concerning the causes of unemployment. One potential member of that consortium dropped out because, he said, the paper had "too much politics and not enough pedagogy". The initiative with conscientization has repeatedly produced conflict and stimulated reaction in many situations.

Relationships and Interchange with Constituencies

The major initiatives cited above were carried out in close cooperation with partners in regional and national bodies. The style of work of the sub-unit has been carefully developed to build programmes with colleagues in the various regions. In 1974 conscientization seminars in Australia, New Zealand, Papua New Guinea and Fiji were all organized by local, regional and national education colleagues. Periodic planning meetings with education secretaries of major regional ecumenical councils and conferences facilitate such joint activities. Contributions made through the LRF provided some financial support for about thirty staff persons connected with educational programmes, chief among them being regional educational and youth secretaries in Africa, Asia, the Caribbean, Latin America, the Middle East and the Pacific. Communication with colleagues around the world has been developed through the *Education Newsletter*, which points to major events, reports and resources that reflect Christian educational activity in churches in all continents, and which stimulates correspondence between readers as well as with the office in Geneva.

Relationships with related programmes of the Roman Catholic Church have continued through regular exchange of information at staff level as well as participation of observer-consultants in major conferences and meetings arranged by the various departments of the sub-unit. One important event was a world conference on "New Trends in Laity Formation" jointly sponsored by the Unit on Education and Renewal of the WCC and the Council on the Laity of the Roman Catholic Church. It met at Assisi, Italy, in September 1974, bringing together about fifty experts to share experiences, to evaluate various practices, to establish a network of contact and collaboration and to suggest directions for future action by the churches.

Renewal

The Emancipation of Women

The concern about discrimination against women has been on the agenda of the WCC since its inception 25 years ago. One of the key topics in the deliberations and discussion in Amsterdam (1948) was the position of women in Church and society. A special Commission, with the task of studying the position and status of women in the various churches, was set up under the leadership of Dr. Kathleen Bliss. A book containing her findings, entitled, *The Service and Status of Women in the Churches*, was published in 1952. A foreward written by Dr. W.A. Visser 't Hooft stated: "It is not only the opinion of Dr. Bliss, but the almost monotonous and impressive *Leitmotiv* [theme tune] of the reports from all countries that (in the words of the Amsterdam Assembly) 'the Church as the Body of Christ consists of men and women, created as responsible persons to glorify God and to do his will', but that 'this truth accepted in theory, is too often ignored in practice'." This statement is still valid and relevant today as we approach the Fifth Assembly of the World Council of Churches.

The first title of this department was the Commission on the Life and Work of Women in the Church, which later, at Evanston in 1954, was changed to the Department on Cooperation of Men and Women in Church and Society. The change of title became necessary in order to move from the traditional concept of a "women's department" concerned with women's organizations predominantly. The Department focussed on the obstacles that were hindering women's liberation: theological, psychological and sociological issues were now studied. The reasoning behind this broader approach was that it was futile to discuss a woman's place and service in the Church without looking at the total society, since the Church does not exist in isolation. The tide of rising expectations for life is clearly moving with the peoples of the world, and it is evidenced by women too. The real question remains whether the Church will ever allow women to be fully human.

After the New Delhi Assembly (1961), the integration of the International Missionary Council with the World Council of Churches took place, and the question of "family ministries" was then added to the mandate of the Department.

In 1971, at Addis Ababa, the Central Committee gave the WCC a new organizational structure, as a result of which the Department had then to operate through two separate "desks": questions of family education were placed in the sub-unit on Education, and the issue of women's emancipation was placed in the sub-unit on Renewal.

Activities over these past seven years arising out of belief in the emancipation of women have been undertaken in response to the mandate which was given at the Uppsala Assembly. The nature and cause of discrimination against women in contemporary society became the theme for a Consultation on Man-Woman Dialogue (see "The Record", no. 3). This consultation explored the identity of Man and Woman, the sharp division of roles in technological society and the prejudices created and perpetuated. The role of women in development was another issue brought into focus by the consultation. In this same context the problem of the ordination of women (see "The Record", no. 12) was explored. Representatives of seventy Member Churches of the WCC discussed the identity crisis of ordained women, urging the WCC structures, theological colleges and Member Churches to examine the barriers against women.

Significant were the Women's Leadership Training Seminars (see "The Record", no. 23) held in Lomé, Togo; Monrovia, Liberia; and Kampala, Uganda; jointly sponsored by the WCC and the All Africa Conference of Churches. The main purpose of these seminars was to help leaders of women's groups to identify problems and to alert them to opportunities for making a Christian witness in Africa and elsewhere in the world; to encourage new concepts of the mission of the Church and of the meaning of justice and freedom; to encourage political and social involvement, and policy making; to encourage creative thinking in church renewal and ecumenism; to consider the place of women in the Church.

Two important ecumenical events should also be mentioned at this point because of their wide implications: the Conference on the Image of Women in the Mass Media (see "The Record", no. 24), and the Consultation on Women's Role in Peace Education (see "The Record", no. 27), sponsored by the Women's Ecumenical Liaison Group (WELG), an organization no longer in existence, but of which the Women's Desk was an integral part. The first conference looked at the full potentiality of women in mass media and drew some relevant conclusions on the media as servants of society. The second consultation, in which SODEPAX was also involved, discussed thoroughly such subjects as neo-colonialism, cultural imperialism, racism, trade and violence.

In June 1974 a world-wide ecumenical consultation on Sexism in the 1970's (see "The Record", no. 42) took place in West Berlin, Germany, bringing together 150 women from 54 countries to explore the world-wide manifestations of sexism‡ in society today and what liberation from sexism could mean for the whole human family. A special issue of RISK, *Words to the Churches: Voices of the Sisters*, Vol. 10 No. 2, 1974, is devoted to the Berlin consultation.

The Women's Desk has been fully involved in programmes in different areas of the world and has attempted to implement the main decisions taken by all of these consultations. Contacts with regional and local groups have been maintained so as to uphold initiatives and promote regular and ongoing programmes. The Desk has also been able to set up study tours for women around the world to visit other countries. It has made contacts with the churches in order to enable them to widen their horizons and to experience what it means to be a part of the world community. Related to this, the scholarship programme provided, especially in developing countries, opportunities for women to obtain further training as well as participation in the life of the Church in other areas. Through the Desk, the Swiss Federation of Protestant Women has made possible, since 1967, scholarships for 25 young women in Togo, and funds were made available for training women as nursery school teachers in Cameroon. Likewise, the World Day of Prayer Committee in the Federal Republic of Germany has granted financial resources to women's groups in rural parts of developing countries in Africa, Asia, Australasia and Latin America. This was in response to the new insights in the WCC towards a more adequate development strategy. Nineteen projects have all been directed at assisting in meeting these needs.

This account is inevitably incomplete. It is a record of the programmes initiated and carried out by a small staff team in Geneva and does not reflect what has been happening in the Member Churches. Some churches have managed to set up special task forces to look at the issue of discrimination against women. To mention a few, the WCC study on Changing

Institutions drew on the work of a group in New York which brought a feminine perspective to bear on the issue. A variety of groups, caucuses and task forces have sprung up around the women's issue, but the important thing about the New York group was that it did not confine its work to women. The concerns of women were related to other important issues such as racism and class. Another piece of work was done by a commission established by the Anglican Communion for the purpose of bringing recommendations on the ordination of women to the Anglican Consultative Council.

Various reports of the World Council over the past few years reveal that a great deal has been done to high-light the theological, sociological and psychological questions that need to be asked about the relationship between men and women. Some churches have tried to put the several discoveries into practical effect.

There are other areas, however, where WCC studies about women have not yet had their impact. A trenchant example was the Fourth Assembly of the World Council at Uppsala in 1968. Women constituted only 9% of the voting delegates at the Assembly. Despite the "pleas" of the Council, the Member Churches generally did not respond by appointing women as delegates. As Dr. Marga Bührig put it: "Making allowance for a measure of exaggeration, one might almost say that these meticulous theological and psychological enquiries into the 'true nature of woman', her intrinsic gifts, the mission entrusted to her by God, and the correct appraisal of the unalterable contrast between man and woman which is part of creation, have perhaps led to an inability or reluctance even to appreciate that 'discrimination' against women even exists, even though its existence is borne out by the facts. It may be that lucid theological insights make people blind to the practical conditions which require change". So while the WCC has taken a definite decision to improve the representation of women at the Fifth Assembly in Nairobi, the programme staff and the committees of the Council remain predominantly male.

Youth Concerns

A highly significant moment at the Uppsala Assembly—and one entirely unplanned by the Assembly's organizers—occurred during the closing service in Uppsala Cathedral. The choir was singing an anthem, Sydney Carter's "When I Needed a Neighbour" (*Cantate Domino* no. 37), when suddenly a group of demonstrators appeared carrying large signs. On the signs were written slogans and imperatives of a quite provocative nature. As the marchers proceeded up the aisles of the cathedral one could read the fine print identifying the sources of the fiery words. They were taken, it turned out, from official enactments of the Assembly, voted by the delegates themselves. And the demonstrators were Youth Participants and a

197

number of young Stewards who had taken part in the Uppsala gathering.

The message to the churches and their representatives, and to the World Council of Churches, was a scorching one: Put up or shut up. Practise what you preach. Over the past seven years, with respect to the concerns of youth, the message has been heeded in some important ways. And in many ways it has not.

From the period of its formation, the World Council of Churches has seen youth as an essential element in its constituency, and at least until 1968 work among Christian young people had been a large element in its programme. It could not have done otherwise. A good number of its former and present leaders have grown up in national or world-wide ecumenical youth movements. Indeed the person chosen to deliver the message of the Youth Observers at the First Assembly of the WCC at Amsterdam was none other than Philip Potter.

Although Potter addressed himself specifically to the issues of concern to the Church in the period immediately following the Second World War, many of his remarks contained—in embryo—some of the main thrusts of the WCC's Youth Department from 1948 until the period under review.

"There can be no doubt that the task of the churches in the evangelization of the young people of this generation is an immense one. We are sure, therefore, that it cannot be attempted by the senior members of the churches without the young people, or *vice versa*. The times demand a forward movement of the *whole* Church, knowing that the vanguard of the attack must be Christian youth, who, at any rate, are in closest contact with other young people".*

The young generation of the 1950's was at first caught up in struggles to repair a war-torn world and to establish, in the emerging societies, or renew, in the older nations, a sense of national identity and purpose. Or they were entangled in the ideological slings and sometimes very real arrows of the "Cold War". In the midst of this the international ecumenical opportunities afforded them by the World Council of Churches were received with genuine gratitude. The work camps, in particular, seemed tangible evidence of doing something useful, and the companionship generated within them was proof that God had made of one blood all the nations of his earth.

Yet to their younger brothers and sisters these responses were not adequate. Glaringly apparent to them was the misery in which most young people lived, about which so little was being done. There were many human needs, as the *New Delhi to Uppsala* report pointed out, "which

*   The text of this address appears in William H. Gentz: The World of Philip Potter. New York: Friendship Press, 1974. Available from WCC Publications, Geneva and New York.

198

require kinds of services other than mere pick and shovel work''. Clearly work had to be done at getting to the root causes of the injustice on international and local levels which were being perpetuated by the structures of authority (including the churches). Yet the problems of each specific situation differed enormously from those of the next. Indeed the complexity of the world-wide youth scene was such that the WCC Youth Department was persuaded to provide the Uppsala Assembly with a special paper on the subject.*

"To draw a profile of youth today is to draw a profile of modern man. . . . We cannot draw a general picture true for all, but we must recognize a few essentials all have in common. All young people are feeling the wind of change, although not all may be equally excited about that prospect. The whole younger generation knows the longing for more adequate structures of society, although the content of their hope may be very different. The whole generation looks for authentic leadership, real imagination, true vision and an open future. Everywhere young people have more power than their elders had in their days because of the increase in their knowledge or the sheer numbers. Even more important, a world-wide younger generation has in common an inter-related future. . . .

"One of the most important phenomena amongst young people today [1968] is the tremendous energy with which they protest against the social and political disorder of our times. There is hardly a country in the world where some form of protest movement is not eminently visible, although the expressions of it differ. . . . In some countries the protest of youth has taken on organizational forms. The unconscious rebellion of the 'unattached' becomes a well-organized political alternative. There is thinking, organization and clarity. Sometimes, the organized protest attracts the 'socially rejecting' even to the extent of changing the concept and image of the organized groups. Sometimes the organized protest takes its own directions. The language of protest has developed its own forms, its hymns and marches, which can have a great attraction also for the non-committed majority of the generation. This can go so far that the original forms of protest become acceptable and have little power left: they become part of the fashion and lose direction. Discernment of the genuine goals of the protest movement remains necessary. . . .

"The protest movements of a younger generation have to be understood in terms of the society to which youth wants to relate but cannot. Romantic applause for protest is as harmful as authoritarian refusal to identify its causes. Without denying that the adolescent also has a responsibility for

*   This paper appeared in Work Book for the Assembly Committees, Uppsala 1968. Geneva: WCC, 1968. Pages 137-52.

the order of society, society should know its own imperfection and, for that reason, invite criticism. Protest in itself, however, is not enough; it has to be evaluated, deepened and translated in a constructive contribution''.

At the time of the Uppsala Assembly the just course in attempting to respond to the vocal young people everywhere apparent seemed to be somehow to integrate youth and their concerns more organically into the whole working of the World Council of Churches. To say so was easy, and may have sounded easy to many, but the doing of it has proved difficult during the period under review. Even in 1968 the Youth Department noted that ''a real integration, which would require or at least allow critical participation, is more than most adults can take and more than most young people can muster''. Added to this problem were two other factors: first, some of the traditional structures by which Christian youth were related to the programmes of the WCC were beginning to experience some difficulties, such as rapid change in leadership and membership, as well as financial instability; and, second, the Constitution and Rules of the WCC had not been devised so as to allow the participation of young people at the highest levels of leadership in any great number (members of the Central Committee, for instance, must have been delegates to the Assembly; at Uppsala the number of delegates under 30 years of age was less than a dozen, or about 1.5%; thus only two of the 120 members of the Central Committee empanelled there were 25 years old or below at the time of their election).

Nevertheless the integration attempt was made. The staff of the Youth Department from 1969 to 1973 was greatly diminished, and due to financial re-allocations the Department lost access to those programme resources used to support the half-dozen people who departed to other assignments. The size of the executive staff was reduced from seven to one during this time, and funds for conducting ecumenical youth work administered by Geneva (outside of the Ecumenical Youth Service and World Youth Projects, both of which programmes were entirely financed by CICARWS with designated grants) were severely limited. Under the integration policy youth concerns and programmes were to be dealt with throughout the World Council of Churches, particularly within the Division of Ecumenical Action (now the Programme Unit on Education and Renewal). Yet, in effect, youth as a constituency was obscured and seemed to become the object of ''benign neglect''.

At the same time, there was a marked increase in regional youth activity. Regional ecumenical youth secretariats were established or strengthened, and many of the programmes and tasks once carried out from Geneva were now administered at the regional level. In Asia, Africa, Latin America and the Caribbean there commenced and continue to take place a greater number of autonomous programmes in response to locally felt needs. In many instances, however, the Geneva youth staff assisted in securing the necessary financial support by way of CICARWS channels. Although there was no correlation between the reduction of youth staff in the WCC and the growth in regional activity, there was, during the period that followed, an increasing emphasis upon one particular area of the ecumenical youth task—that of advocacy and involvement in issues of concern.

Apart from attention to renewal movements involving the younger generation and a number of consultations (see "The Record") specific youth ministries carried out by the World Council during the period under review were effectively reduced to two: the aforementioned Ecumenical Youth Service and the World Youth Projects. Two examples may serve to indicate the character of these programmes.

In 1973, Ecumenical Youth Service sponsored an African/Caribbean study tour that started with attending the inaugural Assembly of the Caribbean Conference of Churches and subsequent travel to various islands in that region. Representatives from Ghanaian, Togolese and Nigerian youth movements discussed and made plans for an exchange of young volunteers from Africa to work with churches and youth movements in the fields of voluntary service and community development—particularly with secondary schoolers—in the Caribbean, including the French-speaking areas.

World Youth Projects in the same period, and after, gave financial support to cooperative youth programmes in Asia where sewing, tailoring and vocational training in transistor repairs—efforts conducted by the churches—were designed to facilitate the employability of youth in that region.

As far as the direct representation of young people in the governing organs of the WCC was concerned, the Central Committee in 1969 resolved "to appoint to the next meeting of the Central Committee within the category of advisers not less than 15 and not more than 20 men and women under the age of 30". The practice was continued at subsequent meetings, and the Younger Advisers have made substantial contributions to debates and decisions. At Addis Ababa specific provision was made for the inclusion of youth in the supervisory committee for the Programme Unit on Education and Communication, and the Structure Committee successfully proposed the requirement that delegations of a certain size or larger to the Fifth Assembly must include a proportion of delegates under 30. Nevertheless, the Central Committee had no authority to augment its own membership in favour of youth, and it has been slow to ensure that a fair number of young men and women be made members of the Council's other Commissions and working groups.

It became apparent midway in the period under review that the hoped-for involvement of youth in all aspects of the WCC's work was not being achieved, and there was nowhere near an adequate response to the challenge so sharply posed by the young participants at the Uppsala Assembly and by their contemporaries in all parts of the world. The Central Committee in 1972 noted the desire of what was then called the Renewal Group ''to be authorized to pick up new concerns and experiment in new areas with a view to achieving'' the discovery of ''where and how God is acting today through traditional or new and radical movements in Church and society, to facilitate communication between such movements, and to stimulate the churches to share in this quest''. The Policy Reference Committee particularly insisted ''that there be a continuing commitment to youth work within the World Council of Churches and that the proposal for a youth team be regarded as a way forward in WCC youth work''.

An Ad Hoc Committee on Youth was set up, and the following year the Central Committee expressed the hope ''that every effort will be made to maintain and develop contacts with the regional activities in this field, so as to secure adequate participation of young people in the Fifth Assembly and more adequate plans for the post-Assembly period''. At its 1974 meeting the Central Committee was not able to agree to the establishment of a special Youth Fund, but it did resolve ''that the General Secretary be asked to examine the situation of youth work in the WCC afresh and bring proposals to the Executive Committee in April 1975''. An expanded staff group has been assigned to carry out this mandate, and a special workshop of youth concerns has been scheduled for the Nairobi Assembly.

What transpired during 1968 and after had and still has wide-ranging implications affecting the ecumenical movement and the Member Churches of the WCC. Massive protests, students and young workers challenging the values (or lack of them) of an industrial social order, just demands for a more humane society and anti-war movements all characterized an unprecedented epoch in the twentieth century that has given way to what the churches and society are now witnessing among the young, namely a quadrangle of moods: neo-conservatism; a silent, uninvolved majority; a confused, searching element; and a minority of activists. The nature and content of these ''moods'' and movements differ markedly from region to region.

If one were to characterize the changes in ecumenical youth work since 1968, one could say that, generally speaking, the younger generation in the North Atlantic is unclear in its directions yet searching for purpose, and their counterparts in the Southern hemisphere are struggling for justice, both within and outside of the churches and the ecumenical movement. These two developments are dialectically related.

At the same time church-related youth work with all its different forms and emphases continues in the Member Churches. Leaders and members of church youth organizations are more often than not critical of the churches to which they belong. It is out of these groups that participants in ecumenical work camps and other forms of voluntary service in many cases come forward.

In the increased complexity and confusion of the 1970's a deep search for meaning is taking place among young people of all regions. This can be illustrated by excerpts from the Taizé‡ Council of Youth's 1974 "Letter to the People of God": "Today we are sure: the risen Christ is preparing his people to become at one and the same time a contemplative people, thirsting for God; a people of justice, living the struggle of men and peoples exploited; a people of communion, where the non-believer also finds a creative place. . . .

"Numerous churches, in the southern hemisphere as in the northern, are spied on interfered with, and even persecuted. Certain of them show that without any bonds with political powers, without means of power, without wealth, the Church can experience a new birth, can become a force of liberation for humanity and radiate God".

Although the youth at Taizé themselves saw that they were of "extreme diversity", they came forth with an enormous response to Philip Potter when he told them that "young people are still regarded as the *avant garde* of the ecumenical movement, and it is their duty to conscientize the Church and encourage it to become the sign of the Resurrection".

Hence the Fifth Assembly of the World Council of Churches must do more than pass supportive legislation in the domain of ecumenical youth ministries. More is called for than merely having a limited number of young people taking part in the ecumenical movement. Youth concerns have gone beyond that stage. The younger generation shares the same attitude as do others in the churches. They want to participate—fully.

Ecumenical youth work is thus paradoxically a necessary and a hazardous affair. When generations no longer share the same mental, spiritual and social values, they need special attention. Yet to isolate youth work is harmful because it tends to endanger the unique quality of the people of God by putting them into divisions of age groupings which are all too often antagonistic to one another. Only by facilitating the freedom of youth work, by responding to it in the entire ecumenical movement or spectrum, and by experimenting in mutual trust, can the churches as a whole be renewed.

In all of this the churches can do tremendous harm or make a tremendous contribution. Harm will be done if the churches continue to speak *about* youth, but never *with* youth. Harm will be done if church leaders do not accept the blame for being responsible for the social environment in which the young live. Harm will be done if the churches require from the younger generation what they themselves do not practice.

An ecumenical youth ministry must be concerned for the whole people of God. Such a youth ministry should never be a nervous effort to keep the young in the Church or win them for the Church without taking into permanent account that they must also be agents for building a better, more liberating society according to the mandates of the Gospel.

Facing the implications of the Fifth Assembly is also to face the challenge of a divided world, a world where there is uneven development, partial counsciousness and many, many questions. The unity of the churches, as the whole people of the Church, is the best testimony to the world that people can be made free and united.

Special Assignments

The Language Policy Task Force

Before the Communication Department left the Programme Unit one major joint initiative took place: the work of the Language Policy Task Force. Appointed in 1971, it brought together the concerns of many who felt that the language policy and practices of the World Council of Churches needed drastic re-appraisal. Including the language services staff and a representative group of other staff, the LPTF brought to the Utrecht Central Committee in 1972 its challenging paper, entitled "The Threat of Monolingualism in the WCC". Relating language to the total activity of the ecumenical fellowship, the report raised fundamental questions about communication. It emphasized that present language policy puts the majority of Member Churches and their participants in the ecumenical movement at a serious disadvantage, because all who do not speak English as a mother tongue operate with a considerable handicap. In short, it said, language is power, and present WCC policy results in an unjust sharing of power.

Urged by the Central Committee to expand and continue its work, the LPTF explored the problem further, to discover a large degree of insensitivity on the part of English mother-tongue speakers, and a rising amount of frustration on the part of others. The language problem therefore opened the door wide to a much larger set of problems for WCC activity: the meaning and processes of communication among people and churches. The

1973 report to the Central Committee therefore stated that "human communication only becomes possible through common involvement in common action", and called in question the entire style of involvement in WCC affairs.

Practical follow-up from the 1973 Central Committee took several forms. Staff discussions opened up various ways of improving and experimenting with the use of language at the Geneva headquarters and in other WCC activities. Language study was further encouraged, and a more careful inventory and use of multi-lingual skills adopted. Proposals for major and minor changes at the Fifth Assembly were made to the appropriate committees, and practical suggestions were made for maintaining and enhancing the use of language services in the Communication Department. Finally, a major recommendation called for special attention up to and during the Assembly, and for a new group responsible to the Central Committee to emerge out of the Assembly to carry further the work begun by the LPTF. Through these activities the WCC became aware of a major problem and set in motion forces to work towards solving it.

Participation in Change

Another special undertaking of the Unit is an action/reflection programme started in 1970 which had its origin in concerns about the poor and the powerless raised by the churches at the Uppsala Assembly. Its purpose was to give the WCC direct linkage with those who are without power. Through wide travel and intensive correspondence, contacts were established and nurtured with more than 80 regional and national coordinators in all continents. Each coordinator has remained in touch with groups in the area, resulting in an extensive network.

This programme, Participation in Change, has established relationships among groups and movements, across national and local boundaries, which are participating in some significant way in producing positive change in Church and society. To the extent possible, it has encouraged a flow of stories, action strategies and experiences of success and failure, theological and biblical insights, and thus helps to provide the support and challenge which come from being in a world fellowship and enterprise instead of being isolated. It is not assumed that there will be many common elements—cultures, backgrounds and histories are so various; but the springboard of Christian faith and hope produces substantial areas of learning experiences.

Participation in Change has made possible an inter-relationship between what is happening at the level of the poor and powerless and what exists at the "higher echelons". This relationship has opened perspectives, encouraged the revision of values, produced a more rounded view of the life of the Church, and has fostered change in attitude and in structures.

Experiments were made with three main types of communication: stories, many of which were published in various issues of *Study Encounter*, cassettes,‡ and word-and-picture descriptions.

Through this programme a new type of ecumenical meeting was tested—meetings of leaders elected by groups of poor and oppressed. One such international gathering was held at Barquisimeto, Caracas, Venezuela, where the participants from six countries were people committed in different communities to the struggle for a new world. The host was a pentecostal congregation where the group experienced the Holy Spirit in Bible study, prayer, praise, the education of disadvantaged children and the delivery of *campesinos* [peasants] from economic oppression. Their store of wisdom is a "memory-bank", not a "book-bank".

Serious thought has to be given by the WCC to the future of this particular approach—this particular means by which people can make up their minds about their destiny—an approach which could transform the churches' relationship to the poor and the powerless.

CURRENT AND EMERGING ISSUES

From its beginning, the Programme Unit on Education and Renewal has found its primary focus in working for liberating education processes and structures with the young, with women, the laity, and those who are involved in innovations designed to extend these processes. The Unit on Education and Renewal has understood the Gospel as calling upon the Church to identify with the oppressed and to work with them to achieve the liberation process, but it can also block it by perpetuating sexist,‡ racist, cultural and class discriminations and dominations. Therefore, the Unit was compelled to engage in analysing the educational processes and shape those processes in which the Church is involved to try to discover which of these efforts contribute to the liberation of the people and the renewal of the Church.

The Unit has been engaged in the search for new ways to raise the consciousness of the people, thereby enabling them to discover and respond to the liberating possibilities of the Gospel and their share in its vision and power. Because the Unit as a whole had come to the conclusion that from such efforts could come an awareness and challenge to the oppressive structures, systems, habits and behavioural patterns that enslave human beings, such awareness can provide positive resources leading towards liberation and renewal not only for individuals but for groups, communities and nations. Education for liberation and renewal in the community thus became the first priority in the Unit's work in the World Council of Churches. To this end the following major issues are presented for critique and development during the coming years (the order of listing implies no priority of importance; all are primary).

Reappraisal of Education

Advanced significantly by the past seven years of work, but not yet completed, radical reappraisal of educational structures and processes now undergoing radical changes is a necessity for the churches in their educational work. Many church educators are quite aware of the changes and have reappraised their work and are moving to reshape it in more useful ways. Church leaders and decision-makers, and those responsible for many traditional church education activities such as theological education, need to be encouraged to broaden and deepen their analysis of the changing situation. Continual reflection upon the Gospel as a liberating goal for human life will frame these efforts in a Christian direction.

Innovations in Education

Where reappraisal has led to new approaches, both within and outside of formal schooling, churches need to experiment with innovations that promise liberation for people and renewal for the churches. Through providing interchange and resources, the WCC can help these innovations to prosper and to share with each other.

Formation of Children in the Faith

Re-appraisal and experimentation have brought promising new ways of nurturing children in the community of faith, and deeper understanding of the harmful effects of certain conditioning processes. The integration of the World Council of Christian Education with the WCC in 1972 brings responsibility for education with those who are young, and calls the WCC to give this work more attention in the years ahead.

Empowerment of the Family

Eroded by various forces, such as urbanization, increasing mobility, and even deliberate policies of some governments, the family struggles today to make its needed contribution to community and to the liberation of persons. Powerful forces in society bombard persons in family relationships, and modern families have a hard time combatting them. New patterns of intimacy, new attempts to establish communal and group support, new potenial for liberation through counselling and psychological insight all challenge the churches to study carefully what is happening in family life today and to develop more adequate ways of empowering the family as a way of liberating persons and renewing human community.

Laity in Mission

The ecumenical theological education of the whole people of God: baptized Christians need good education opportunities to develop into mature discipleship. Christian education for children and a simple biblical literacy need to be balanced by adult analysis of what it means to live and act in a Christian manner in today's world. Youth need to be aided in their searching for responsible and authentic life in community. Women need to be aided in their break-out from exploitation and domestication. All Christians need broader awareness of the international and national structural forces by which their private lives are shaped. Christians need ethical, theological and spiritual education into political, economic and social insight and activity worthy of their Lord and his liberating good news. Parochial consciousnesses and consciences need opening out into the broadest ecumenical reaches of God's world and people. The churches desperately need the liberating activity of informed laity. The WCC needs to concentrate its work upon liberating education with adults, especially in non-formal settings.

Doing Theology

From struggles and experiences of oppression, exploitation and powerlessness come dramatic awareness of the liberating Gospel of Jesus Christ. Reflection upon these struggles sharpens the Christian sense of what God is doing in human life and leads into further action from which comes further learning. Education for liberation and community within the Church provides an arena for doing theology, and for discerning the specifically Christian challenges and contributions in education. In the process of struggle and reflection, Christians together do theology as they discover what it means to be Christian in their lives. Rather than limiting theology to specialized and designated experts, the Christian community itself, men and women and young people in the context of their struggles, aided by educational processes that help them become more aware of their historical and personal situation and of the movement of the liberating Christ among them, develop their theological understanding as they practice their Christian lives together in action. Behavioural sciences and communal cultural values can help, as can insight into socio-economic systems and practices. The theological and ethical call comes to the churches to participate fully in actions that empower the powerless, that help them gain awareness of their situation and of the Gospel of liberation as they work together in community to shape their lives.

Participation in Change

The vitality of faith and the impressive styles of life of the groups and movements at the base, contacted through this programme, indicate:

(a) The continuing service which may be offered by the Unit on Education and Renewal through providing links between groups and movements which are often very isolated, and which need support and challenge within the world church fellowship;

(b) The need for the whole Church to pay heed to the theological insights, action and reflection concerns and political awareness of awakened "Christians at the base". The contribution of little-educated and powerless people is essential for the renewal of the total Church; and

(c) The lack of representation of such people on the committees and Commissions of the WCC and its staff is a continuing weakness.

Keeping Pace with Youth Change

The changing character of youth as a community, a mood, and an age grouping (with no common denominator in any part of the world—what is considered "youth" in the Western world is looked upon as being a "child" in other cultures) requires a compatible kind of programme in order to be relevant to that community, mood and grouping.

Youth Participation

It is necessary to establish ways by which the younger generation can more deeply and fully take part in the ecumenical movement globally, regionally and locally. In this the WCC has the responsibility to promote programmes reflecting this need, but it also has to do so in its own life by advocating the full participation of the younger generation in all its life and work.

Congregational Renewal

In the last few years many "probes" have been made into new developments in forms of Christian community. On the one hand there are indications that the life of the local congregation is receiving renewed attention in the traditional churches, as the place in which people can find a caring community, and in whose liturgy they can express and celebrate their faith. A major conference on Worship and Evangelism, planned by this Unit in May 1975, at Windsor, England, will help focus more sharply the concern of this Unit for liturgical renewal. Contact has been made and is being maintained with charismatic‡ movements, Christian communities outside or alongside the institutional churches, and radical action-oriented groups. The real potential of such renewal movements both within and outside the local congregation is not yet appreciated or clear, but one can affirm a sense of excitement and hope that the Christian community under the inspiration of the Holy Spirit is indeed discovering new forms of corporate existence.

RISK

Edited from within the Programme Unit on Education and Renewal, the magazine RISK informs the ecumenical constituency of the new issues that are constantly emerging as challenges to Christian concern.

5

communication

At the Uppsala Assembly in 1968 the Department of Communication celebrated its first birthday. It had been created by the Central Committee the previous year in an attempt to integrate and centralize the various communication efforts of the World Council of Churches. Three former entities were involved. First was the Department of Information, charged by the Evanston Assembly with the responsibility ''for making known the activities of the World Council through the church and secular press and other media, also serving the churches by providing them with news about the life of their sister churches''. To this was added the WCC Publications Office, which had been established in 1956 as a desk within the Finance Office to handle orders and subscriptions for all the publications then edited in the various departments of the WCC. Similarly the Language Service was brought into the Department in 1968.

Growing Pains

In 1971 the WCC Structure Committee proposed the creation of a special Programme Unit on Education and Communication, linking the Communication Department with the then existing Division of Ecumenical Action and the Office of Education. The rationale of this proposal seemed sound at the time: the programme function of the Department of Communication was to be predominantly in the field of ecumenical education. Implementing the proposal, however, turned out not to be practicable. The Department in both its service and programme functions was in fact related to all departments in the WCC, and any specific affinity with one or other Unit was better expressed in closer working relationships rather than structual changes. The Central Committee in Geneva 1973 therefore decided to tie the Department structurally with the General Secretariat and to re-approve the Department's own aims and functions.

Aims and Expectations

At that session of the Central Committee an analysis of the Department's task was presented. It included the following observations·

"We were conscious first of the threefold role of the Department. The first is to be the '*spokesman*' of the World Council and its works, the channel by which information about our life and work is made available in the appropriate professional ways to the communications media. Second, the Department has a task of '*strategizing*'. Presenting the Council comprehensively throughout all the media, combining faith, witness, justice, service, education and renewal through word, sound and image is part of that strategy, as is the task of enabling all the churches to share in the development of mutual understanding and renewal. Fundamental to all this is the LISTENING process. Third, the Department has a '*reflector*' role in taking seriously some of the opportunities the mass media present for building up the community of mankind as well as exposing the obstacles which prevent it.

"The task is enormous, and, as we never tire of pointing out, has to be accomplished by a small staff with limited resources. Hence our concern first to define in the functions those tasks which we see as the specific priority work for the Department and second to make clear those areas where the job is no less urgent but where wider collaboration with other agencies is called for. We continue to affirm that for us work with the media is the most important priority for the Department's time and energies, and one which demands the use of skill, tact, and patience.

"Aware of how important communication strategies prove to be when the Council becomes involved in difficult or controversial issues, we are convinced that it would be irresponsible to reduce work in those areas which help to make the Council better known to a wide audience in the churches and among the public at large." The World Council of Churches as a world-wide network of communication is able to communicate and stimulate communication only to the degree to which the Member Churches enable the Council to do so.

Thus, both the formulation of the task of the Department and its practical implications are intimately linked to the programme of the World Council of Churches as a whole and to the creative process of learning and sharing in and among the Member Churches which may possibly lead to a common vision for the role that the churches play in shaping the future of mankind.

In evaluating and assisting the work of the Communication Department a number of factors need to be borne in mind.

World Council communication has to address itself both to churches— within and outside the membership of the WCC—and to the world at large, using the channels of mass communication. Many churches view the mass media with suspicion because the social and political concerns of the World Council and its Member Churches are given much more attention than theological reflection, that is, the theological frame of reference within which actions are taken or decisions are made. Sometimes this suspicion is unfounded, because there are many producers, reporters and journalists in the mass media who try successfully to interpret the Church's concerns precisely in the light of its own presuppositions and convictions. In any case, the thorn remains in the flesh: the definition of relevancy, the selection of what is relevant about the churches and the ecumenical movement is not an exclusive prerogative of the churches and should not be such. This places a particular task on all ecumenical communication around the world: it is not just telling the story of what happens in and with the churches, but also recounting the history of God at work in the churches and the world at large.

Another factor which needs to be borne in mind is that ecumenical action, in fact that this Council of 271 churches itself, has become more and more controversial as concerns in the field of racism and development, for instance, have grown to be an integral part of the WCC programme. This is true in view of both institutions outside the constituency and Member Churches as well. Certain governments, for instance, have launched massive campaigns against the WCC, distributing ''information'' —in fact horrendous distortions—about the WCC in such a dimension that even united efforts on the international and national levels were not always able to cope.

Within and among the Member Churches, we find an increasing number of conflict situations which in one way or the other involve staff or Central Committee actions taken with regard to social and political issues. It is obvious that WCC communication has to recognize these situations in terms other than mere conflict management aimed at restoring immediate consensus. Consensus is not a pre-requisite for communication, rather communication is an indispensable condition for consensus.

Conflicts need to be exposed and lifted to a level of visibility and reflection on which participation and learning can take place. There is an increasing need for conflict orientation in our communication efforts which the Department has tried to recognize and certainly will have to take very seriously in the period following the Assembly.

Ecumenical Action as News

The demands of radio, television and the press are for quick information, background documentation and on-the-spot interviews. And at the same time, the WCC Member Churches want to know more, and faster, about situations and developments in the churches in other parts of the world, and expect this information to be provided.

The three years immediately after the Uppsala Assembly were a time of innovation and creativity for the *Press Office* as it attempted to respond to these demands. A period of acute financial crisis followed, during which it was necessary to reduce the French and German news desks and allow the post of Senior Press Officer — which was created and filled at the Uppsala Assembly — to fall vacant. However, many of the policies and practices put into effect in the first three years continue to this day. In spite of severe financial limitations, the Press Office has extended its liaison function with the secular and church press, and has served the Member Churches and staff of the World Council. A Reuters telex service was installed in the Ecumenical Centre by means of which WCC personnel can receive news of developments as they occur and thus are able to respond immediately. Reuters, for its part, began to pick up more stories related to the WCC and the churches, and to distribute them around the world. Closer cooperation with Reuters and other international wire services has increasingly put electronic technology at the Council's disposal at minimal cost. In addition, personal ties have been developed with other international journalists assigned to the Geneva offices of the United Nations, and contacts with leading newspapers throughout the world were established on the occasion of staff visits. Emphasis was also put on inviting journalists and broadcasters to visit the World Council headquarters in Geneva to have a look around for themselves and write their own stories. The Director of the Communication Department held regular "briefing" sessions in several countries so that those who write regularly about Council activities could bring themselves up to date.

Production of the Ecumenical Press Service (EPS) has continued, supplemented by *This Month*, a publication which was issued until October 1974 as part of EPS but also sold separately at low cost and at quantity rates. Its purpose was to provide ecumenical material to lay people and local churches. Four articles reflected the Church at work in four different continents. The news round-up covered World Council and world confessional family developments during the past month, and the Periscope section contained news of the churches in capsule form. Experience with both the feasibility and the limitations of this publication has formed the basis for launching the new monthly magazine ONE WORLD (see below).

Simultaneously, the office for *Radio and Television* has increased its effectiveness on the level of newscasts. Working conditions at the Ecumenical Centre were improved by the appointment of a full-time sound technician in 1969. Studio output has increased as a result, and the section has thus been able to give better service to local and foreign radio journalists on assignment to WCC headquarters, especially at major conferences or events like the visit of Pope Paul VI. This is also true for large meetings held elsewhere than Geneva. Services provided in such cases include liaison between staff and participants on the one side and the media representatives on the other. The radio office has done its best to meet the increasing demands of broadcasters: at the Utrecht Central Committee meeting in 1972 the office arranged 90 radio and television interviews; at the Central Committee meetings in Geneva (1973) and Berlin (1974) some 130 interviews were set up on each occasion.

As the interest of the media in ecumenical news grows, one problem becomes clear: attention is reserved almost exclusively for actions taken or positions declared on the part of the World Council with regard to controversial issues. As a result of this attitude, understandable in itself, the public all too easily gets a picture of the ecumenical movement (and the WCC as its instrument) which does not do full justice to activities and developments which by their very nature are bound to attract less attention than the controversial ones.

There is no reason to complain about this state of affairs. There is no reason for complacency either. On the one hand, a news editor cannot afford to ignore the interests of his audience — nor the existing or supposed lack of interest. On the other hand, the WCC must realize that an effort to communicate some of its more delicate and complicated concerns may very well be crowned with success, at least occasionally.

Interpreting the Ecumenical Movement

For some time the Communication Department has been struggling to provide a more adequate means of handling the necessary interpretation of the ecumenical movement and the work of the World Council of Churches, in order to make an understanding of the life and work of the ecumenical movement more accessible to the Member Churches and their congregations. This must include interpretation of what lies behind the decisions of the World Council and the provision of background information on the thinking that has led to particular actions. A comprehensive approach is required with regard to the World Council of Churches as a whole and also in the use of the various media.

How has the Department been able to meet this need? The next few pages give an account of the work which has been done over the past seven years, with particular attention given to the efforts toward comprehensiveness.

At the request of the Communication Committee, the Central Committee at Addis Ababa (1971) instructed the General Secretary to review the situation of WCC *Periodicals*. A staff group from the various programme units was established, with the Director of Communication as Chairman. Its discussions resulted chiefly in the clarification of the related but different functions of the existing journals: debate (*The Ecumenical Review*, *International Review of Mission*); provocation (RISK); documentation (*Study Encounter*). The one suggestion for major change in the existing situation was to prove divisive: namely that *The Ecumenical Review* and *International Review of Mission* should give way to a single quarterly journal of debate and scholarship which could range over the entire field of interest in the ecumenical movement as a whole. A letter circulated to all national councils and existing subscribers produced a limited and evenly divided response. Opinion within the Commission on World Mission and Evangelism, however, both before and at its Bangkok meeting, was largely hostile to the idea. The Central Committee in 1972 therefore resolved that while "looking forward to the time when a single quarterly can debate in a common context the varied aspects of the ecumenical movement, the separate identities" of the publications be "maintained for the time being"; and in 1973 it agreed that the report on the Council's programme of periodicals "be regarded as a working paper up to the Assembly in 1975"

Meanwhile the Central Committee agreed to establish a joint Editorial Office which would assume responsibility for *The Ecumenical Review* and *Study Encounter* together with any books the Council would publish; provide editorial advice and assistance to RISK and to any WCC Unit requesting its help; and coordinate all contacts with printers. This in turn involved the appointment of a Publications Manager with professional experience in publishing who would be responsible for sales and subscriptions, as well as contacts with publishers in several language areas. On the policy side, a staff coordinating group on periodicals was established with the Deputy General Secretary for Programme as its chairman, to allow representatives of all units to consult on overall plans and priorities.

The launching of the monthly magazine ONE WORLD was a major step towards an integrated, interpretative approach to WCC periodicals. Key concepts for the new magazine are a comprehensive presentation of the concerns of the ecumenical movement in which theological discussion and renewal questions are given a place alongside social action reports; a simple style which can enable insights and activities to be shared among a wider cross-section of the Council's constituency; an interpretation of key decisions and discussions, and space for the necessary controversies to emerge. Successor to the EPS *This Month*, ONE WORLD has the added advantage of providing in one place what has previously been found in a range of different materials addressed to diverse constituencies within the churches. ONE WORLD has been and will continue to be a forum where all the constituencies can come together for mutual exchange and benefit.

The review of periodicals launched in 1971 has therefore had some results. But the questions raised have by no means been fully resolved. The Assembly will need to pay some attention to the relative priorities of the communication media served by the Council's periodicals, to the balance of the various functions mentioned above, and especially to the ways in which these periodicals could be of more active help to the ecumenical efforts of the Member Churches.

In the field of book publishing, the period since 1968 has seen above all the taking of initiatives from the Council to interest publishers in different language areas in taking into their own lists the book manuscripts arising out of the Council's work. In Spanish, thanks to the appointment for several years by the Spanish Evangelical Church of a literature secretary, contact was made with a large number of publishers in Spain and Latin America. Some 20 books associated with the WCC were published as a result of these contacts, and a public was reached hitherto largely unaware of the ecumenical movement.

In German, numerous discussions with interested publishers in the Federal Republic and Switzerland eventually led to the founding in 1972 of a standing group of ecumenically interested publishers under the auspices of the Arbeitsgemeinschaft Christlicher Kirchen. This group includes almost all the leading religious publishers, Catholic and Protestant. At an annual meeting during the Frankfurt Book Fair information is given about forthcoming projects, publishers express their respective interest in these, and a small executive committee is elected to adjudicate where necessary. As a mechanism this is undoubtedly useful, but it does not cover the need for a more dynamic presentation of WCC projects to publishers who could, if interested, take an active share in shaping the manuscripts. The churches in the German Democratic Republic, through the Evangelische Verlagsanstalt Berlin, are also beginning to share in the publishing of some WCC manuscripts.

English, so dominant in the conference life of the WCC, has been a more difficult language for book publishing than German or Spanish. Contacts with publishers in Britain and the United States have revealed considerable interest in principle but very much less desire to accept actual manuscripts. Religious publishing is felt to be a difficult field on the whole, and World Council manuscripts signed by unfamiliar names, especially when they are symposia from conference reports, are regarded as particularly unsellable.

French is also far from easy. The Geneva Protestant firm, Labor & Fides, has continued to be a useful partner, and the Centre de Littérature Evangélique (CLE) in Cameroun has shown considerable interest— especially in any project that concerns Africa. Among the publishers in French there seems to be more openness among the larger general houses with religious sections in their lists than among the specialist religious publishers.

Contacts have also been pursued among Dutch, Italian and Scandinavian publishers ranging over the whole field of WCC interests, and with a number of Christian publishing houses in Africa and Asia with a view to projects of particular interest in their areas.

In the case of the more interesting conferences, the aim has been to concentrate less on having the "official report" published than on inviting a number of qualified authors to write books conveying the importance and the thrust of the subject in their own styles and for their own public; the desire is not so much to present publishers with a ready-made manuscript as to invite their active help in choosing the author and advising on the approach to be taken in order to reach a worthwhile book. These aims, if realized, would certainly result in much better communication than we usually get at present. But they are demanding: of publishers because not all houses are used to taking such initiatives, especially not the small religious houses, and not at the international level; and of the Council, not because every conference does not have enough fresh thinking or experience behind them to deserve a full book, but because the planning of the book has to be seen well ahead of time as an undertaking in its own right, not just as an adjunct of the conference.

A special undertaking of the Publications Office in these years deserves mention. In October 1972 an exhibition of books and journals of ecumenical interest in French was mounted in the Ecumenical Centre in Geneva, with the help of the Union d'Editeurs Français. A large and vivid display was accompanied by a programme of events, among which a lecture by Roger Garaudy and a guitar recital by Francis Bebey were special highlights. But the number of visitors and quantity of sales were seriously disappointing.

On the *radio* side, in 1970 a beginning towards an integrated approach was made with the regular production of a monthly interpretation service on tape, INTERVOX. It is a joint venture of the WCC, the Lutheran World Federation, the World Alliance of Reformed Churches and the World Association for Christian Communication. INTERVOX is issued in the three languages regularly used by the WCC and is carried by some hundred radio stations throughout the world. In 1974 the processing of the German edition of INTERVOX was changed by agreement with the Association of West German Radio Stations in order to speed up the transmission of material from Geneva to the FRG, and in order to broaden the service by offering raw material (unedited interviews, commentaries, etc.) for immediate use. Specializing in "signs of renewal" of the Church and in the Church's involvement in matters of society, justice and peace, an INTERVOX issue usually contains four or five items. Geographical balance is a matter of constant concern; an increasing number of correspondents abroad help to maintain ecumenical standards.

Ever since the regular production of radio programme elements in the

Ecumenical Centre started in 1966, the focus has been on their possible use by radio stations in those countries where the three regular WCC languages are understood. It was only occasionally that the limitation in finance and personnel allowed for attempts to reach the people in the context of their parish life. Much more could have been done in the way of informative or educational programmes on sound cassettes‡ to be used as discussion-starters, for example. Unfortunately, the staff and equipment available to the section is too limited to undertake this kind of cassette production on a larger scale. The experience gained with the two cassettes on the theme "Salvation Today" has confirmed the usefulness of such productions and at the same time has made it clear that a much bigger promotional effort is required. One must reckon with a further and accelerated development away from the traditional one-quarter inch tape towards the compact cassette, which is easier to store and to handle by the consumer. The question is whether the WCC can keep up with these developments.

The WCC's *sound archives* had to be organized while the "normal" work of the radio office went on. Hundreds of tapes—some of them dating from the years before the founding Assembly at Amsterdam—had to be processed (sometimes even to be identified), to be copied if the original had become too brittle, and to be indexed. This work is almost completed, and the archive is up to date.

In *television*, the department's main activity is advising and stimulating outside agencies. It is gratifying that so many television stations produce programmes—or programme elements—related to the ecumenical movement. The general tendency is away from colourful and folkloristic presentations of the movement, which characterized so many of these productions in the earlier days, and towards a concentration on the hard questions arising from the Church's social and political involvement. TV programmes produced over the last years have been numerous and have covered a wide range of ecumenical interest in the fields of development, inter-church aid, combatting racism, mission today, and international affairs in general. Although a number of productions, for instance in Europe with Eurovision, exceeded the boundaries of one area, the usual practice is that these programmes are shown once or twice in a particular geographical region and are not known to others. It is quite clear that the World Council of Churches is in an outstanding and central position where the information about programmes can be stored, and the possibility of sharing these programmes with other geographical areas can be provided. Thus it is foreseeable that the World Council will more and more take on the function of a data bank for religious and ecumenically related TV programmes. In order to develop this function and thus to render a more comprehensive service to individual TV producers, the Department clearly needs to make more use of the new types of equipment in the field of video-cassettes which have been developed over the last two years.

Another question regards the content of the point of view from which the respective TV programme is being produced. Naturally the number of actual co-productions is very limited, and the advisory capacity of the Department is largely in the area of selecting material and helping with ideas. As a result, one sometimes finds it difficult to recognize the "professional ecumenist's" viewpoint in the treatment of a particular programme. However, these programmes are quite often a way for the churches to be confronted with the way others look at them and so to be forced to take a fresh look at themselves and at questions and events, some of which the churches have not rethought in contemporary terms.

There has been a major change in attitudes to *film, the arts, and visual communication* in general within the Member Churches and beyond. The central place of the arts in the Uppsala Assembly was a major breakthrough. A large world meeting had never before included such an array of art, music, dance, theatre, photo shows, and especially modern films (features and shorts) in its programme. At Uppsala they were an integral and central part of the agenda. Some delegates were shocked by individual films, paintings or folksongs, but almost everyone was grateful for the exposure to what contemporary artists were saying about the Church and the world.

This interest has increased in the period since Uppsala, and it seems that we have come full circle from the early years of the Council, when there was opposition to such things as illustrations in booklets or styles of layout and modern graphics, and where there was a special suspicion about films and other visual and performing arts. The embarrassment now arises from the fact that planners of meetings are eager to have art shows, films, original music as replacements for some of the speeches and the "sacred" mimeographed papers. This dramatic change in attitude is welcome, but seldom is the desire to use new forms of non-verbal communication matched by the understanding that it takes a great deal of time, money and professional talent to produce them.

The past seven years have turned out to be increasingly "electronic" in their communication aspects. The Uppsala film "Behold All Things New", which had already focussed on the important role of non-written communication, was given the ecumenical award at the first International Christian Television Week in Monte Carlo, 1969. Several other WCC productions and co-productions have been recognized in international film and television festivals on more than fifty occasions. Prizes included the Human Rights Award "Film of the Year", London; best contribution to international communications, Hollywood, and so on. These awards served a very practical function, since they gave wide publicity at a time when there was virtually no money available for promotion of such programmes.

Advice to the Member Churches and secular groups has become a central part of the work of the Film and Visual Arts section. The head of this section serves on the Film and TV Council of UNESCO, with the WACC and on Interfilm, as well as participating in juries at major film festivals. There is now a strong group of church and secular film experts who share their information and cooperate closely with the World Council. This has become of the most useful functions of the Department. In many ways, this role is more useful and creative than direct involvement in the production of new films.

The *photo service* has continued to grow and become more specialized. Much of the distribution is now based on the monthly *Photo Oikoumene*, which serves as a continuing catalogue of pictures and is widely used.

Experiments with exhibitions such as the Corita Kent art show, which came to Geneva and parts of which were later sent across Europe and as far away as Australia, the photo exhibition on racism which was seen in many places, including the AACC Assembly in Lusaka, 1974, illustrate what could be done on a more regular basis if staff and funds were available. The Film and Visual Arts section of the Department has suffered from a major overload of work. Many requests to produce films from the Member Churches, UN agencies, and others, had to be turned down, even though they carried with them a production budget.

WCC Language Service was a title adopted a few years ago as a more adequate indication of the range of services provided by the group than the former title of "Translation Section". Now a sub-section of the Department of Communication, the Language Service exists to serve the WCC in the field of language. A small team of eleven provides a permanent translation service, organizes interpretation for conferences and meetings, promotes and helps to organize staff language courses and generally encourages a fuller awareness of the importance of languages at all levels of the ecumenical movement. It provides specialist advice on language problems both for WCC staff and outside enquirers.

The staff is also responsible for the Ecumenical Vocabulary published in view of the Nairobi Assembly. This is a service not only to the Geneva staff of the WCC but also to the Officers and decision-making bodies, as well as to a wide national, regional and international ecumenical public. It is intended as a useful and even indispensable working tool for all engaged in speaking, writing or translating ecumenical materials. Where so large a body of people is involved, using a variety of languages, some terminological reference point is needed if even a minimum of consistency and clarity is to be secured.

One of the most important new features of the Ecumenical Vocabulary is the inclusion of Spanish alongside the other three languages ordinarily in ecumenical use. The permanent staff is constantly engaged in collecting and noting changes in terminology with a view to further publications.

The Language Service has undergone a fundamental change in the working pattern and direction of the service, from a mainly pragmatic approach to one of action and reflection. The modern linguistic renaissance and the new horizons that this has opened up in the field of language had already prepared the way for this change by creating a new outlook among linguists. But it was not until the establishment of a WCC staff task force on language policy that conscious ecumenical reflection was focussed on the interconnection between ecumenism and language and on the role and style of the WCC as a language-using agency of a multilingual ecumenical constituency. (See Chapter Four, pages 204-205.) The Language Service has played its part in the work of the task force particularly with regard to practical experiments with language courses to help staff members to extend their language capacities.

In addition, first requests have come from one or two national and regional bodies for advice and help in establishing new patterns of language service.

The rejection of the mechanical, "black box" view of translation, in conjunction with the exacting demands made on translators in today's language explosion led the Language Service to arrange for a first experimental in-service training seminar where specialist translation problems were examined with the aid of an interdisciplinary team from Strasbourg University. This has since been repeated and has shown how vital it is, not only for the translators themselves but also for the ecumenical movement, that they keep abreast of the rapid developments in the scientific study of languages and draw on the special insights of linguists, sociologists and theologians.

Eugene Nida of the United Bible Societies has recently pointed out with reference to nations what is also true of ecumenical bodies: "nations must have some kind of linguistic unity if they are to succeed as living institutions, but this can be accomplished not by eliminating minority languages but by encouraging multilinguism". If ecumenism is to become a vital dimension at every level of church life, this direction must not be lost sight of. A multilingual ecumenical movement will need its linguists in the future. The problems of communication in a multilingual movement will always be in part linguistic problems. The organization of solutions to these problems will not be possible from Geneva alone, but neither will it be possible without focussed reflection and action for the purpose of stimulating awareness and experiment at regional and national levels and also listening to and profiting from the linguistic discoveries now being made in many places throughout the world.

Identifying Priorities

In looking ahead and trying to identify priorities for the Department of Communication one has to strike a balance between three factors: dreaming out loud; evaluating present and future limitations in personnel and finances realistically; and projecting past experiences. For the Department of Communication the combination of these three factors seems to focus priorities in two areas:

First, a sustained and enabling contact with communicators in the mass media. The Uppsala Assembly produced a report on the churches and the mass media, calling upon the churches for a better understanding of and involvement in the structures of mass communication. Little or nothing was done to implement the specific recommendations of that paper although at the time it was widely acclaimed, often quoted and favourably compared with the Second Vatican Council document on the same subject. Some of these recommendations still express priority concerns on at least two points: (a) the need for an increased familiarity of mass communicators with the ecumenical movement and the WCC; and (b) the need for closer contacts and cooperation among mass communicators from various parts of the world in the field of what is usually called "religious" communication. For the period after the Nairobi Assembly both of these concerns need to find a place·in the programme and budget of the Communication Department. Close cooperation and a workable division of labour with the World Association for Christian Communication (WACC) goes without saying.

The second set of priorities is in the field of intensified communication with and among the Member Churches of the WCC. General Secretary Philip Potter indicated this in his report to the Central Committee at Geneva in 1973 when he said: "We need to give far more urgent and sustained attention to the ways in which the World Council can become an organ of communication between the churches as they seek to fulfill their common calling".· As the World Council is a fellowship of churches, and as churches all over the world are more and more ready to express their desire to communicate with others by appointing   part-time or full-time staff to do this, intense cooperation and collaboration with church communicators on the part of the WCC becomes a "must". Small beginnings made by involving consultants from this part of the WCC constituency in the work of the well-functioning Departmental Committee need to be built up and widened. New forms of consultation, particularly in view of specific programmes of the WCC, need developing. In this context communication with churches in Africa, Asia and Latin America requires special emphasis and attention. The whole problem of developing non-elitist and indigenous communication systems is intimately linked with the fact that in these regions knowledge about the ecumenical movement and churches in other parts of the world is often fragmentary, superficial or even erroneous. The WCC and its Department of Communication will have to contribute their share in the task. Community among 271 churches rests with the ability of their Council to communicate.

6

finance and central services

The Disturbing Financial Picture

Reporting on the finances of the World Council of Churches during the period since 1968 is to paint a picture of continuous, cumulative, growing difficulties and problems. This is, of course, merely a reflection of what many of the Member Churches themselves have undergone. It has been possible to meet these problems and to carry the work forward to the present date. But to an important degree this has been achieved by taking certain emergency measures and by securing special non-recurring contributions. The Member Churches have demonstrated their commitment to fellowship in the World Council by trying to increase their financial support and to make special contributions. But at the moment it is difficult to make confident forecasts for the period following the Fifth Assembly in Nairobi. The programme of the World Council and its effectiveness will depend on the priority which the Member Churches place on ecumenical work and the extent to which they are willing and able to provide the financial support needed for that programme.

Progress has been made in seeking (to quote the phrase used at the 1973 Central Committee meeting) to express "the oneness of the World Council in its financial procedures". For a long time—and for reasons which will become clear later on in this chapter—the Central Committee has felt that the organizational unity of the WCC should be reflected in unified methods of financial cultivation and shared responsibility for expenses.

However, it still remains necessary to speak separately about the various budgets, each with its own separate and designated financial support, under which the operations of the World Council are conducted. It was already clear at Uppsala, and stated in the report of the Financial Committee to the Assembly, that difficulties must be foreseen in the financing of operations under the General Budget in the succeeding years. Since 1971, the difficulties have become widespread, and they arise in respect of all other budgets as well: those of the Commission on World Mission and Evangelism, the Commission on Inter-Church Aid, Refugee and World Service, the Office of Education, the Programme to Combat Racism and the Commission on the Churches' Participation in Development.

There are three main problems which (although they are closely inter-related) must be considered separately: inflation; the world monetary crisis; and the financial difficulties of the Member Churches themselves.

Inflation

Most Member Churches know from their own experience the difficulties presented by the high rates of inflation in the present period. In the early years of the life of the World Council, the annual rise in expenses, by reason of inflation, was so small that operations could be maintained without asking for increased contributions each year. This has progressively ceased to be true and is now entirely impossible.

Since the founding of the WCC in 1948, the increase in the cost of living index in Switzerland has been as follows:

5 years	1948/53	4.6%
5 years	1953/58	7.6%
5 years	1958/63	10.7%
5 years	1963/68	18.4%
5 years	1968/73	31.1%

But the increase year by year over the last eight years has been as follows:

1967	3.5%
1968	2.2%
1969	2.3%
1970	5.4%
1971	6.6%
1972	6.9%
1973	11.9%
1974	7.6%

To illustrate the problem in another way, the total General Budget expenditure in 1968 was a little more than Swiss Francs 4,600,000. Inflation between January 1968 and January 1974 was 37.6%. Thus, to carry out the same activities in 1974 would— merely because of increase expense caused by inflation—involve expenditure of about Swiss Francs 6,330,000.

only the first major development. Whereas there were fixed rates of ex-

The World Monetary Crisis

The second major problem is the decline in the value of many currencies in terms of Swiss Francs as a result of the continuing world monetary crisis. For the World Council, this problem first became acute from May 9, 1971, when the Swiss Franc was revalued by 7%. That was, however, only the first major development. Wheras there were fixed rates of exchange between all major currencies until 1971, that system collapsed and most exchange rates are now left free to fluctuate in response to market and other influences. This development has had three major consequences for the World Council: the value of contributions from the Member Chruches and their agencies expressed in terms of Swiss Franc value has declined substantially; it has become extremely difficult to present financial forecasts for coming years; and it has become necessary to revise the financial and accounting procedures of the World Council to meet the new situation.

The contributions of the Member Churches to the General Budget in 1973 produced, in total, Swiss Francs 4,918,137. At the rates of exchange effective in September 1974, the same contributions would produce Swiss Francs 4,785,458; at the rate of exchange applicable in 1968, the same contributions would have produced Swiss Francs 5,758,532. Thus the 1973 contributions would have produced nearly Swiss Francs 1,000,000 (or about 20%) more at the rates of exchange applicable in 1968 than they would have produced at the rates of exchange applicable in September 1974.

The Financial Problems of the Member Churches Themselves

The problem of the increasing rate of inflation is common to most countries and many Member Churches are finding that their income, even if it is not declining, is not increasing sufficiently to compensate the effects of inflation. It is therefore encouraging to be able to report that, in spite of their own problems, the Member Churches have increased their contributions to the General Budget. Member Churches which have made since the Uppsala Assembly the minimum requested increases in contributions to the General Budget, have increased their contributions by at least two-thirds between 1968 and 1973. In terms of their own currencies, the Member Churches in all countries other than the Federal Republic of Germany and the United States of America have increased their contributions by 69%. The Evangelical Church in Germany. has generously increased her contribution by a greater percentage. The Member Churches in the USA, which bore the preponderant share in financing the work for the first twenty years of the life of the World Council, have themselves experienced financial problems in recent years. Their contributions to the General Budget in 1968 amounted to $ 582,833. Their contributions in 1973, including some late payments received after the 1973 books were closed, amounted to $ 699,356. Those figures show an increase in terms of US Dollars of 20%. The picture is, however, very different in terms of Swiss Francs. At the rate of exchange then applicable, the 1968 contribution represented Swiss Francs 2,494,523. By reason of the decline of the value of the Dollar, the 1973 contributions represent Swiss Francs

2,137,756. Thus, in terms of Swiss Franc value, the US contributions show a decline of Swiss Francs 356,767, or more than 14%.

The Difficulty of Presenting Summarized Financial Statements

In past periods, financial developments have been illustrated by summary tables showing total income and expenditure year by year under each budget. There are a number of reasons why it is not feasible to do this for the period since 1968. The increase in costs by reason of inflation distorts any comparisons. The content and presentation of budgets has been modified during the period: responsibility for some expenses previously included in the General Budget has been accepted by other budgets; some expenses previously borne by the Service Programme Budget of CICARWS have been transferred to the Project List and support sought on a project basis; some expenses previously carried by CWME—Programme Askings have been transferred to CWME —Operating Budget; and so forth. Changing and fluctuating rates of exchange distort any presentations of total operations in terms of one currency. From the inauguration of the World Council in 1948 until 1971, the rate of exchange between the US Dollar and the Swiss Franc remained unchanged at $1 = Sw. Fr. 4.28. Financial presentations were therefore normally made in terms of US Dollars, using that fixed rate of exchange. To meet the problems arising from the world monetary crisis, it was decided in 1971:

(a) that for operations—mainly headquarters administration—involving expenditure predominantly in Switzerland, the Swiss Franc should be taken as the basic currency; and

(b) that for other operations—such as CICARWS/CWME Project List, the specialized funds (TEF, EDF, ACLD), etc.—the US Dollar should be taken as the basic currency.

Experience has shown that those decisions were wise and necessary. One consequence is, however, that—not because of any action by the World Council but by reason of the world monetary crisis—the presentation of summarized statements of figures year by year becomes virtually meaningless and could cause mis-interpretation. In the presentations which follow and which indicate developments under each of the budgets during the past period, the story is told in words and not in the form of tabular statements.

A.   The General Budget

At the Uppsala Assembly in 1968, the Finance Committee stated flatly that the maintenance of operations under the General Budget "calls for the earnest attention of all Assembly participants". Indeed it was disclosed that expenditure in the three years 1966/68 was expected to exceed normal income by about Sw. Fr. 1,450,000 and that this problem had been overcome only by omitting allocations to reserves for three years (about Sw. Fr. 640,000); by securing special contributions of about Sw. Fr. 600,000; and by using a surplus brought forward from preceding years. The Finance Committee reported that, in the period following the Uppsala Assembly, "resources adequate for the financing of the work will not be available unless there is a considerable increase in total Member Church contributions".

The General Budget covers the expenses of Central and Executive Committee meetings; allocations to a reserve for the expenses of Assemblies; the operations of the General Secretariat, and of the sub-units on Faith and Order, Church and Society, Renewal and Renewal movements, Laity and Adult Education and the Ecumenical Institute; half the expenses of the New York Office, a major part of the expenses of the Commission on International Affairs and the Communications Department; and a part of the expenses of the sub-unit on Dialogue with People of Living Faiths and Ideologies, the Secretariat of the Programme to Combat Racism, the Portfolio for Biblical Studies, the Library and the Department of Finance and Central Services. It is financed by the basic contributions of the Member Churches.

It has already been mentioned that, especially in terms of their own currencies, Member Churches have continued to demonstrate their commitment by increasing their contributions. Nonetheless, in the years since Uppsala, activities of the highest priority have been maintained only by undertaking a series of emergency measures: special contributions have been secured; economies have been sought at all points and staff and programme have been held down or reduced; and expenditure has been closely reviewed to examine whether some expenses previously borne by the General Budget could legitimately be transferred to or be shared by other budgets; and, where it was found that this could be done, appropriate transfers have been made.

In the eight years 1968/75, total General Budget expenditure will have been about Sw. Fr. 48,000,000 (an average of about Sw. Fr. 6,000,000 per year). Normal income in the same period will have been about Sw. Fr. 42,000,000. Expenditure has thus been financed to the extent of about Sw. Fr. 6,000,000— or around 12.5%—from special gifts. The major special contributions have been: about Sw. Fr. 1,700,000 from Member Churches mainly in the USA and the Federal Republic of Germany for the travel expenses of participants, mainly from the Third World, to meetings of the Central and Executive Committees, the Unit Committees, and the like; about Sw. Fr. 1,800,000 as special allocations from the Evangelical Church in Germany; about Sw. Fr. 350,000 from the Landskirchen in Germany to compensate the revaluation of the Swiss Franc; about Sw. Fr. 405,000 from individuals in the USA in response to an appeal by the General Secretary; about Sw. Fr. 600,000 as a special grant from the Russian Orthodox Church; and about Sw. Fr. 300,000 in special transfers from CICARWS. Hearty thanks are due, and have been expressed, to those who by such gifts have helped to make it possible to carry forward the work in this period. Recent economic developments and the problems faced by the Member Churches at this time do, however, unfortunately suggest that it is unlikely that comparable special contributions can be secured in the years that lie ahead.

Throughout the period under review, maximum endeavours have been made to exercise economy at all points. *Ad hoc* measures, such as the decision to transfer the Central Committee meeting in 1972 from Helsinki to Geneva, have been taken. Staff has been reduced in some areas, for example the staff of the New York Office and in what is now the Unit on Education and Renewal. On the other hand, the Central Committee has found that in order to carry out its mandate, strengthening of staff was necessary at some points, for example, General Secretariat, and Communication Department; and there has been added to the General Budget a participation in the expenses of the Secretariat of the Programme to Combat Racism, and in the expenses of the sub-unit on Dialogue with People of Living Faiths and Ideologies.

Some expenses previously borne by the General Budget have been transferred to or are now shared by other budgets: for example, CICARWS and CWME now contribute towards the costs of Central and Executive Committee meetings; other budgets and other organizations with offices in the Ecumenical Centre now contribute to the costs of the Library; a major part of the expense of the Secretariat on Dialogue with People of Living Faiths and Ideologies is now borne by CWME. It has been found possible to secure annual contributions of about Sw. Frs. 175,000 towards the expenses of the Ecumenical Institute, reducing the expense falling on the General Budget. Expense has been further eased by securing seconded staff to fill some positions, notably a position on the Secretariat on Faith and Order, a position generally related to the work of the Unit on Faith and Witness, and the position of one member of the teaching staff of the Ecumenical Institute. The position of a second member of the teaching staff of the Ecumenical Institute is financed by a grant from a foundation.

It is for these reasons that a report on General Budget operations 1968/75 can be summed up in three seemingly contradictory statements: normal income has not been sufficient to maintain the authorized programme and activities under the General Budget; economies, restraints on programmes and reductions in staff have been found necessary, but nonetheless the basic programme and activities have been maintained; and there is now a reasonable prospect that operations can be financed to the end of 1975.

The Nairobi Assembly and the Member Churches by their own actions after the Assembly will have to decide whether the degree of priority given by them to the work which they carry out together as a fellowship of churches in the World Council of Churches is such that they will increase their contributions to a level sufficient to finance the carrying forward of the agreed programme of work which falls under the General Budget.

In the light of these facts, the Central Committee adopted the following resolutions at its meeting in 1974:

"(a) that all Member Churches be urged to take any possible action to increase their contributions to the General Budget in 1974 and 1975;

"(b) noting that there are still some Member Churches which make no contribution or which make an unreasonably small contribution, that all such Member Churches be urged to take speedy action to correct this situation;

"(c) that the Member Churches in the USA be asked to seek to raise by one-third from the level of their 1973 contributions the total of the US support for the General Budget for 1976;

"(d) that the Member Churches in Germany be asked to seek to raise their contribution for 1976 by one-third from the 1973 level; and

"(e) that the request to the Member Churches in all other countries from the Central Committee in 1973 to seek to raise their contributions for 1976 by at least 50% from the level of their 1973 contributions be confirmed."

Income adequate to finance General Budget operations will not be assured unless resolution (b), above, is taken seriously by many Member Churches; those few Member Churches which still make no contribution accept the responsibility to contribute in the future; and many Member Churches agree to make a greater increase than the minimum increase of 50% suggested in resolution (e).

When adopting the above resolutions, the Central Committee recognized that the Member Churches in the USA have, from the constitution of the World Council until very recently, been called on to provide an unreasonably high proportion of the total financial support for the General Budget. Furthermore, in the last few years, the contributions of the Evangelical Church in Germany have risen to an unduly high proportion. It is for that reason that the Central Committee called upon the Member Churches in the USA and in Germany to seek to raise their contributions by one-third and upon the Member Churches in all other countries to seek to raise their contributions by at least 50%. If all Member Churches respond to those requests, it would still be true that the sharing of financial responsibility would be roughly as follows: Member Churches in the USA 37.5%; the Evangelical Church in Germany 35%; and all other Member Churches 27.5%.

In addition to the resolutions mentioned, the Central Committee further resolved "that all Member Churches be requested, in the period following the Fifth Assembly, to plan for an annual increase in contribution sufficient to compensate the effects of inflation and maintain the real value of their support". This resolution is a "sign of the times".

B. Programme Projects

Early in the life of the World Council, it was found that a number of Member Churches and their agencies could make special contributions—in addition to their basic support—towards particular programmes and activities. Procedures were therefore developed for the seeking of resources for "Programme Projects". Those procedures have been continued in the period since the Uppsala Assembly, and considerable supplementary support has been received. Indeed, the provisions for programme within the General Budget in respect of the sub-units financed under that budget are completely inadequate, and the work of those sub-units is made effective only by those additional resources obtained under programme project procedures. The study on the Future of Man and Society in a World of Science-Based Technology and the world conference on that subject which took place in Bucharest; the Berlin Conference on Sexism in the 1970's; all of the work in the field of Family Education; the efforts of the Joint Working Group of the World Council and the Roman Catholic Church, and other joint activities with Roman Catholics; the study on Violence, Non-violence and the Struggle for Social Justice; all of the Humanum Studies; and various smaller programmes and consultations have been financed outside the basic budgets through resources secured in this way.

C. Commission on Inter-Church Aid,
Refugee and World Service

The financial operaitons of CICARWS can be divided generally into four categories: the Service Programme—those activites which the churches have agreed should be conducted centrally by the Commission itself; the Service to Refugees—the largest single item within the Service Programme; the CICARWS/CWME Project List—a submission to the churches and their agencies of the projects of the churches around the world for which support is needed; and emergency appeals for help to the victims of natural and man-made disasters and for rehabilitation programmes after those disasters.

Service Programme

As with the General Budget of the World Council, inflation and the world monetary crisis have given rise to serious problems for the Service Programme Budget of CICARWS. Particularly in 1972/73, normal income was inadequate to cover needs. Economies and adjustments were made. Some staff positions were eliminated (such as the Secretary for Literature and Health). Some items were taken out of the Service Programme, and support for them is now sought on a project basis (the rest centre at Casa Locarno is one example). Some agencies made special contributions of a non-recurring nature to help to meet the immediate crisis and permit the work to be carried forward. The complications arising from exchange rates are clearly illustrated by the figures for the Service Programme. Service Programme income in 1968 was $1,630,625 or Sw. Frs. 6,979,075, and $2,308,200 or Sw. Frs. 7,252,226 in 1973. Thus there was an increase in income of about 41.5% in terms of US Dollars but an increase of only 3.9%—far from adequate to cover inflation—in terms of Swiss Francs. Since a substantial part of the Service Programme expenditure is in Swiss Francs or in currencies which have moved with the Swiss Franc rather than the US Dollar, this means that, especially when inflation is taken into account, the resources available for Service Programme activities in 1973 were less than in 1968.

Service to Refugees

As reported in Chapter Three, the emphasis in the work of the Service to Refugees has been changing over the past few years. The traditional resettlement activity continues but has declined, and the decentralized work for refugees (as in the Middle East and Africa) has grown. The expenditure for the field offices engaged in resettlement was $671,965 in 1968 and $698,918 in 1973; with inflation and the reduced value of the US Dollar, the figures actually reflect a reduction in this activity. The allocation of Service Programme resources for the Service to Refugees remained around $500,000—525,000 per year in the years 1968/73. In the 1974 Service Programme Budget, it was necessary to raise the allocation to Service to Refugees to $725,000. There is, in addition, special income from intergovernmental and governmental agencies to complete the financing of the total budget, which includes the expense of the Administration and Resettlement Office in Geneva.

Project List

The resources handled under the Project List have grown in US currency figures from about $7,500,000 in 1968 to about $13,000,000 in 1973. No commitments are entered into in excess of resources received or reasonably assured. This activity does not give rise to budgetary problems, but the increased volume does, of course, create an increased work-load for the Geneva administration.

Emergency Appeals

There has been a considerable growth in this activity over the period. The resources handled rose from less than $3,000,000 in 1968 to over $10,000,000 per year in 1972 and 1973. There were large programmes for the Nigeria emergency in 1970/71 and for Bangladesh in 1972/73. Here again expenditure is limited to the resources available and, as with project activities, the activities in respect of emergency appeals give rise to no budgetary problems but do increase the amount of work in the Geneva headquarters.

In General

Here again, the picture can be summed up in a few seemingly contradictory statements: there has been a significant growth in the resources available both for project activities and for emergency programmes; the programme and activities under the Service Programme have been carried forward; normal income has not been adequate for the maintenance of Service Programme activities, and there have been some staff reductions; some activities have been transferred from Service Programme support to project support; economies have been sought at all points; and special non-recurring supplementary contributions have been secured. The continuance of the work does, however, depend on the willingness of the Member Churches and their agencies to increase their support and, in particular, to make regular annual increases adequate to compensate the effects of inflation.

D. Commission on World Mission and Evangelism

Operating Budget

The CWME has two separate but interrelated patterns of financing: the Operating Buget; and Programme Askings. In addtion there are separate budgets for the three sponsored agencies: Theological Education Fund; Agency for Christian Literature Development; and Christian Medical Commission. An indication of the order of magnitude of the operations is given by the following figures for total contributions received in 1973:

Operating Budget	Sw. Fr.	912,408
Programme Askings	Sw. Fr.	2,288,714
TEF		$410,869
ACLD		$456,874
CMC	Sw. Fr.	1,403,669

The Operating Budget includes the basic administrative costs and salaries of the Commission, and the main source of support is the contribution income from affiliated councils. Normal income was sufficient to cover the budget in the three years 1968/70, but, as with other budgets, financial difficulties began with the year 1971. Contribution income from affiliated councils is at present insufficient to cover the total Operating Budget but the Commission has agreed that if support for the Operating Budget is insufficient to cover total expenses, resources can be transferred from "Programme Askings—Undesignated" (see the next paragraph) to cover any shortfall. The Commission does not, however, consider this to be a sound solution The Operating Budget should be financed by the contributions of the affiliated councils, and there is need for a substantial increase in those contributions if this is to be achieved.

Programme Askings

The procedure for seeking resources under "Programme Askings" was initiated before the Uppsala Assembly in recognition of the fact that mission boards, societies, and the like, were willing to provide additional resources for particular programmes and activities. Funds have been made available for a variety of programmes in different parts of the world through these procedures. Furthermore, the total amount received in response to Programme Askings has grown considerably over the years. The detailed list of items to be included in Programme Askings is reviewed regularly by the Commission and includes programmes related to CWME, some aspects of the work of other Units of the World Council which are of direct concern to CWME, and the programmes and activities of others, notably Regional Councils. Support is received both in designated contributions for particular items in the list and in undesignated contributions. The activities under Programme Askings are conducted in a manner which ensures that expenses and commitments are not entered into in excess of assured resources.

The three sponsored agencies—TEF, ACLD and CMC—operate

under separate budgets. The Central Committee, on recommendation from CWME, appoints a representative committee of specialists for each agency, which is responsible for planning the work of the agency and for keeping activities within the limits of finances available.

E. Commission on the Churches' Participation in Development

This Commission was established in 1970 in response to the new emphasis given to the development concern at the Uppsala Assembly and on the basis of a recommendation from the Montreux Consultation on Development held earlier that year. At the same time, Member Churches and agencies were asked to contribute to the newly established Ecumenical Development Fund, from which this work is financed. During the initial period, attention was concentrated on establishing guidelines for the action of the churches and the World Council, and on securing support for the activities planned; expenses were relatively low, but income was nonetheless inadequate to cover them, and a moderate deficit was accumulated. The work then developed, and support grew. In 1973, expenses totalled $1,820,987, and a balance of $712,191 was carried forward to 1974 on the Ecumenical Development Fund. Support was, however, somewhat unbalanced, with an unduly high proportion coming from the Federal Republic of Germany. The approved budget for 1975 comprises expenditure of Sw. Frs. 1,781,100 and international operations totalling $2,010,500, and, while it is hoped that the FRG support will be maintained, strenuous efforts are being made to secure increased support for the Ecumenical Development Fund from other countries as well.

CCPD has, among other things, studied the possibility of assisting the Member Churches to participate in development by using for development goals some of the capital resources under their management. On the basis of recommendations developed by this study, the Central Committee in August 1974 decided to approve a plan for the establishment of an Ecumenical Development Cooperative Society, once the minimum initial resources needed (Sw. Fr. 15,000,000 or about $5,000,000) are assured. The Central Committee affirmed its conviction that the proposed society "has the potential to be an effective instrument for the promotion of justice and development among the poor communities of the world and a proper means of redeploying a part of the investment resources of the churches". The Central Committee further decided that the World Council shall become a founding member of the society. Work is in process towards gaining assurance of adequate initial support, so as to proceed as rapidly as possible to the establishment of the society, which will be an independent legal entity but related to the World Council.

F. Office of Education

The Uppsala Assembly gave general approval to the establishment of this office with the understanding that it would be "financed apart from the General Budget". The importance of this office was increased when, in 1971, a plan for the integration of the World Council of Christian Education with the World Council of Churches was adopted and implemented.

While plans were being developed for the integration of the World Council of Christian Education with the World Council of Churches, the two bodies established the Education Renewal Fund (ERF) which was designed to give assistance to educational projects of study, experimentation and change. During its mandate, 1970/73, more than 70 projects totalling over $1,000,000 were supported by various church agencies which responded to requests that were presented through ERF.

The decision to create a separate budget for the Office of Education was based on the conviction that agencies within the churches—education agencies in particular—would be willing and able to contribute to the support of the work. It was also anticipated that, following integration, the income preciously received by WCCE would continue and would represent a further source of support. Contributions to the budget of the Office of Education have in fact been received—particularly from North America—and there is continuing income from WCCE sources, though smaller in amount than had been hoped. It has, however, not yet been found possible to build up a regular and reasonably assured annual flow of contributions from a representative range of Member Churches adequate to support the budget Special contributions have been secured to complete the financing of the budget, which for 1974 amounts to Sw. Fr. 559,850. There is reasonable assurance that enough income will be received to cover all' expenses to the end of 1974. Endeavours to secure adequate continuing support for this budget continue, and the matter will need to be reviewed again at the Fifth Assembly.

G. Composite Statement of Needs

It will be clear from the foregoing sections of this chapter that the World Council does not operate on the basis of one budget but of a number of budgets, each with its own flow of designated support. The need for this range of separate budgets arises from the need to relate to internal structures of the Member Churches themselves; agencies within the churches contribute to the work in designated fields of activity—such as relief,

236

inter-church aid, or mission—but cannot make undesignated contributions towards supporting the World Council in general.

The problem of seeking ways in which the oneness of the World Council can be expressed in its financial procedures has been discussed and examined regularly during the period under review, as has already been pointed out. The Structure Committee, in reporting to the Central Committee in January 1971, proposed adopting the procedure of presenting one composite statement of needs covering all activities for which financial support is to be sought. It did not prove easy to devise a form of presentation which was helpful or easily understood. The two composite statements issued in April 1972 and April 1973 were found to be of limited usefulness. A revised and simpler form of presentation was submitted to the Central Committee in August 1974 covering needs for 1974 and 1975. A Composite Statement of Needs for 1975 and 1976 in the revised form, or in a still further improved form, will be laid before the Assembly.

H. Ecumenical Centre Properties

It was reported to the Uppsala Assembly that Sw. Fr. 5,000,000 had been borrowed to finance the purchase of the property adjoining the Ecumenical Centre as a protection against possible future needs. The Assembly gave authority for gifts to be sought to pay off the loan, so that the World Council might become effective owner of the property. Endeavours to secure gifts for this project or to establish a fund-raising campaign were unsuccessful, and it became necessary to recognize that the period was not a good one in which to raise a large capital fund for such a purpose. By reason of the rise in property values, it was found possible to retain 10,000 square metres of the property (2.47 acres) and to sell the remainder for a price sufficient to repay the loan, cover all expenses (mainly interest) and leave a cash profit of Sw. Fr. 729,328. Sincere gratitude is due, and has been expressed, to the three Member Churches which guaranteed the loan and also generously renounced the shares to which they were entitled in the cash profit.

There has been no need to enlarge the Ecumenical Centre properties during the period but it has been necessary to use 21 offices in a building on the adjoining property already referred to. It has been possible to negotiate the continuing use of those offices, following the sale, for the three years to the end of 1976, and further extension of the period may be possible. But if and when it is necessary to vacate that building, a major problem is to be anticipated. Extension of headquarters properties will be necessary, and resources are not available to finance such an undertaking.

I. Ecumenical Institute Properties

Transformation work was carried out on one of the properties—Petit Bossey—at a total cost of Sw. Fr. 438,930. Nearly half of the cost was covered by an unexpected legacy in favour of the Ecumenical Institute. The remainder of the cost was covered by taking a mortgage loan of Sw. Fr. 230, 000 on the Institute's properties. The annual interest and amortization costs are borne by the budget of the Institute.

J. Reserves

The World Council has, throughout its existence, operated with only minimal reserves. At December 31, 1973, the balances in reserves available to support normal operations in the event of unforeseen problems were

General Reserve	Sw. Fr. 1,227,320
CWME Working Capital Fund	476,577
Office of Education—	
Unrestricted Capital Fund	142,203
CICARWS—Service Programme Reserve	3,550,409

The balances represent six weeks' to three months' expenditure at present levels under the related budgets for the first three reserves and about five months' expenditure in the case of CICARWS. Furthermore, following a decision taken in 1967, the resources in the above reserves are placed in investment portfolios under professional management; there was a further decline in the value of World Council investment portfolios over the first nine months of 1974—as is true of virtually all investment portfolios at this time—and the reserves have been further eroded.

In the case of the General Reserve against emergency needs in General Budget operations, the record is as follows: after the Amsterdam Assembly in 1948, the World Council started with a balance of about Sw. Fr. 21,000 in this reserve; by annual allocations, it was built up to about Sw. Fr. 1,147, 000 (or the equivalent of four to five months' expenditure under the General Budget) at the end of 1961; annual allocations have been continued, except for the three years 1966/68, when they were omitted because of the inadequacy of income to finance normal operations; exchange losses because the reserve is to an important degree invested in US Dollars and losses because the decline in the market value of shares has cancelled out most of the allocations to the reserve since 1961; inflation has caused a growth in the Swiss Franc amount of annual expenditure under the General Budget. As a result, the General Reserve is substantially lower, when expressed as a percentage of annual General Budget expenditure, in 1974 than it was in 1961.

There is a further reserve in respect of the Office of Education, the Restricted Capital Fund (at December 31, 1973 Sw. Fr. 507,889), but there is a requirement that its capital be kept intact. The income is used for the normal operating budget of the Office of Education.

K. Provident and Retirement Funds

Operations have continued normally under the Provident and Retirement Funds, which are independent legal entities, constituted as foundations under Swiss law. There is, however, need to mention two significant developments. It has been decided by referendum in Switzerland that the provision of retirement rights by employers shall be made obligatory, and legislation to that effect is now being drafted. When the new legislation is available, it will be necessary to restructure the foundations to meet the new legal requirements. Secondly, the actuarial soundness of all retirement schemes is being adversely affected at this time by the high rate of inflation—a rate of inflation higher than the return which can be earned on invested capital. Either or both of these factors may make it necessary to consider increasing the percentage of salary contributed to the Retirement Fund, in order to ensure that it is actuarially sound.

The Work of the Department of Finances and Central Services

There have been significant changes in the work of the Department during the period—some with a view to improved performance and some in response to outside developments. For a while—particularly in 1973—the accounting records fell into arrears, with inconvenience to all concerned, by reason of the additional work-load arising from the world monetary crisis. Those arrears have now been largely over-taken.

One major development during the period was the initiation and development of an Electronic Data Processing Section to handle accounting and other work by computer. Recognizing that this was "the way of the future", expert outside help was secured to examine whether the volume of work was sufficient to justify such a step and, after a positive report has been received, to advise in choosing the most appropriate equipment.

Staff were engaged to prepare systems, equipment was hired and the handling of accounting records by computer started on January 1, 1971. Other uses—CICARWS project records, salaries and publications subscriptions lists (billing and mailing)—were then introduced. After satisfactory initial experience and further study of the economics of the operation, it was decided in June 1972 to purchase the computer on terms under which most of the rent paid in the initial period was treated as partial payment of the purchase price. CICARWS, recognizing that the need for a computer arose primarily from the volume of operation and the imformation needs of that Commission, generously provided the resources to finance both the studies and the initial preparatory costs as well as the purchase cost of the computer.

It was bad luck that the new system for handling accounting records—based on fixed rates of exchange—was developed just before the world monetary system—also based on fixed exchange rates—began to collapse in 1971. When the collapse began, various interim measures were adopted to

239

meet the resulting problems, but it was finally necessary to decide that from January 1, 1973, operations must be conducted on the basis of daily market exchange rates. The year 1973 was particularly difficult, since time was needed to develop new appropriate computer systems. Revised systems which greatly facilitate the handling of this difficult problem took effect on January 1, 1974.

The collapse of the world monetary system has, of course, also greatly increased the work load of the Treasury Section. Daily listings of market exchange rates are issued. Conversion calculations at the appropriate rate must be made for all transactions involving two currencies. And the task of managing a Revolving Portfolio of liquid resources totalling at all times about $ 20 Million is nerve-wracking. It is necessary to follow the development of the world monetary situation from day to day, to seek expert advice at frequent intervals and to make decisions as to where and in what currencies funds shall be held. These tasks are added to the normal routine responsibilities of keeping records of all resources, effecting all payments which the World Council wishes to make by remittances to almost all parts of the world, and ensuring that funds are immediately available when large payments are requested without prior notice but also that balances on current account are kept at acceptable levels and that, as far as possible, liquid resources are placed in interest-earning time deposits.

The other elements of the Department's work have gone forward without such significant and time-consuming changes. Following the retirement of the Business Manager in 1973, Administrative Services and Business Management were combined in one section. The Central Services Section carries responsibility for purchasing, shipping and insurance and for providing central services for office supplies and equipment, mail, telephone and telex, duplicating and offset printing—with offset gradually replacing stencil duplication—and the cleaning and maintenance of buildings and grounds. The same section is responsible for the organizing of the larger meetings—a heavy responsibility when such meetings are as numerous as in 1974—for the reception and visitors' services, and for relations with travel agents and the cafeteria management. The Payroll Section is responsible for the payment of salaries and for all questions related to salary deductions—relations with tax and social security authorities, with the health insurance company and with other retirement funds—for the payment of rent on apartments leased by the World Council, for confidential cash records, and for the administration of the Provident and Retirement Funds.

In accordance with the proposals of the Structure Committee, accepted by the Central Committee in January 1971, a Staff Finance Coordinating Group was established with a representative from the General Secretariat, the Finance Officers of the three Programme Units and of the Ecumenical Institute, and senior staff from the Department. This group is responsible for the compilation of the budget from the needs as reported by the Programme Units and other sub-sections within the structure and for the discussion of all problems related to the financial operations of the World Council. The Composite Statement of Needs, mentioned above, was developed by the work of the Staff Finance Coordinating Group, which has proved a most valuable addition to the administrative structures of the World Council and for the work of the Department. A study of the operations of the Department was made by outside experts at the end of 1973, and a review and (where appropriate) modification of the pattern of work in the light of that report is in process. Responsibility for relations with the Member Churches regarding support for the General Budget, which until 1974 was carried by the Director of the Department, has now mostly been transferred to the General Secretariat.

Conclusions (without Predictions)

The activities of the World Council have continued in the period since the Uppsala Assembly in 1968. New responsibilities have been accepted and carried, notably the Office of Education, the sub-unit on Dialogue with People of Living Faiths and Ideologies, the Programme to Combat Racism, the Commission on the Churches' Participation in Development, and the Ecumenical Development Cooperative Society now in process of formation. The continuing growth in membership, with new Member Churches almost wholly in the Third World and largely unable to make significant financial contributions, increases the responsibilities and the work of the World Council. Increasing opportunities for joint activities with the Roman Catholic Church also lead to increased work and expenses.

The Member Churches have continued to demonstrate their conviction that the work of the World Council is important to them by increasing their contributions and seeking to raise special contributions, notwithstanding the financial difficulties of the past few years, so as to continue working together in the fellowship of the World Council to meet the challenges and opportunities of this period.

It is, however, clear that at the present time no one can venture any confident forecasts of developments in the period that lies ahead. The problem arising from the world monetary crisis, intensified by the effects of the increase in oil prices in late 1973, are as yet unsolved. The high rate of inflation is a major cause of wide-spread concern, and governments are seeking to find ways to combat this problem but with little success so far. It is not possible to foresee how the international and the various national economies will develop in the coming years or how those developments will affect the finances of the Member Churches.

On the other hand, it is clear that the Nairobi Assembly will face challenges to continue and strengthen existing work in many fields and to take up new problems of particular urgency for the period following the Fifth Assembly. It is even more necessary this time than at earlier assemblies for the Member Churches and their delegates to be fully conscious of the fact that carrying out the decisions which they take at the Fifth Assembly will be dependent on their subsequent action in making available the necessary financial resources. There will be need for a significant increase in contributions in order that normal income may be brought into balance with current expenditure, for regular annual increases thereafter sufficient to compensate the effects of inflation and for new resources to finance those activities, should the Fifth Assembly decide to place new responsibilities on the World Council.

lexicon

The following word list contains technical terms and names of persons perhaps not familiar to all readers, as well as words too newly coined to appear in most convenient dictionaries or whose use here differs considerably from common definitions. No identification is made of living persons. As an additional aid to readers the full titles are given of all acronyms used in this report, with indication (where appropriate) of whether they are an organ of the United Nations or the World Council of Churches.

* * *

AACC — All Africa Conference of Churches.
ACLD — Agency for Christian Literature Development [WCC].
ACTS — Advisory Committee on Technical Services [WCC].
Anatta [Pali] — "The doctrine of the impermanence of the separative ego, [which] when taken to its logical conclusion produces the doctrine of *Sunyata*, the Void. All manifested things, when analysed and taken to pieces, are found to lack continuous form or unchanging substance. . . The Buddha analysed the thing called man and proved it to contain no single permanent factor, nor anything resembling a changeless and immortal 'soul'. This, however, has been narrowed by later Buddhists to a doctrine of 'no soul' for which there is neither Scriptural authority nor the support of sense." (Christmas Humphries: *Buddhism*.)
Bonhoeffer, Dietrich (1906-1945) — A German pastor and teacher, he was one of the most outstanding and influential theologians of this century. He was a leader in the Confessing Church, which opposed the "Reich Church" dominated by the German State. Arrested by the nazis in 1939, he was executed by special order of SS leader Heinrich Himmler at the Flossenburg concentration camp on April 9, 1945, a few days before it was liberated by the Allies. "It would be a superficial understanding of Bonhoeffer that considered him simply as a man caught in the events of his time, like a fly in a spider's web. He himself understood his career as the continually deepening response to a vocation that finally demanded everything he had. The best-known of his books published in his lifetime was *The Cost of Discipleship*, and perhaps the word 'discipleship' is the key to his theology. What does it mean to be a disciple? Whereas his Lutheran training had stressed 'grace alone' as that which makes the disciple, Bonhoeffer

shifted emphasis to obedience. He made a famous distinction between 'cheap grace' and 'costly grace'. Cheap grace is nominal Christianity, grace 'sold on the market', 'thrown away at cut prices', to quote Bonhoeffer's biting words. Costly grace is obedient discipleship, and he understood this particularly as obedience to the Sermon on the Mount''. (John Mcquarrie)

Casa Locarno — A rest home run by the Swiss churches and supported through the Commission on Inter-Church Aid, Refugee and World Service.

Cassette — A small cartridge containing unlooped magnetic tape and designed for automatic use on insertion into a tape recorder or player designed to receive it.

CCA — Christian Conference of Asia.

CCC — Caribbean Conference of Churches.

CCIA — Commission of the Churches on International Affairs [WCC].

CCJP — Committee on the Church and the Jewish People [WCC].

CCPD — Commission on the Churches' Participation in Development [WCC].

CEC — Conference of European Churches.

CEVAA — Ecumenical Community for Apostolic Action (Communauté Evangélique d'Action Apostolique).

Charismatic [from the Greek *charisma*, a ''grace'' or ''favour'', especially a gift of God's grace] — The *Charismatic movement* is a term used to describe churches and Christians who lay ''stress on an experience called 'the baptism in the Spirit' as a second stage (after conversion) in the life of holiness. . . . It is now fairly well-known that clergy and lay[people] within the Roman Catholic Church and all of the main Protestant denominations have claimed to have received a 'baptism in the Spirit' with attendant manifestations, such as speaking in tongues, powers of healing, exorcism, and other practices . . . .*Charismatic gifts* is a phrase properly used to describe *all* the endowments with which the Holy Spirit enriches the Church. . . .'' (Report of the Special Committee on the Work of the Holy Spirit, The United Presbyterian Church in the USA.)

CICARWS — Commission on Inter-Church Aid, Refugee and World Service [WCC].

CLLT — Course for Leaders of Lay Training [WCC co-sponsorship].

CMC — Christian Medical Commission [WCC].

Conscientization — A term [*conscientização* in Portuguese] popularized by Paulo Freire, and which may be defined as ''a consciousness-raising which commits itself to changing reality''. (H. Volkomener) ''A conscientizing—and therefore liberating—education is not that transfer of neatly wrapped knowledge in which there certainly is no knowledge; it is a true act of knowing. Through it, both teacher and pupils simultaneously become knowing subjects, brought together by the object they are knowing. There is no longer one who thinks, who knows, standing in front of others who admit they don't know, that they have to be taught. Rather, all of them are inquisitive learners, avid to learn''. (Paulo Freire)

CWME — Commission on World Mission and Evangelism [WCC].

DFI — Dialogue with People of Living Faiths and Ideologies [WCC].

Diakonia [Greek] — Service, attendance on a duty, deaconship. Campare I Corinthians 12:5: "and there are varieties of service, but the same Lord (*kai diaireseis* diakoniōn *eisin, kai ho autos Kyrios*)''.

EACC — The former East Asia Christian Conference, now the Christian Conference of Asia.

Ecclesiology — Until recently this word was used in English to denote "the science of church building and decoration''. Nowadays, especially in ecumenical circles, the word used to describe any or all of the following: the study of doctrine concerning the Church; the study of church order, especially the development of church law and governance in various systems or types; or (more loosely) an understanding of what the Church as an institution means in the lives of its people.

ECLOF — Ecumenical Church Loan Fund [WCC].

ECOSOC — Economic and Social Council [UN].

Ecumenical Patriarchate — "The Patriarch of Constantinople [modern Istanbul, Turkey] is known as the 'Ecumenical' (or universal) Patriarch, and since the schism between east and west he has enjoyed a position of special honour among all the Orthodox communities; but he does not have the right to interfere in the internal affairs of other churches''. (Timothy Ware: *The Orthodox Church*)

EDF — Ecumenical Development Fund [WCC].

EKD — Evangelical Church in Germany (Evangelische Kirche in Deutschland).

Encuentro [Spanish] — "Encounter" or "meeting", and hence a particular technique of informative visitation first developed in conjunction with the Lima 1971 Assembly of the World Council of Christian Education. "Planned according to suggestions from Latin Americans themselves, the *encuentros* served as intensive research opportunities into how education takes place in that culture and how church education fits into that larger context. The word *encuentro*. . . could not be translated easily, for the Spanish word signifies the deep involvement of participants with each other in an encounter or meeting. The aim was to explore, *to learn* inductively about education in the specific context of a Latin American city with its political, economic and social situations and tensions, and its larger educational systems within that whole. In that light the delegates studied the particular practices of church education, parish and otherwise." (William B. Kennedy: "Encuentros: a New Ecumenical Learning Experience", *Study Encounter* Vol. VIII no. 2, 1972 [SE/24])

EPS — Ecumenical Press Service [WCC].

ERF — Educational Renewal Fund [WCC].

ESP — Ecumenical Sharing of Personnel [WCC].

EYS — Ecumenical Youth Service [WCC].

FRG — Federal Republic of Germany.

Fry, Franklin Clark (1900-1968) — An American church statesman, President of the Lutheran Church in America and its major predecessor from 1944 onwards, he was Chairman of the WCC Central Committee from 1954 until his death. Dr. Fry played a leading role in church relief work after the Second World War and was renowned as a church parliamentarian.

Hare Krishna Movement — A form of Hinduism practised largely in the West, its mostly young adherents are highly visible on the pavements of major cities, dressed in garnet or saffron robes, the males among them wearing shaven heads except for a long top-knot. These persons are popularly called "Hare Krishna" because of the chant, in the Sanskrit language, which they ceaselessly chant and which begins with those words. The Hindu god Krishna, a personable, blue-skinned deity of acknowledged charm, is an *avatar*—or incarnation—of the god Vishnu. Some sophisticated Hindus claim that Jesus Christ is yet another *avatar* of the same god.

Humanum [Latin] — "Everything that is of men and women and children; human nature". (Eric Partridge) Perhaps derived from the well-known phrase of the Roman playwright Terence, *Humanum nihil a me alienum puto*, "Nothing that is human do I consider foreign to me".

IDOC — An International Documentation service based in Rome and devoted to distributing and generating documentation and analyses on issues of justice, order and liberty, with a special commitment to gathering information from the Third World.

ILO — International Labour Office [UN].

JWG — Joint Working Group of the Roman Catholic Church and the WCC.

Kimbangu, Simon (1889-1951) — Born at Nkamba in the Central Congo (now Zaire), Simon Kimbangu was a man of peasant background who for a while worked as a catechist at the Baptist Mission. "During an influenza epidemic in 1918 [he] heard the voice of Christ calling him to 'witness to your brethren and to convert them'. After resisting the call for three years, he began healing the sick and preaching against witchcraft, and thousands of Congolese began flocking to Nkamba. He lasted six months before missionaries and the Belgian authorities, fearful of a popular revolt, had him arrested. The prophet spent the rest of his life in prison in what is now Lubumbashi, where he died in 1951 at the age of 62. His ideas were outlawed, and his close associates exiled to remote regions. The deportations had the reverse effect of spreading the movement. . .The Kimbanguist Church holds to a literalistic interpretation of the Bible, the principle of nonviolence and a strong conviction that the Holy Spirit was working through an African. It believes in baptism by the Spirit rather than by water, though infants receive a blessing with water that has baptismal overtones. . . . Students of the Kimbanguist Church have explained its remarkable growth by the fact that it gave expression to [Zairean] cultural forms at a time when missionary-founded churches were slow in recognizing the need for indigenous liturgies and the development of local leaders''. (Edward B. Fiske: *The New York Times,* February 24, 1971.)

LPTF — Language Policy Task Force [WCC].

LWF — Lutheran World Federation.

MECC — Middle East Council of Churches.

NCC — National Council of Churches, or National Christian Conference.

NCCCUSA — National Council of Churches of Christ in the United States of America.

NGO — Non-Governmental Organization.

Niles, Daniel T. (1908-1970) — A Ceylonese Methodist, and one of Asia's most distinguished contemporary Christian thinkers, Niles was for a time General Secretary, and then Chairman, of the East Asia Christian Conference. He served a number of years as secretary in the Department of Studies in Evangelism of the WCC. At the Fourth Assembly of the Council he preached the opening sermon, and later in the Assembly he was elected one of the WCC's six Presidents. A prolific author, D. T. Niles's study of indigenous religions in Sri Lanka is reflected in his book, *Sir, I Would See Jesus.*

OAU — Organization for African Untiy.

Oikoumene [Greek] — The inhabited world; as in Romans 10: 18: ''and their words unto the ends of the world (*kai eis ta perata tēs* oikoumenēs *ta rhēmata autōn*)''.

Oldham, Joseph Houldsworth (1874-1969) — Anglican layman of Scottish and Irish ancestry, he was Honorary President of the WCC 1961-1968. ''He was the first and most distinguished secretary of the International Missionary Council. He carried chief responsibility for the Oxford Conference of 1937 on Church, Community and State. During the

Second World War he launched and edited the *Christian News-letter* and created the Christian Frontier Movement. He was one of the most influential advisers in the formation of the British Council of Churches, the World Council of Churches, and the Commission of the Churches on International Affairs". (Norman Goodall: *The Ecumenical Movement*)

Parameter — In mathematics, "a variable or an arbitrary constant appearing in a mathematical expression, each value of which restricts or determines the specific form of the expression" (*American Heritage Dictionary*); hence, figuratively, that which restricts or determines the shape and direction of a discussion or an argument.

PCR — Programme to Combat Racism [WCC].

Privatistic — Refers to the tendency of church ministries to families, especially in Protestant churches, "to presuppose and to be directed towards the nuclear [small-unit] family. But the nuclear family is beginning to be questioned. While enhancing the personal and private character of life, its privatization has limited harmfully its role in society and has made it essentially a conservative force resistant to change. Under the pressure of over-population, the smaller family provides a more limited field for its important socializing processes and requires the socializing power of larger forms of community". (*Family Power*: A Report on a Consultation of an International Ad Hoc Advisory Committee of the Office of Family Ministries. Geneva: WCC, 1973; mimeographed)

RAM — Rural Agricultural Mission [WCC].

RCC — Roman Catholic Church.

Sahel — A zone, not a political unit, of North Central Africa south of the Sahara and Libyan Deserts, stretching from near the west coast nearly 4,000 miles to the mountains of Ethiopia, with its widest part nearly 1,000 miles. Comprised of major portions of the republics of Mauritania, Senegal, Mali, Upper Volta, Niger and Chad, it consists of desert, grassy steppes and extensive plains. The delicate ecological balance of this region whose normal average rainfall is 40 cm. has in recent years been upset by droughts which have caused widespread famine. Ethnologically it is inhabited by Negro peoples under Muslim influence.

Sexism — Conscious or unconscious discrimination against persons because of the sex to which they belong. This term, analogous to *racism*, is usually applied to discrimination against women. The conscious belittling of women, or the relegation of them to an inferior status, when practised by men, is sometimes called "male chauvinism". The word *sexism* should not be confused with the word *sexuality*, and it has nothing whatever to do with prurience.

Socialization — "Every human being is conditioned, especially in his early years, through family relationships, peer-group activities, and in school and work experiences. Our attitudes, prejudices, ways of perceiving and communicating are all shaped by a process that the behavioural scientists call 'socialization'." (*Education Newsletter*, Vol. III No. 2, June 1974. Issued by the Office of Education, WCC.)

SODEPAX — Committee on Society, Development and Peace [WCC/RCC]

Sub-proletariat — The bottommost stratum of the lowest class of the community, indigent wage earners and labourers, frequently of a different cultural background that the dominant class of a society.

Syncretism — The artificial and deliberate combining of distinct theological and ritual elements of two or more discrete and well-acknowledged religions to produce yet another and distinct religion. The Baha'i faith, with headquarters in Haifa, Israel, is a genuine example. Illegitimate use of the term among Christians is wide-spread and generally is employed by foreigners to describe the incorporation into local Christian behaviour of indigenous concepts and usages alien to the outsider and of which he or she disapproves.

Taizé — "An ordered community of brothers" coming from a dozen different countries and from many different denominations, including—with the agreement of the Archbishop of Paris—Roman Catholics, with headquarters in "Taizé, a tiny village in Burgundy. . . The aim of the Community of Taizé is to serve God in life, work and worship. The experiment was started in 1939 by Roger Schutz, then a young theologian active in the Swiss Student Christian Movement. Now Prior of the Community, Schutz's concept of the brotherhood of celibacy, common ownership and obedience has been slowly worked out in the Reformed tradition. . . . Prayer, worship, inner silence and action are all essential to the Taizé way of life". (William D. Boyd and David Alexander in *Presbyterian Life*, January 19, 1957)

TEF — Theological Education Fund [WCC].

UIM — Urban Industrial Mission [WCC].

Ujamaa [Swahili] — "Society, social units, group, community or extended family" and hence used to describe the form of socialism practised in Tanzania, especially communal villages. "Traditional *ujamaa* had three basic principles: (1) brotherly love and respect; (2) the sharing of the most important sources of wealth; and (3) the sharing of productive labour. . . . [It is this] basic nature of community life that Tanzanians have inherited from their fathers and are now modifying to suit the needs of a modern people. . . . *Ujamaa*, when used in the context of Tanzania's socialism, is not a mere ideology, nor does it refer to a scientific system". (Thomas Musa in Dossier Section III, page 25. See also Dossier Section VI, pages 51-53.)

UN — United Nations.

UNCTAD — United Nations Conference on Trade and Development.

UNELAM — Movement for Latin-American Evangelical Unity (Movimento pro Unidad Evangelica Latino-Americana).

UNESCO — United Nations Educational , Scientific and Cultural Organization.

WACC — World Association for Christian Communication.

WARC — World Alliance of Reformed Churches.

WCC — World Council of Churches.

WCCE — World Council for Christian Education.

WELG — Women's Ecumenical Liaison Group.

WSCF — World Student Christian Federation.

WYP — World Youth Projects [WCC].

YMCA — Young Men's Christian Association.

Yoga [Sanskrit] — (1) A Hindu discipline aimed at training the consciousness for a state of perfect spiritual insight and tranquillity. (2) A system of exercises practised as a part of this discipline to promote control of the body and mind.

YMCA — Young Women's Christian Association.

Zen [Japanese] — "Founded as a School of Buddhism by Bodhidharma (Japanese: Daruma), who reached China from South India in A.D. 520. . . . The purpose of Zen is to pass beyond the intellect. . . . The process of Zen is a leap from thinking to knowing, . . . and the Zen student uses all scriptures and any philosophy which helps to make and use the bridge. . . . Yet even Zen has produced its own technique for the 'sudden' path to Satori, the Zen name for Enlightenment. The two most famous devices are the *mondo*, a form of rapid question-answer between Master and pupil which aims at so speeding the process of thought that it is suddenly transcended, and the *koan*, a word or phrase insoluble by the intellect, which is often a compressed form of *mondo*. Neither has any meaning for the rational mind, else it would not be Zen." (Christmas Humphries: *Buddhism*.)

index

Accra, Faith and Order Meeting (1974), 73, 80, 82

Addis Ababa, Central Committee Meeting (1971), 25, 39, 41, 43, 44, 65, 99, 117, 149, 179, 195, 201, 214

Adler, Elisabeth, 154

Advisory Committee on Technical Services [ACTS], 146

Africa, 24, 32, 47, 55, 58, 66, 80, 88, 92, 93, 94, 96, 100, 102, 104, 107, 109, 111, 113, 126, 130, 131, 153, 159, 165, 167, 168, 172, 173, 175, 176, 181, 188, 189, 190, 191, 194, 195, 196, 200, 201, 223, 232

Agency for Christian Literature Development [ACLD], 94-95, 227, 234, 243

Agriculture, 87, 97, 131, 148-150, 170

Ajaltoun, Multilateral Dialogue (1970), 103, 107

Algeria, 31, 129, 138

All Africa Conference of Churches [AACC], 159, 165, 173, 183, 184, 189, 190, 195, 243

Aluko, S.A., 113

Amsterdam, First Assembly (1948), 23, 153, 194, 198, 238

Angola, 85, 144, 158, 174

Ankrah, Kodwo, 165

Apartheid, 132, 157, 172, 176; see also Racism

Appleton, George, 106

Argentina, 87, 147, 192

Arnoldshain, Executive Committee Meeting (1970), 41, 44, 140

Asia, 24, 32, 37, 47, 54, 55, 58, 92, 93, 94, 96, 100, 102-104, 107, 109, 111, 113, 130, 153, 157, 159, 167, 171, 176, 181, 188, 191, 194, 196, 200, 223

Assembly Planning and Preparations, 41-42, 65-68, 228

Australia, 24, 44, 96, 156, 191, 192, 196

Austria, 129

Bangkok, Conference on Salvation Today and CWME Assembly (1972/3), 13, 54, 70, 82-84, 86, 88, 90, 91, 99-100, 160, 175

Bangladesh, 164, 165, 166, 170, 233

Banking, 157; also see Finance and Central Services

Beaupère, René, 61

Behrhorst, Carroll, 97

Bergen, Consultation on World Educational Crisis (1970), 181, 188-189, 193

Berlin, Central Committee Meeting (1974), 29, 44, 66, 154, 156, 213, 235

Conférence on Sexism in the 1970's (1974), 15, 186, 188, 196, 231

Biblical Studies Portfolio, 15, 52-56, 228

Birch, Charles, 111n.

Black Theology, 14, 90, 185, 186

Blake, Eugene Carson, 31, 38, 45, 138, 139

Bliss, Kathleen, 194

Bonhoeffer, Dietrich, 17, 20, 243-244

Bortnowska, Halina, 83

Bossey, Ecumenical Institute at, 15, 50, 52, 56-60, 179, 187, 188, 228, 229, 238

Boumedienne, Houari, 129, 138

Brash, Alan, 45

Brasil para Cristo Church, 22

Brazil, 83, 84, 130, 178

Broumana, Christian-Muslim Consultation (1972), 101

Browne, Eleanor Kent, 11

Bucharest, Conference on Science and Technology (1974), 114-115

Buddhism, 100, 102-103, 105, 243, 250

Budget, General, see General Budget

Budgets, Programme, 18-19, 156, 227, 231, 234-237

Bührig, Marga, 197

Burma, 169

Burundi, 159, 163

Cameroon, 148, 149-150, 196

Canada, 10, 75, 156, 173

Cantate Domino, 77, 197

Canterbury, Central Committee Meeting (1969), 25, 43, 44, 109, 138, 153, 154-155, 160, 161

Cardiff, Church and Society Consultation (1972), 114, 116, 118

Caribbean, 24, 91, 94, 148, 150, 153, 191, 194, 200, 201

Caribbean Conference of Churches [CCC], 24, 150, 244

Carter, Sydney, 197

Casa Locarno, 174, 232, 244

Catholicity, 72, 77-79

CCIA, 14, 18, 33, 37, 42, 90, 122, 123, 124, 125, 126, 127-139, 158, 165, 228, 244, 248

CCPD, 14, 18, 33, 37, 42, 90, 122, 123, 124, 125, 126, 127, 139-152, 158, 167, 171, 224, 235, 241, 244

Centre de Litterature Evangelique, 216

Centre Saint-Irenee, 61

CEVAA, 88

Charismatic Movements and Churches, 35, 57, 65, 72, 187, 244

Chile, 31, 87, 125, 126, 142, 172, 173

Chimaltenango Development Project, Guatemala, 97-98

Cho, Kiyoko Takeda, 45

Christian Conference of Asia [CCA], 26, 157, 159, 244, 245

Christian Literature Fund, 94

Christian Medical Commission [CMC], 15, 96-98, 234, 244

Christians in the Technical and Social Revolutions of Our Time, Church and Society Conference, Geneva (1966), 13, 108, 134, 160

Church and Society, Studies on, 13, 42, 69, 70, 91, 108-119, 228

Church Union, 10, 72, 74-76

Church Unity, 8, 19, 23, 34, 69, 72-80, 121

Churches in Mission, CWME Study, 85

CICARWS, 14, 18, 34, 39, 42, 88, 122, 125, 126, 127, 128, 158, 162-177, 184, 189, 190, 200, 201, 224, 229, 231-233, 238, 239, 244

Colombo, Multilateral Dialogue (1974), 103-104

Common Witness and Proselytism, Joint Working Group Study, 37, 81

Communication, 19, 21, 26, 28, 30, 42, 64, 65, 66, 67, 94-95, 122, 128, 183, 196
  Department of Communication, 42, 48, 58, 178, 180, 181, 182, 204, 205, 210-223, 228, 229

Composite Statement of Needs, 224, 236-237, 241

Computer, 239, 240

Concepts of Unity and Models of Union, Faith and Order Study, 13, 76

Conciliar Fellowship, 76, 79-80

Conference of European Churches [CEC], 174, 244

Confessing Christ Today, Assembly Section, 51, 67, 84, 86

Confessional Families, 74

Congregational Renewal, 209

Conscientization, 15, 86, 145, 150, 184, 187, 192-193, 244-245

Conservative Evangelical, 35, 53, 84

Constitution and Rules of the WCC, 23, 35, 43, 200

Cooperation of Men and Women in Church, Family and Society, Department of, 178, 179, 194

Corporations, Multinational, 130-131, 156-157

CWME, 13, 18, 24, 42, 55, 69, 70, 71, 82-98, 99, 100, 158, 168, 175, 224, 227, 229, 233-235, 245

Czechoslovakia, 31, 55, 172

Dar es Salaam University, 193

De Silva, Lynn, 102

Decentralization, 26, 31-33

Derr, Thomas S., 112

Deschner, John, 161

Development, 130, 164, 167
  Commission on the Churches' Participation in Development [CCPD], 14, 18, 33, 37, 42, 90, 122, 123, 124, 125, 126, 127, 139-152, 158, 167, 171, 224, 235, 241, 244

Diakonia, 124, 175, 245

Dialogue with People of Living Faiths and Ideologies [DFI], 14, 33, 37, 42, 58, 69, 70, 80, 87, 95, 98-108, 120, 228, 229, 241, 245

Disarmament, 129, 130

Disaster Response, 14, 16, 123, 163, 170-171, 233

Doing Theology, 50, 51, 57, 208

East Asia Christian Conference [EACC], see Christian Conference of Asia [CCA]

Ecclesiology, 23, 38, 51, 245

Ecology, 56, 112, 113; see also Environment

Economics, 16, 130, 134, 140; see also Finance and Central Services

Ecumenical Action, Division of, 14, 178, 181, 184, 200, 210

Ecumenical Centre, 31, 37, 60, 213, 229, 237

Ecumenical Church Loan Fund [ECLOF], 169, 245

Ecumenical Courier, 64

Ecumenical Development Cooperative Society, 143, 235, 241

Ecumenical Development Fund [EDF], 147, 150, 151, 227, 235, 245

Ecumenical Institute, 15, 50, 52, 56,60, 179, 187, 188, 228, 229, 238

Ecumenical Patriarchate, 30, 245

Ecumenical Press Service [EPS], 213, 246

Ecumenical Review, 23n., 30n., 38n., 51, 54n., 75, 77, 113n., 117n., 118n., 214, 215

Ecumenical Sharing of Personnel [EPS], 39, 88-89, 90, 91, 175-176, 246

Ecumenical Youth Service [EYS], 178, 182, 200, 201, 246

Edinburgh, World Missionary Conference (1910), 14

Education and Renewal, Programme Unit on, 14, 42-43, 47, 51, 54, 174, 175, 178;209, 210, 229

General Secretariat, 12, 30, 31-47, 48, 53, 210, 214, 228, 229, 240, 241

Genetics, 33, 111

Geneva, 31, 62, 63, 162, 201, 213, 220, 221
  Central Committee Meeting (1973), 29, 44, 117, 182, 213, 222
  Church and Society Conference (1966), 13, 108, 134, 160
  Executive Committee Meeting (1970), 41, 44
  Executive Committee Meeting (1975), 44

Geneva University, 55, 57, 59

German Democratic Republic [GDR], 44, 172

Germany, Federal Republic of [FRG], 39, 147, 159, 196, 226, 228, 230, 246

Education for Mission, 89

Education Office, 14, 15, 18, 42, 89, 158, 174, 178, 180, 181, 182, 184,

252

187, 188-194, 207, 210, 224, 236, 238

Education Renewal Fund [ERF], 192, 193, 227, 236

Egypt, 142

Encuentros, 183, 184-185, 190, 245-246

Environment, 33, 110; see also Ecology

Ethiopia, 147, 148, 149, 152

Eucharist, 23, 73, 79

Europe, 24, 54, 55, 59, 88, 96, 100, 164, 166, 167, 172, 173, 176, 190, 192

European Conference on Christian Education, 190

Evangelical Church in Germany [EKD], 31, 39, 44, 147, 159, 228, 245

Evangelism, 37, 52, 84, 86, 88, 90, 100, 120, 141

Evanston, Second Assembly (1954), 40, 62, 99, 153, 178, 194, 210,

Exhibitions, 156, 217, 220

Faith and Order, Commission and Secretariat, 9, 13, 35, 36, 37, 42, 52, 54, 55, 69, 70, 71, 72-82, 91, 102, 175, 179, 228

Faith and Witness, Programme Unit on, 42, 47, 51, 54, 69-121, 175

Familia '74, Assembly on the Family (1974), 15, 185, 187, 189

Family Ministries Office, 175, 181, 182, 186, 189, 191-192, 195, 207, 248

Fellowship among the Churches, 16-22, 23-44, 69, 75, 79, 89, 90, 120, 163, 167-168, 177, 212, 222-223

Fertilizers, 131

Fiji, 85, 193

Film and Visual Arts, 219-220

Finance and Central Services, Department of, 18-19, 48, 157, 158, 224,-242

Food, 16, 126, 132, 152

France, 58

Frankfurt Book Fair, 216

Freire, Paulo, 137, 184, 186-187, 244-245

FRELIMO, 158

Fry, Franklin Clark, 8, 246

Fund for Reconstruction and Rehabilitation in Indochina, 171

Future of Man and Society in a World of Science-Based Technology, Church and Society Study 13-14, 33, 70, 71, 108, 109-116, 231

Gallis, Marion, 142n.

General Budget, 16, 18-19, 39, 56, 58-59, 63-64, 224, 225, 226, 227-231, 232, 236, 241

Ghana, 80, 113, 142

Gill, David M., 110n.; see also Assembly Planning and Preparations

Giving an Account of the Hope that is in Us, Faith and Order Study, 13, 54, 70, 81-82, 91

Glass, Bentley, 113

Gospel, 19, 49, 53, 69, 70, 79, 81, 82, 85, 86, 87, 90, 91, 94, 96, 106, 120, 128, 134, 153, 177, 192, 204, 208

Graves, Charles, 61

Greece, 165, 175

Groscurth, Reinhard, 9

Guatemala, 93, 97

Hallencreutz, Carl F., 99

Hardoy, Jorge, 113

Hare Krishna, 105, 246

Helsinki, 43, 229

Hinduism, 102-103, 105, 106, 250

Hooft, W.A. Visser 't, 7, 62, 153, 194

Human Rights, 14, 16, 33, 50, 57, 125, 127, 129, 132, 134-136

Humanum Studies, 15, 48-52, 55, 231, 246

Ideologies, 8, 33, 34, 53, 71, 104, 105, 108, 115

IDOC, 61, 246

Ife University, 113

Images of the Future, 110

India, 8, 10, 44, 157

Indians (Native Americans), 156

Indochina, 16, 34, 63, 125, 128, 138, 139, 202

Indonesia, 55, 66, 92, 148

Inflation, 225

Inter-Chruch Aid, Refugee and World SErvice, Commission on [CICARWS], 14, 18, 34, 39, 42, 88, 122, 125, 126, 127, 128, 158, 162-177, 184, 189, 190, 200, 201, 224, 229, 231-233, 238, 239, 244

International Affairs, Commission of the Churches on [CCIA], 14, 33-34, 42, 50, 60, 90, 122, 123, 124, 125, 126, 127;139, 158, 165, 228, 244, 248

International Bureau of Education, 186

International Missionary Council [IMC], 69, 85, 91, 127, 153, 195, 247

International Review of Mission [IRM], 214, 215

Interuniversitair Instituut, Utrecht, 61

INTERVOX, 217

Ireland, 37

Islam, 101-102, 106, 124; see also Muslims

Israel, 129; see also Jewish People

Italy, 55, 175

Ivory Coast, 142

Japan, 45, 85

Jenkins, David, 48

Jesus Christ, 8, 10, 16, 17, 22, 33, 35, 49, 51, 52, 65, 66, 67, 70, 78, 79, 82, 95, 99, 106, 116, 120, 121, 142, 208, 246

JESUS CHRIST FREES AND UNITES, Nairobi Assembly Theme, 7, 21, 58, 67, 160

Jesus Movement, 187

Jewish People, 100-101, 103, 104, 105, 106
    Committee on the Church and the

Jewish People [CCJP], 54, 100-101, 244

Joint Working Group of the WCC and the Roman Catholic Church [JWG], 36, 37, 231, 246

Jonah, 136

Justice and Service, Programme Unit on, 14, 42, 47, 54, 91, 122-177

Kenya, 66, 75

Kimbangu, Simon, 24, 246-247
Church of Jesus Christ on Earth by the Prophet Simon Kimbangu, 24

King, Martin Luther, 117

Klostermaier, Klaus, 102

Korea, 55, 87

Koyama, Kosuke, 113

Laity and Adult Education, 37, 178, 180, 181, 182, 184, 186, 190-191, 207-208, 228

Laity Formation Consultation, Assisi (1974), 54, 189

Language Policy Task Force [LPTF], 51, 54, 186, 204-205, 247

Language Service, 205, 210, 220-222

Latin America, 24, 46, 58, 86, 92, 93, 94, 96, 109, 111, 113, 116, 150, 156, 165, 172, 173, 176, 183, 189, 196, 200, 223

Lausanne University, 54, 55

Lebanon, 101, 103

Leisure Tourism, 180, 191

Leuenberg Agreement, 75

Liberation Theology in Latin America, 15, 90, 185, 186

Life and Work Movement, 62, 69, 122, 179

Library, 60-61, 228

Lima, Assembly of WCCE (1971), 180, 183, 185, 190

Limits to Growth, 110, 113, 114

Lutheran World Federation [LWF], 75, 187, 190, 247

Madagascar, 142

Malaysia, 142, 169

Massachusetts Institute of Technology, 113

Material Aid, CICARWS, 176

Mathews, James K., 41

Mehl, Roger, 9

Mello, Manoel de, 84

Mexico, 83, 85

Middle East, 24, 31, 34, 55, 58, 124, 125, 128-129, 130, 138, 168, 172, 173, 194, 232

Middle East Council of Churches [MECC], 24, 179, 247

Migrant Workers, 131, 176

Migration Secretariat, 126, 158, 176

Mission and Evangelism, see World Mission and Evangelism, Commission

Monetary Crisis, 16, 39, 130-131, 224-227

Montreux, Consultation on Development (1970), 140, 141, 147, 148, 167, 235

Mozambique, 126, 158, 174

Muslims, 66, 101-102, 103, 124, 170; see also Islam

Nairobi, Fifth Assembly (1975), 7, 8, 11, 18, 21, 23, 36, 39, 51, 54, 55, 56, 58, 61, 63, 65-68, 105, 119, 124, 127, 152, 176, 177, 194, 197, 202, 220, 222, 224, 230, 242

Namibia (South West Africa), 158

National Christian Councils [NCC's], 24, 31, 32, 37, 42, 45, 60, 63, 97, 169, 179, 181, 185, 247

National Council of Churches of Christ in the USA [NCCCUSA], 63, 65, 247

Near East, see Middle East

Near East Council of Churches, see Middle East Council of Churches

Nemi, Consultation on Human Environment (1971), 113, 116

Netherlands, 144, 147, 148, 159

New Delhi, Third Assembly (1961), 8, 11, 33, 77, 79, 99, 153, 178, 195

New York, 62, 129, 197

New York Office of the WCC, 11, 60, 61-65, 228, 229

New Zealand, 44, 96, 147, 156, 191, 193

Nida, Eugene, 221

Nigeria, 34, 125, 163, 170

Niles, D.T., 44, 247

Nineveh, 136, 137

Non-Governmental Organizations [NGO's], 129, 158, 193, 247

North America, 24, 55, 85, 96, 163, 164, 172, 182, 189, 236

Northern Hemisphere, 20, 202

Notting Hill, Consultation on Racism, (1969), 153

Nurture, Christian, 19, 183

Nwosu, Ben, 113

Oikoumene, 17, 20, 247

Oil, 114, 152

Oldham, J.H., 17, 153, 247-248

ONE WORLD, 213, 215

Orthodox Churches, 24, 47, 57, 84, 86, 164-165, 172, 179, 182, 183, 186

Oxford, Conference on Church, Community and State (1937), 153

Pacific Area, 88, 92, 191, 194

Palestinians, 34, 129, 139, 172

Papua New Guinea, 180-181, 185, 192, 193

Participation in Change Programme, 14, 16, 50, 57, 58, 187, 205-206, 208

Patterns of Relationships Between the Roman Catholic Church and the

WCC, Joint Working Group Study, 37-38

Paul VI, Pope and Bishop of Rome, 31, 37-38, 213

Peace Churches, Historic, 119

Pentecostals, 35, 86, 206

Periodicals, WCC, 214-216, 218

Personnel Office, 46

Peter, 81

Philippines, 87

Photo Oikoumene, 220

Pimen, Patriarch of Moscow and All the Russias, 31

Poland, 83, 172

Political and Economic Choices, 16-18, 49, 78, 89-90, 110, 135

Portugal, 16, 173

Potter, Philip, 13, 31, 36, 45, 64, 136, 198, 203, 222

Poverty 2000, 142

Press Office, 212-213

Primal World-Views, 104

Priorities Committee, 39, 40

Programme Projects, 19, 146, 156, 227, 231

Programme to Combat Racism [PCR], 14, 33, 42, 90, 117, 122, 123, 124, 126, 152-162, 224, 228, 241

Programme Units, Organizing of, 14, 42, 45, 59, 69-72, 90-91, 122, 125-127, 154, 178-182, 210

Project List, CICARWS/CWME, 125, 166, 170, 227, 231, 233

Protest Movements, 173-174, 184, 199-200, 202

Provident and Retirement Funds, 239, 240

Publications Office, 64, 210, 216-217

Racism, 34, 78, 80, 124, 154, 176, 206, 248; see also Programme to Combat Racism

Radio and Television Office, 213-214, 217-218

Raiser, Konrad, 12, 45, 215

Randers, Jorgen, 113

Rao, K.S., 83

Raw Materials and Development, UN Special Assembly, 130-133, 139

Refugees, 184
    Secretariat for Refugees, CICARWS, 126, 171-174, 232

Regional Councils of Churches, 24, 31, 32, 37, 42, 45, 89, 181, 185, 234

Renewal, 19, 42, 183, 185, 186, 228; see also Education and Renewal

Reserves, 238

Reuters, 213

Rhodesia, Southern (Zimbabwe), 87, 138, 158

RISK, 83, 178, 181, 182, 184, 185, 191, 196, 209, 214

Role of Christians in Changing Institutions, CWME Study, 50, 85

Roman Catholic Church, 24, 35-38, 53, 72, 74, 77, 96-97, 167, 182, 183, 186
    Council on the Laity, 189, 194
    Ecumenical Institute in Jerusalem, 61
    Federation for the Biblical Apostolate 54
    In the Ecumenical Scene, 24, 35, 36, 37, 38, 53, 72, 74, 76, 77, 97, 150, 183, 186, 194, 248
    Justice and Peace Commission, 37
    National Conferences of Catholic Bishops, 97
    Relations with, 31, 36-38, 72, 74, 96, 167
    Secretariat for Promoting Christian Unity, 36, 37, 77
    Week of Prayer, 36, 77
    Vatican Council, Second, 36, 74, 78

Roszak, Theodore, 113

Rural Agricultural Mission [RAM], 87, 248

Russia, see USSR

Sahel, 123, 152, 170-171, 248

Salvation Today Conference and Study, 13, 54, 58, 70, 82-84, 86, 90, 91, 100, 160, 175, 218

Santos, Antonio Jose, 83

Scholarships Programme, 59, 174, 179, 180, 182, 188, 190

Science and the Quality of Life, 49, 50, 56-57, 71, 110, 111, 112, 115

Secularism, 86

Seeing Education Whole, 180, 189

Seventh-Day Adventists, 36, 76-77

Sexism, 15, 188, 196-197, 206 248

Sexism in the 1970's Conference (1974), 15, 186, 188, 196, 231

Smith, Huston, 105

Social Service Portfolio, CICARWS, 175, 189

Socialization, 189, 248

Society, Development and Peace, WCC-RCC Committee [SODEPAX], 37, 150, 180-181, 196, 249

South Africa, Republic of, 55, 138, 153, 156, 158

South West Africa, see Namibia

Southern Africa, 34, 53, 126, 138, 157, 160, 164, 176

Southern Hemisphere, 20, 24, 178, 202

Special Fund, PCR, 155-156, 159

Spirituality, 8, 33, 102, 103-104, 105, 120

Sri Lanka (Ceylon), 103, 142, 191

Staffing Matters, 45-47

Strasbourg University, 61

Structure Committee, 41, 43, 46, 65-66, 122, 125-127, 163, 179, 201, 237, 240

Study Encounter, 52n., 54n., 103n., 111n., 114n., 116n., 165, 183, 187, 206, 215

Sudan, 16, 125, 129, 138, 165, 170

Sustainable and Just Society, 115

255

Sweden, 173
Swiss Federation of Protestant Women, 196
Swiss Franc, 225, 226, 227, 228, 232, 238
Switzerland, 187, 225, 227
Syncretism, 103, 104, 107, 249

Taize, 203, 249
Tanzania, 85, 142, 192, 249
Teams, CICARWS Personnel Desk, 175
Technical Services, 125, 146, 243; see also Advisory Committee on Techical Services
Technology, 33, 49k 56-57, 71, 104, 105, 109-116, 120, 146, 147
Television, 108, 213-214, 218-219
Thailand, 87, 100
Theological Education Fund [TEF], 15, 88, 91-94, 227, 234, 249
This Month, 213, 215
Thomas, M.M., 7, 113
Togo, 183, 195, 196
Toronto, Central Committee Meeting (1950), 23
Torres, Camilo, 83
Tribalism, 159
Trinidad, 169, 191

Uganda, 85, 172, 183, 195
Ujamaa, 85, 189, 249-250
UNELAM, 159, 250
Unemployment, 131
United Bible Societies, 52, 54, 221
United Kingdom, 10, 132, 159, 185
United Naitons, [UN], †24, 127, 129, 132, 133, 134, 142, 144, 173, 186, 193, 220, 242, 250
United States of America [USA], 10, 44, 45, 55, 61-65, 85, 156, 159, 173, 191, 192, 226, 228, 230
United States Conference for the WCC, 64, 65
Unity of the Church and the Unity of Mankind, Faith and Order Study, 13, 33, 71, 78-80, 161, 162
Uppsala, Fourth Assembly (1968), 7, 11, 14, 16, 18, 19, 23, 24, 25, 30, 33, 36, 37, 38, 39, 41, 42, 45, 48, 56, 60, 62, 69, 72, 73, 78, 85, 91, 99, 105, 122, 128, 134, 136, 137, 139, 143, 146, 152, 153, 163, 167, 170, 180, 191, 195, 197, 199, 210, 222, 224, 227, 231, 234, 235, 237, 241
Urban Industrial Mission [UIM], 87, 168, 249
Uruguay, 148, 180

USSR, 165
Utrecht, Central Committee Meeting (1972), 27, 28, 34, 43, 44, 45, 50, 70, 156, 157

Vatican Council, Second, 36, 74, 78, 222
Verghese, T. Paul (Metropolitan Paulos Mar Gregorios), 112n.
Vietnam, 125, 128, 171, 173
Violence, Nonviolence and the Struggle for Social Justice, Church and Society Study, 14, 33, 44, 108, 116-119, 158, 231
Vischer, Lukas, 161
Visits and Visitation, 30, 31, 32, 213
Visser 't Hooft, W.A., 7, 62, 153, 213

Waldheim, Kurt, 132
Weber, Hans-Ruedi, 54
Week of Prayer for Christian Unity, 36, 77
Willebrands, Jan Cardinal, 36, 38
Women's Desk, 181, 182, 183, 184, 188, 194-197
Women's Ecumenical Liaison Group [WELG], 183, 196, 250
Women's Liberation, 16, 33, 41, 47, 80, 108, 179, 181, 183, 194-197, 207-208
World Alliance of Reformed Churches [WARC], 75, 250
World Association for Christian Communication [WACC], 95, 219, 222,
World Bank, 152
World Council of Christian Education [WCCE], 15, 178-179, 183, 190, 193, 207, 236
World Day of Prayer, 196
World Mission and Evangelism, Commission on [CWME], 13, 18, 24, 42, 55, 69, 70, 71, 82-98, 99, 100, 158, 168, 175, 224, 227, 229, 233-235, 245
World Student Christian Federation [WSCF], 60, 77, 179, 180, 186, 193
World Youth Projects [WYP], 182, 200,
Worship, 66, 104

YMCA, 54, 180, 186, 193, 250
Yoder, John H., 118
Youth Concerns, 15, 37, 41, 45, 178, 179, 180-181, 182, 187, 188, 197-204, 207, 209
YWCA, 54, 180, 186, 193, 250

Zambia, 142, 182
Zimbabwe (Southern Rhodesia), 87, 138, 158